MORE THAN THE EAR DISCOVERS

MORE THAN THE EAR DISCOVERS

GOD IN THE PLAYS OF CHRISTOPHER FRY

Stanley M. Wiersma

LOYOLA UNIVERSITY PRESS
Chicago, 1983

ISBN 0-8294-0442-2

Printed in the United States of America

For

Robert Gittings and Jo Manton,
loyal champions of the plays of Christopher Fry
and the first to discover in them
more than the ear discovers.

"Influences and origins are sometimes hard to pin down, and are often forgotten. For instance, I was looking through my old school copy of Sir Thomas Browne the other day—written on the fly-leaf was 1925. It is much underlined (I don't know that I have read it since that time, or certainly not for very many years) and I was surprised to find some of the underlined passages, since forgotten, reminded me of lines in the plays. 'Even that vulgar and Tavern-Music. . . . There is something in it of Divinity more than the ear discovers: it is an Hieroglyphical and shadowed lesson of the whole World and creatures of God'—that doesn't seem far from the Countess's description of the gipsy music in the Golden Bull tavern in *The Dark is Light Enough*. But whether I should have written the speech if I had never read *Religio Medici*, who can tell?"

Christopher Fry, in a letter to SMW,
22 August 1966.

TABLE OF CONTENTS

Preface

It has always seemed to me that drama, poetry, and religion are natural allies (even if the Puritans did commit the error of closing down the theatres). Each of these three things reaches its highest level of achievement and insight when combined with the two others. One thinks, of course, of the Elizabethan period, or—going farther back—of ancient Greece.

I have my times when I daydream about the advent of a supremely gifted writer who would do for our times what Shakespeare did for his—unite at top power the twin forces of poetry and theatre. Through the combination of verse and dramatic form, the profoundest religious and philosophic insights would naturally find their expression.

I have dreamed this daydream for a long time. And I do not stand alone in nursing the hope that these three—drama, poetry, religion—would one day rediscover their natural affinities and prove that drama, poetry, and religion are stronger united than separated. At times I have observed some signs of a poetic-religious-dramatic crystalization, though the role of religion is likely to be less than that of the other two.

In this century Maxwell Anderson proved that there was a market for poetic drama, even if the poetry was often clumsy and sadly lacking the grace and grandeur of a Shakespeare. Still, the customers came and paid.

My hope was that he would be the John the Baptist preparing the way for a greater one. It did not turn out that way. Anderson simply faded away. More successful, I suppose, was T. S. Eliot, who knew something about drama, poetry, and theology—all three. Toward the end of his life he turned to verse drama for most of the writing he wanted to do. Eliot had many things going against, him such as an almost total lack of practical stage experience. But he also had something going for him, for these late-born plays proved capable of holding audiences that did not automatically respond to poetry—and still less to theology. In any event these plays are now part of the permanent repertory of the century, and so poetic drama is not totally extinct.

One could go on listing other gallant attempts at poetic drama. Sometimes they are more *tours de force* than actable plays—one would say this of some of Auden's work. But to sum it up, the end of the first half of the century bequeathed us the half success of several writers venturing into poetic drama, but no success that seems likely to merit Horace's bronze.

What went wrong? One answer is that the attempt was hopeless from the start. I confess that at times I believe this. I have been asking for a drama, written in verse, and preferably religious (if not theological) in the way it reads life. At other times as I pour myself a drink to recover from the TV news, this world of ours looks incurably prosaic, and I cynically observe that "Every period of history gets the drama it deserves." From a prosy world comes prosy drama.

Such for my less hopeful moments. But most of the time I refuse to believe so dour a picture, and I keep alive in my heart the vision of the rebirth of the poetic drama. And I trust that with this reborn drama would necessarily come a release of religious insight.

And now I arrive at my main point. There was a moment when I thought my dream had come true. This was the advent of Christopher Fry on the British and American stage. It was like a friendly enemy moving in to disarm old rulers and hail the new. Soon, in one season there were four Fry plays on Broadway stages. And then, almost before the scholars had time to analyze this amazing phenomenon, it was as though a magician had whisked his handkerchief away and the game was over. I can still remember the one time I met Fry: he talked excitedly about *Curtmantle*, his next play; but as time went on, one delay followed another. I had the sense of new hopes quickly fading.

So to speak, I had smelled something in the air. What I had smelled was history's movement to a new period. Around midcentury there had been much talk of an intellectual religious revival, as exemplified by such writers as C. S. Lewis and Charles Williams; this atmosphere also worked in favor of Fry. Then came one of those abrupt mutations to which the stage in particular is so prone.* A hardbitten neo-naturalism swept the British and American stage. Suddenly, in the course of a few years, there seemed no further place for Fry. It was as crudely simple as that. If Fry had been overesteemed during his brief years of triumph, he was overneglected when the pendulum swung against him.

Other midcentury Christian writers, such as Lewis, Williams, Tolkien, and Sayers, have been more than adequately footnoted by the scholars, and a good start has been made in trying to see them whole. Perhaps it was Fry's sudden and almost total disappearance from public view that diverted the scholars away from him, toward writers who were more visible and seemed more exciting.

Professor Wiersma has now done what someone should have done decades ago. A brilliantly clear and incisive writer, and a man equally at home in literary criticism and theology, he has dared to look at Fry's corpus and see it whole. He is equally at home analyzing a play as play or a theological parallel as theology, and at ease most of all in helping the reader to see each literary work as a seamless unit.

This is a very difficult enterprise. The danger is that theology will swallow drama or drama will follow theology. It is a tribute to Dr. Wiersma's poise that he never loses his balance. Consistently, calmly, he keeps his composure throughout the book and thereby **helps us readers see Fry in all his fullness.**

Religion plays a role in one mode or another in all of Fry's plays. Sometimes they constitute a kind of parable. But to say merely that is to say little. What counts is what a writer does with these religious-literary forms. Fry sets them to dancing and singing, so that the whole landscape and sky awake and rejoice in the goodness of existence. (Here perhaps is one key to Fry's fall from popularity: he is too hopeful for this grim age.)

With growing awe, I have been jotting down some of the themes that Dr. Wiersma finds in Fry's plays. A very incomplete list: sainthood, incarnation, multiple vision, history and myth, the role of women, atonement, resurrection, law and sin, trinity, pacifism, spirititual evolution—but I choose to break off here, lest my little

*Lewis and Williams have become cult figures, but drama is a more public thing, requiring greater agreement between the members of the audience.

preface be longer than the author's book. Just as Fry's sensibility is undivided, so is Dr. Wiersma's perception of Fry.

This is an important book—important in its content, and with a significance extending beyond itself. It may well signal a turning point in popular and scholarly attitude toward Fry. For I see his works as either fading quietly and completely away or as returning —perhaps almost overnight—from a long hibernation in the cold world. Was Fry a fluke who briefly bewitched a dazed stage? Or was he indeed the poetic dramatist of enduring stature we had waited for? If the latter, I see in Dr. Wiersma's book the source of a new understanding of Fry which will encourage the lords of the theatre to re-examine his work.

In any case, the necessary book has been written, and brilliantly, and so the chips are down. Readers who choose to explore a Fry play will find they have here in one volume all that they need to know about the playwright in order to make up their own minds about him. They can explore Fry with the adroit aid of one who understands him profoundly.

The rehabilitation of Fry could conceivably be more than an isolated event. The man delights us, but he also teaches, and his teaching makes the world new. Through his work we see and sense the beauty of holiness and the holiness of beauty. We look at the world with fresh eyes. There is no better guide through this new world than Stan Wiersma.

—Chad Walsh

Acknowledgments

The body of Chapter 4 appeared in *Modern Drama* 8 (1965), 293–302; the explication at the end of 4 appeared in *The Explicator* 37 (1979), 29–31. Chapter 6 appeared in *The Grand Valley State College Review* 2 (1975), 17–32; Chapter 8 in *Ariel* 6 (1975), 17–32; and Chapter 9 in *The Christian Scholar's Review* 7 (1977), 119–137. Parts of Chapter 12 appeared in *Modern Drama* 13 (1971), 432–447. All appear here with slight emendation. Permission has been granted by all previous publishers.

Permission has also been obtained from Oxford University Press for all quotes from Fry's plays published by Oxford University Press.

Permission has also been obtained from the authors quoted in Chapter 14.

PRELIMINARY NOTES AND QUERIES 1

An Interior Dialogue

1. Q. Is Christopher Fry a theologian?
   A. No.
2. Q. Why should there be a book about his theology then?
   A. Anybody who thinks about God at all has at least an implied theology. Fry's thinking about God is inventive and adventuresome.
3. Q. Fry has made up a theology of his own, then?
   A. Fry has inherited the traditional theology of Western Christianity, and now he has modified it to suit his contemporary needs.
4. Q. He knows the Anglican Catechism and then goes from there on his own?
   A. He reads much more than the Catechism. He reads older religious writers like Johannes Eckhart and Sir Thomas Browne. He reads more recent religious writers like Nikolai Berdyaev and Søren Kierkegaard—especially Kierkegaard. And, of course, the Bible. He knows the Bible very well indeed.
5. Q. So he is a theologian after all?
   A. No. He does not study theology in the systematic way he would if he were a professor of theology or even a theological student. He has a rough-and-ready interest in church history and in the history of dogma; he has a fascination with the mystics outside the mainstream of

western Christianity and with Celtic Christianity. He has profound respect for the Bible, both as literature and as revelation. But all of his interest and fascination and respect is rough-and-ready—not superficial, but not directed at clarifying the issues, advancing new hypotheses in some narrow sub-discipline, or writing scholarly articles. A theologian, after all, is a skilled professional academician. Fry is a playwright.

6. Q. So Fry does not write his theology down?
   A. He has written at least four essays that in a broad sense could be called theological: "How Lost, How Amazed, How Miraculous We Are," "Comedy," "Death," and "Looking for a Language."[1]

7. Q. So then, obviously your method is to get his explicit theology from the essays and then illustrate those ideas from the plays?
   A. No. The theology implied in the plays is much more comprehensive than the theology in the essays. The theology in the essays serves as a control, but not as the basis for the book. Each play is allowed to speak for itself, with a chapter apiece on each major play. Sometimes the essays give a clue to the meaning of a play.

8. Q. The plays and the essays are your chief sources then?
   A. The plays are the chief source, but a fifteen-year correspondence with Fry, supplemented by a number of visits, is even more important than the essays. The essays are his intellectualized reflections about God and related matters, but the plays, letters, and conversations come closer to communicating his existential relationships to people, to the world, and to God.

9. Q. You feel you really know Fry then?
   A. He and I began corresponding after the essay on *A Phoenix Too Frequent*, my first published essay on Fry.[2] I had attempted to show that St. Paul's Epistle to the Romans was a source for *Phoenix*. I sent him a copy of the essay, he wrote back expressing appreciation for it and agreeing that Romans had been a source. We have corresponded ever since. During the summer of 1969

my family and I lived in England. We first met the Frys at a private production, the first, of *A Yard of Sun* on July 11. During that summer we visited some five times after that initial meeting. In 1973, my family and I again lived near the Frys, near Chichester, from January until June. I met Fry regularly, most often to discuss the first draft of one or another of the essays in this book. During the summer of 1976 I again lived in Fry's neighborhood and visited with him. His ethos as person—the sound of his voice, for instance—is useful for getting at the voices of the characters in the plays, not to mention the theology embedded in what they say.

10. Q. If he has read all of these essays on the plays and criticized them, is yours the authorized interpretation?

A. Not at all. Sometimes when Fry disagrees with my interpretations of his plays and formulations of his ideas, he persuades me and I make changes. Just as often, when Fry disagrees, he leaves me unpersuaded. For better or worse, the book is mine. Fry's opinions in conversations and letters are useful input, but the book remains my interpretation of the plays and the theology implied in them.

11. Q. Your book is written, then, to interest theologians in the plays of Christopher Fry?

A. If that is one of the results of my book, I shall be very happy. Actually, however, I am attempting to get the literary-critical establishment which dismissed Fry in the early sixties to see that their dismissing him resulted from an anti-theological bias. Establishing an a-theological basis for drama and for all of life, the establishment is as theological as Fry himself, in spite of its disclaimers. The Death-of-God movement in the sixties and its spinoff in a secular ethos did nothing to damage God, but it did damage some of God's followers, Fry included. Today, nothing is deader than the Death-of-God movement, but Fry's reputation has not rallied.

Immediately after the war, in 1950, Fry was on the cover of *Time*[3] and four of his plays were on Broadway at once—an honor no other playwright has experienced.

The popular audience then intuited the need for a new theology for a new world, and recognized it in Fry's plays: there were reassuring links to the theology of the past without involving a confining dogmatism or a scientifically disproved cosmology or a joyless puritanism. In short, Fry's rip-roaring comedy had implications to nourish the human spirit wounded by war. The time is coming again—it always does—when a new theology—really, a reinterpretation of the old one—will be necessary, and in this connection I think Fry's theology can be a help.

12. Q. Were there really four plays on Broadway at once?
    A. *A Phoenix Too Frequent, The Lady's Not for Burning, Ring Round the Moon* (translated from Anouilh), and *Venus Observed* all played between spring, 1950, and spring, 1951.

13. Q. Isn't *Lady* his most successful play?
    A. At the boxoffice, yes. Still, its ideas are less explicit than those of his other plays. It is the most consistently trivialized of all his plays, especially by amateur acting companies and college troupes. One feature of the organization of this book is that it makes it possible to crack *Lady*.

14. Q. How?
    A. The nine other plays are discussed first, chronologically. Next a summarizing chapter distills the archetypal form from all of the others. Then that archetypal form is applied to *Lady*, the play that everybody thinks is self-evident.

15. Q. Is that the extent of the book then?
    A. No, two chapters follow that: a summary and systemization of Fry's theology and, finally, a brief defense of it.

16. Q. Two summarizing chapters? How does the summary before *Lady* differ from the summary after it?
    A. The first gets at the archetypal form in diachronic order, the second at the intellectual-theological content in a synchronic organization.

17. Q. How are the nine chapters on plays other than *Lady* organized?

A. An essay on each play in chronological order, except that *Lady* is postponed until after a chapter that distills the archetypal form from the other nine.

18. Q. Isn't it unsatisfying, using a chronological order and then making a major exception to it?

A. Yes, but the work remains literary criticism as well as theology, and for that reason the book needs a critical problem to focus on, like getting *Lady* interpreted in the light of the other plays. The dual purpose, literary criticism and theology, works against a tidy organization.

19. Q. Are all of the plays of one type that they can be summarized so tidily, both as to literary form and theological content?

A. No. There are the plays which explicitly name God, written for performance in or near a church: *Boy with a Cart* (1939); *The Firstborn* (1946); *Thor, with Angels* (1948); and *A Sleep of Prisoners* (1951). All the other plays are written for performance in the secular theater and do not explicitly name God. The most important subgroup in these secular plays is the seasonal comedies: *The Lady's Not for Burning* (1949) for spring, *A Yard of Sun* (1970) for summer, *Venus Observed* (1949) for autumn, and *The Dark Is Light Enough* (1954) for winter. In addition, there is the one-act comedy, *A Phoenix Too Frequent* (1946), and the tragedy, *Curtmantle* (1961). So really, there are three types of plays: liturgical, comedy, and tragedy. I might add in this connection that the earlier critics, starting with Derek Stanford, considered the summer comedy in the seasonal plays to be *Phoenix*, since *Yard* was so long in coming. Before it had appeared, Fry identified *Yard* to me as the summer comedy.[4] Incidentally, from now on the following abbreviations will be standard: *Boy, Thor, Firstborn, Sleep, Lady, Yard, Venus, Dark, Phoenix, Curtmantle.*

20. Q. Wouldn't it be more satisfying to organize the book ac-

cording to the types of plays?

A. *Curtmantle* and *Phoenix* do not make a couple, except as "Other Plays." They would dangle as awkwardly in a generic organization as *Lady* in the organization chosen. Besides, for revealing the growth in Fry's theological perspective, a chronological organization is better. The one chronological lapse is to focus the whole book on the interpretation of *Lady*.

21. Q. Isn't Emil Roy's book[5] organized chronologically as well, and haven't the chronological points been made as well as they need to be?

A. Roy's book has taught us all very much indeed. The facts about Christopher Fry's life are as completely put down there as any person needs to know them in order to get at the plays. The history of each play on the stage, including players, directors, and critical reception, is all usefully recorded there. Besides, a sound and basic strategy of literary interpretation obtains in Roy's book; for analysis of plot, character, and theme the book is excellent. It even brings up Fry's religious ideas now and then. What it fails to grasp is that Fry's evolving religious ideas determine the need for each new work—either a new theological problem to work through or a new approach to a problem confronted before. The perception of the theological problem in each play determines the form of each play. Too often Roy's interpretations seem as though Fry's plays are formally and aesthetically autonomous, with Fry's theology thrown in—or creeping in—for good measure. Roy is too trapped in the methodology of old-style new criticism to see that the theology in each play determines the literary form.

22. Q. But certainly Nelvin Vos's earlier work on Fry is not subject to that same limitation, and it, too, is laid out chronologically.

A. Vos forges his critical instrument[6] to show how different Fry is from Thornton Wilder as humanist and from Ionesco as existentialist. In Vos's view, Fry becomes an inventive and creative spokesman for Christianity against the other two; his creativity lies mainly in how palatably he puts orthodoxy—almost as though Fry were an even more clever reincarnation of G. K. Chesterton as apologist. Vos's method, totally appropriate for his comparative purpose, does not do justice to Fry's struggle in sifting and winnowing his inherited orthodoxy or to the inventive shape Fry's theology takes.

23. Q. And what about you? Dutch Calvinist? Member of the Christian Reformed Church, one of the most traditional of churches and a tenured faculty member in a college supported by that church? Can you agree with everything Fry says and not be a hypocrite?

A. Theology needs to be rethought for our time if it is to survive our time. And so, although I generally agree with Fry's approach, agreeing or not agreeing is not my purpose in this book. My purpose is to explain as accurately as I can what Fry's theology is, as shown in his plays. To the extent that I disagree here or there, to that extent Fry and I are part of a family quarrel. Some essays for a Christian audience will be the project following this one, explaining where I disagree. This book pleads for the reasonableness of Fry's approach; to sprinkle my incidental dissatisfactions all the way through would dissipate its purpose.

24. Q. You are a Calvinist. Didn't you say somewhere that Fry is a Quaker?[7]

A. Yes, I said so, but Fry has never been a Quaker. All his life he has been associated with the Church of England, his father being a lay reader.

Christopher Fry was born "Arthur Hammond Harris" and took his maternal grandmother's maiden name, Fry, when he was seventeen. When I first knew Christopher Fry, in 1969, I asked him whether he was of the famous Quaker Fry family, including Elizabeth Fry, the prison reformer. His answer was affirmative. A whole lot fell into place: Fry's concern with violence in all of his plays and his living in Bedford as a child and his attending school there.

When I saw Fry again in 1973, he and his friend

Robert Gittings warned me about making much of Fry's Quaker connections. It seemed they suspected that Fry's side of the Fry family was not related to the Quaker side of the Fry family. The hard evidence appears in *Can You Find Me*, Fry's autobiographical account of his childhood:

> I was brought up believing the Frys were Quakers, and certainly if there is anything I have always 'felt in the blood and felt along the heart' it is this. Perhaps at some time they were. I'm reluctant to deny it after living with the belief so long and so compatibly, but the evidence is slight. There are deeds of 1701 and 1826 relating to the Quakers' burial ground at the east end of Axbridge, and years ago a cousin showed me a letter, since lost, written by one of the Frys in the mid-nineteenth century, which used the second person singular throughout, 'thees' and 'thous' of the Friends. In one of my Uncle Charlie's sketch-books illustrating the story of his life, he has written underneath a painting of his grandfather's house: 'Winscombe, centre of the Quaker religion'. But Peter and Joanna were buried in the Axbridge church, with a plaque on the wall to say so; and their son, Thomas Homfray, has a handsome stained-glass window to his memory in the church at Winscombe. It displays at its centre the coat of arms which this unoffending clan had somehow acquired; and very strange and unexpected it is. The nature of the Frys was steady, God-fearing, kindly, unassuming, and mildly humorous; but the coat of arms shows a mailed arm holding a sword, and on the sword is impaled the bloody head of a Moor. The motto reads: *Virtute et Numine.*[8]

The violent coat of arms is compelling evidence that Fry's Fry relatives are not related to the Quaker Frys. The extent to which Fry's thinking for so long that he was a Quaker by birthright influenced his ideas about violence, his change of name, or his insistence that "the Kingdom of Heaven is within you"[9]—the extent of that influence is not knowable, not even, perhaps, by Christopher Fry himself.

And so, contrary to all that is written about Fry's essential Quakerism in essays—critical, biographical, and popular, some of them by me—the answer is "No, Christopher Fry is not a Quaker and has never been."

25. Q. To get the design of Fry's theology, a reader ought to read your book straight through. It makes no sense to read the whole book unless the reader has also read the ten Fry plays. Only theologians are interested in the design of anybody's theology. How many theologians have read all of Fry's plays? Who will read your book?

A. Any person, theologian or not, who knows all of Fry's plays would have some interest, it would seem, in the coherent body of thought that Fry develops throughout his plays. My book is designed primarily for such a reader. A secondary use of the book, however, is to be a critical reference work on Fry. Anybody who has read only one play of Fry's will find a chapter written on that play, reading which chapter does not necessarily presuppose knowing all of the previous chapters in the book. It will probably be used more by people needing a line on a particular play than by people looking for the archetypal pattern of Fry's theology. The last two chapters are available for anybody who wishes to get at Fry as theologian without getting at Fry as playwright, although I hope there will be very few of these.

26. Q. Are you working, then, as a literary critic or as a theologian?

A. As a literary critic, trying to find the principle of wholeness in each of Fry's plays, which turns out to be a theological principle in every case. Then those theological principles together make a consistent pattern. To the extent that the whole book demonstrates that consistent theological pattern, to that extent I am working as a theologian. The way I get at each play, however, is very much in the tradition of literary criticism.

27. Q. Again, if every play holds together on a theological principle, isn't Christopher Fry a theologian?

A. Was Flannery O'Connor a theologian?

Was John Milton a theologian?
Was Isaiah a theologian?
Was Jesus the Christ a theologian?

28. Q. That is no answer. Is Fry a theologian?
    A. Well . . . no, I think. Still no.

29. A. Are you a theologian?
    A. No.

30. Q. How can you write a book about theology and not be a theologian?
    A. No comment.

SHOULDER TO SHOULDER WITH GOD 2

The Boy with a Cart

The first section of the prologue to *Boy*[1] identifies humanity's job as division and God's as provision. People divide the open country into fields; let some grow burdened and others lie fallow; plow one and graze cattle on another. People make distinctions between barn and stable, between cow and horse; between scythe, flail, and harrow—between harvesting, threshing, and seeding; between sheepshearing, milking, and mowing—getting clothing from animals, food from animals, and food for animals; between sowing and pruning, between what happens before plants sprout and after. In short, dividing things is humankind's distinctive labor, "older/Than knowledge." It is necessary work, but not the same work as God's.

God provides what people divide. In spring "the bud and shoot/ With pointing finger show the hand at the root"; bud and shoot are as opposite from root as anything can be within a vegetable organism. Moreover, the finger points two ways at once: points toward heaven as its source and toward the earth as its source. Only to a divider are the two directions different. God the provider surrounds both the heavens and the earth, and the barriers between them fall away. Thus, "Sky and root" are "in joint action," and the bleating lambs "ally" with sunlight and sprouting leaves. Joint actions of creatures becoming allied in himself is God's characteristic work. God provides, which means that God does the opposite of dividing. He links together what no mortal would have considered possible.

The second section of the prologue shows humankind still as the divider. Each person has one's own doorway, one's own garden gate, one's own private world of private memories and private shadows. The garden gate represents division from the next-door neighbor, and gossip represents the division of next-door neighbors from the third party gossipped about. The neighbors are not united in love but in common hostility toward someone else.

When April comes, God the provider breaks down barriers in all directions, and people get an inkling of work other than division. People begin to learn more from each other, "More than the gossip that comes to us over our gates." Gossip—facts or falsehoods taken to be facts—divides. More than interest in facts—real or fabricated—is involved when people see an old man "cracking" his memory for "dry milk," when they see an old woman "dandling shadows." In the middle of the gossip session, suddenly what is being gossipped about is less important than the isolation of the person gossipped with. Barriers crumble, and in such moods "we have felt/Heaven ride with Spring into the meadows." Heaven and nature, person and person are all destroying barriers—but only for a glimmering moment. The momentary intuition of spring does not last even as long as July.

The third part of the prologue presents the idea with greater urgency: we dividers want to join in God's work as provider, to break barriers down. The greater urgency is conveyed in the narrowing time references. Not only in spring, but also in the morning and evening, we hanker to share in God's work:

> We have felt the joint action of root and sky, of man
> And God, when day first risks the hills, and when
> The darkness hangs the hatchet in the barn
> And scrapes the heavy boot against the iron.

But discerning divinity is not the same as sharing in divinity's work. The human woodcutter remains human, hanging the hatchet in the barn in the evening, and humanity as woodcutter is different from humanity as housekeeper—the woodcutter must scrape off his boot before he may come in. We divide and are divided in spite of our discerning of divinity.

Discerning divinity and hankering to share in its work are the stock in trade of all pantheists and romantics, who are torn between hankering for lack of boundaries on the one hand and feeling trapped in a civilization that demands boundaries on the other. Could it have been the same William Wordsworth who inveighed against the railroad and who invested heavily in railroad stock? Hankering for unity and lack of barriers is not enough.

Still, it is better to be inconsistent and hanker for God than consistent and secular, and Fry makes the hankering compelling. We have, he says, "Guessed at divinity working above the wind,/ Working under our feet." We have guessed at the possibility of extremes being brought together. We have watched the miracle of the swift perpendicular flight of the lark:

> "Or at the end/Of a furrow, watching the lark dissolve in sun,/We have almost known, a little have known."

And all winter we have seen the Milky Way, but in spring the blackthorn bush blocks the view from our window, and suddenly the stars turn to flowers and the flowers to stars:

> . . . we have seen
> The blackthorn hang where the Milky Way has been:
> Flower and star spattering the sky.

Near and far cease to matter, it is all so urgent, but we cannot break out of our dividing. We are caught in the Platonic dualism of flesh and spirit, of Wordsworth's nature poetry and his railroad stocks. The demand within us to break down barriers and to join God's work is urgent, but we cannot break away the barriers which are necessary to civilized life. And hence our perceptions of God's providing are dulled: "We have discerned," and "guessed," "almost known," "a little have known," but only a little.

The fourth part of the prologue identifies dividing with death. The month is October and a falling star is burning itself out:

> Coming out from our doorways on October nights
> We have seen the sky unfreeze and a star drip
> Into the south: experienced alteration
> Beyond experience.

Death wrenches things apart; death is the great divider. All of humanity's distinctions and divisions have death in them, and winter. The evil in the universe is all related to the evil in humankind:

> . . . the jibbing, man destroying, denying,
> Disputing, or the late frost looting the land
> Of green.

That winter should come "looting" like a thief connects humanity's moral evils with the painful evils of nature. Lightning is the thief's "rifle" which destroys root and blade; floods come as murderers. The human tendency to divide is all of a piece with nature's divisions. And yet, despite human malignancy, which seems to have spread to the universe, "We have felt the grip/Of the hand on earth and sky in careful coupling" and "In root and sky we can discern the hand."

The real problem as presented in the first four sections of the prologue is that humankind feels intimations of God's providing, feels urgency to share in God's providing in addition to doing the distinctively human dividing, does share in God's providing on an elementary level. But God's work remains essentially foreign to humanity—except for the story of St. Cuthman. The conclusion of the prologue, in sketching what the play will be about, makes clear that the barriers between God's work and humanity's work can fall aside. The bondage to a Platonic dualism, with its restless yearning for unity, can be broken.

To be sure, Cuthman remains a divider: here and there, this occupation and that, space and time. He pulls a cart with his mother in it over five—not four or six—counties. He starts as a shepherd and ends as a carpenter. But in addition to being a divider, Cuthman is a provider. As an everyday provider he provides a living for himself and for his mother. More remarkably, he provides a church for his adopted town, Steyning. In the process of providing, he brushes all kinds of barriers aside and brings together what ought to be brought together and keeps together what might easily drift apart. The providing that a father does for a family keeps the family alive only incidentally; the separated members of the family could remain alive under other sponsorship. Keeping the family together is the father's task as provider; providing is the opposite of dividing. Thus any father participates in God's work on an elementary level, as long as the family stays together. In Cuthman, however, the skill at providing turns so advanced that the impossible happens: the human divider and God the provider are no longer to be distinguished from each other. "It is there in the story of Cuthman, the working together/Of man and God like root and sky. . ." The rest of the play explains in seven episodes how the impossible becomes possible.

EPISODE 1 (pp. 2–3):

As the first episode opens, Cuthman sees no difficulty in adjusting people's ways to God's ways. Weary of tending sheep because of his father's delay in letting him go home, Cuthman commits the sheep to God so he can have a quiet dinner. He draws a circle around the sheep and says, "God guard them here, if God will guard them." To the sheep he says, "Give no trouble," and the sheep do not break through the circle. It is the Eden of Cuthman's experience:

> This is the morning to take the air, flute-clear
> And, like a lutanist, with a hand of wind
> Playing the responsive hills, till a long vibration
> Spills across the fields, and the chancelled larches
> Sing like Lenten choirboys, a green treble;
> Playing at last the skylark into rising,
> The wintered cuckoo to a bashful stutter.
> It is the first day of the year that I've king'd
> Myself on the rock, sat myself in the wind:
> It was laying my face on gold. And when I stood
> I felt the webs of winter all blow by
> And in the bone-dry runnel of the earth
> Spring restart her flood.

Youth, spring, and Eden are all metaphors for each other in the first episode.

EPISODE 2 (pp. 3–10):

Episode 2 overlaps with Episode 1, for the messengers of Cuthman's fall hear him speak of youth, spring, and Eden without Cuthman's knowing what Eden is. Two neighbor women come to the pasture to confront Cuthman with the news that his father has died. The fall, here, is not a moral fall, but an encounter with pain. The chorus, The People of South England, articulates the meaning of the fall while Cuthman mourns silently:

The day is pulled up by the root and dries,
And the sun drains to the hollow sea.
Heaven is quarried with cries.
Song dies on the tree.

Then the chorus asks questions: "How is your faith now, Cuthman?" "Is God still in the air/Now that the sun is down?" "Can faith for long elude/Prevailing fever?" Cuthman answers that, indeed, he has "stayed too long with the children." He had not made his peace with time, accepting only "a brushwork sun skidding ahead of me/And not the dealer of days and the docker of time."

Cuthman's new awareness of death, pain, and time immediately reduces his power over the external world and alienates him from nature:

The circle is broken and the sheep wander.
They pull the branches of the myrtle under:
Nibble the shadow of the cypress, trample
The yew, and break the willow of its tears.
This is no grief of theirs.

His innocence about time and pain gave Cuthman a power over himself and nature which he did not appreciate. Now, having experienced pain, he appreciates the power but no longer has it. One has power over nature as long as one feels comfortable in it; alienated from it, one loses the power.

But the fall is not merely encountering evil as pain; it is also making moral decisions. Cuthman's decision to charm the sheep in a circle was motivated by his desire for a pleasant lunch hour. No sooner has Cuthman's father died than the roof is sold over his head, there is no money, and he is responsible for taking care of his old mother. His confidence in himself and his rapport with the outside world have vanished. Shall he bring the sheep home? He wants to know, only to be told there is no longer a home to bring them to. The issue is no longer whether his lunch hour will be pleasant or not. Encountering need, he encounters the possibility for evil. It is no accident that "And lead us not into temptation" begins with *and* and follows hard upon "Give us this day our daily bread" in the Lord's Prayer. Lack of bread makes people steal. As it turns out, Cuthman does not steal, but the plan he concocts is even stranger. Those who favor the blandness of life-adjustment as the cure for moral and social ills might wish he had stolen.

The idyllic days in the pasture had not yet really been the union of root and sky. God had done providing aplenty, but Cuthman had done too little dividing. Root was included in sky for Cuthman; he saw no distinctions. His fall makes a more mature relationship with God possible. That is why the chorus celebrates the "dereliction of a mild morning":

> Out of this, out of the first incision
> Of mortality on mortality, there comes
> The genuflexion, and the partition of pain
> Between man and God; there grows the mutual action,
> The perspective to the vision.
> Out of this, out of the dereliction
> Of a mild morning, comes the morning's motive,
> The first conception, the fusion of root and sky;
> Grows the achievement of the falling shadow,
> Pain's patient benediction.

The shadow is God's blueprint for Cuthman to realize; without pain Cuthman would achieve nothing.

EPISODE 3 (pp. 10-15):

Another way to put it: without pain Cuthman's reactions would have been more typical. He is forced by calamity to decide how to support himself and his mother. He could steal or work, but instead he does "something after his own heart." Episode 3 opens with the neighbors deploring what Cuthman decides. They would have understood theft better:

> What will the old woman do,
> Dear heart, with no roof over her head, no man,
> No money, and her boy doing nothing
> But make a cart?

The avoidance of pain, both psychological and physical, determines a person's needs and gives urgency to one's moral choices. The privateness of pain makes moral decisions arising out of the pain private, never quite what the neighbors would have expected.

Not even family understands the privateness of a person's response to pain. Hard upon the complaint of the neighbors,

Cuthman and his mother leave town. Cuthman is responsible for his mother and she loves him, but she cannot understand the privateness of his decision. She has told the villagers, "We are going away; Cuthman has found work to do," even though she knows he has not. Grief and pain have not brought her to urgent and personal moral decision; she is perfectly understandable when she complains that "there's no one to look after me except a fool of a son, and he wants to trundle me all over the world like a load of fish." While Cuthman obviously has the patience of a saint in dealing with his opaquely bourgeois mother, she certainly has her patience with him too. She is only an ordinary Christian, no saint whose legend will be dramatic substance ten centuries later. But unlike the other ordinary Christians of the village, she cannot ignore or ridicule Cuthman because he is her son.

Grief begins the process of sainthood in Cuthman, a process which divides him from other people, even from good people like his neighbors and his mother. Cuthman is learning what it means that humanity divides. Root and sky cooperate, but there is no way to get humankind to participate in the cosmic cooperation unless it first recognizes its tendency to divide and unless it learns how to reconcile its division with God's provision. Cuthman's naive inexperience was the condition for his original problem-free trust in God's provision.

EPISODE 4 (pp. 15–23):

The division between an ordinary Christian mother and a visionary Christian son is difficult enough. The division between the visionary son and the hostile non-Christian world is even more severe. This more severe division is the burden of Episode 4.

The ropes on the cart break and Cuthman's mother falls out of the cart, stiff and sore. Some mowers, busy at haying, laugh at the misfortune. They laugh even harder when Cuthman proposes to make some new ropes from withies.

At this point God intervenes. He causes a rain shower to wash away the hay of the mowers, even though Cuthman and his mother gather withies nearby in bright sunshine, wearing "the sun like a coat." Cuthman

felt the mood
Of the meadow change, as though a tide

Had turned in the sap, or heaven from the balance
Of creation had shifted a degree.
. . . .
At that place, and then, I tell you, Mother,
God rode up my spirit and drew in
Beside me.

At that moment Cuthman knows that where his new rope of withies breaks he must build a church. From the laughter Cuthman knows that the withies will break, but the laughter and the breakable withies help him find his purpose. The shower of rain is God's response to the hostile laughter of the mowers, but Cuthman's response to the laughter and to the shower is his vow to build a church where the withies break.

The tension between mother and son is progressively resolved. The saint recognizes his mother's everyday needs and gives them the priority over his own, if not in his heart, at least in his relationship with her. He realizes that she cannot be as interested in his projects as he is:

There, where they break,
Where God breaks them, you shall set up
House again and put clean paper on
Larder shelves.

He mentions his mother's housekeeping before he mentions his own chief concern. And when he declares to her his intention to build a church where prayer will be valid, he brings it up as a place for his mother to pray in: "a church to pray in/When you have put your broom away, and untied/Your apron." Cuthman has learned that saints cannot be spiritual snobs. Saints themselves are dividers; and although he aspires to be a provider, along with God, he cannot scorn people who remain dividers.

EPISODE 5 (pp. 23–29):

The withies break, and the evening turns a friendly face in the person of Old Tawm, who is trying to escape his over-protective children, who pursue him with extra clothes and coax him in from the evening air. Their solicitations have turned him crotchety: "What do they think I was born into this world for if it wasn't to die of it?" When Old Tawm's daughter giggles at Cuthman's being with an old woman, Tawm shows greater understanding than his daughter does: "You've got no understanding of geography, daughter. All the places in the world have their own ways and this young man is doing so because it's his way."

All kinds of role complements and role reversals take place at once. Cuthman's mother and the audience learn that if Cuthman had stayed at home with his mother, being solicitous for her, old age would have had other limitations for her, since Old Tawm is bored by his children. Tawm wants nothing more than involvement; Cuthman's mother could do with a little less involvement than Cuthman provides her. The two roles of the elderly complement each other.

Besides, Cuthman and his mother complement each other in handling the neighbors. When the withies break and the travellers stop, the villagers from Steyning gather around, but Cuthman cannot think of a thing to say. The mother is far less embarrassed: "They're welcoming us. It's like old times. It was just like this when your father brought me home on the back of his horse." All Cuthman can say to the questions of the villagers is, "I've come to build a church." His mother is far more adept at making friends with the villagers than he: "It's an idea that my boy has; he has got it very much at heart. But I don't know what we can be looking like; I can't imagine at all. You must take us for tramps. Before my husband died I always hoped that one day we'd see the country together, but it really is very tiring." She knows just how to give her single-minded son's project its due and yet change the subject before it puts off the villagers. Her bourgeois chit-chat, so foreign to Cuthman's concerns, is just right for smoothing the way between Cuthman and the community.

The upshot of his mother's diplomacy is that Cuthman is offered a job as a shepherd. From one point of view Cuthman is back where he started; from another, everything has changed. Before, being a shepherd was a way of helping his father; now, being a shepherd is the means to keep his mother and him alive while he builds the church. Before, God kept the sheep for Cuthman when he was having lunch—God helped Cuthman; now God is helping the whole community of Steyning through Cuthman. Had it not been so innocent, Cuthman's early possessiveness toward God would have been selfish. Suffering and conflict have brought human dividing and divine providing closer together:

God be on the hill, and in my heart
And hand. God guide the hammer and the plane.
As the root is guided. Let there be a church—

The tools for dividing like hammer and plane remain necessary, even for saints.

Episode 5 makes clear that Fry's preoccupation with root and sky is not doctrinaire pantheism. Such pantheism always insists on a false and absolute antithesis between civilization and nature. The absolute pantheist Cuthman was at the beginning would have seen the hammer and plane as threats; but Fry sees hammer and plane guided by God as much as roots are guided. Being civilized is as natural for a person as being a tree is natural for a tree. Unnaturalness is separating either civilization or nature from God and hence separating them from each other. Before his father's death Cuthman was a doctrinaire pantheist, and he is so no longer; but he still has more metamorphoses to undergo.

EPISODE 6 (pp. 29–36)

The problem with being a saint is to bring the internal relationship with God into harmony with the external world, both nature and society. Cuthman had not yet earned his harmony with nature when he charmed his sheep into not straying during his lunch break; Cuthman had not yet earned his harmony with society when the village women came to tell him of his father's death. He took his harmony with nature for granted, and he was snobbish toward the nice neighbors with long noses. Nature showed its hostile side in death, and society's hostility precipitated Cuthman's decision to leave town.

"Nice neighbors with long noses" first brought Cuthman the news of his father's death in Episode 2. The theme of "nice neighbors" is carried forward by Cuthman's mother, exemplifying secular society's lack of comprehension of the saint but its good-natured tolerance just the same. The theme of "long noses" is carried forward by the hostile mowers, exemplifying secular society's unjustified hatred of saints. Cuthman is learning to appreciate society in the person of his mother, in spite of her lack of comprehension, and to endure the enemies.

Cuthman is also learning to trust nature, in spite of death and evil. That the cart ropes break shows the hostility of nature; that the rain shower punishes the mowers shows the friendliness of nature.

When the withies break, this comes as a sign from God that a church needs to be built at Steyning; when the ropes broke earlier, this came as a sign of the hostility of nature. Cuthman's attitude has changed so that the breaking of the withies is a sign of God's goodness; but if Cuthman is right about the withies, then the breaking of the rope the first time and the death of the father were also signs of God's goodness. His response to these earlier evils makes the present good possible. The complexity of the problem is that evil remains evil, even though God's grace and a saint's vision can change evil into good.

These four themes all converge in Episode 6: belonging to nature and being at odds with nature, belonging to society and being at odds with society.

Cuthman cannot build a church single-handed. Even if he could, the building would only look like a church but would not be a church. Churches need community. And Cuthman has mobilized the entire community to help him build. A farmer donates ground, a builder bricks, a woodman timber; and after their own work is finished each day, all the villagers help with the building, filling every evening with song. Cuthman belongs to the community.

But in another way Cuthman does not belong to the community. The Fipps family—Alfred, Demiwulf, and their mother—is disenchanted. Not only do they refuse to work, they also agitate against Cuthman in the community and steal his oxen. The opposition is much more focused and organized than was the earlier, more casual taunting of the mowers. Cuthman and his mother had only to walk away from them; they had no power to impede the journey. But the Fipps family can do political damage to Cuthman's project, and they do tangible damage by stealing the oxen. Cuthman cannot walk away from the society with which he is at odds.

That Cuthman and his project are part of the community shows God's providing. That any specialized project, no matter how sound, alienates part of the community is the result of human dividing. Innocent dividing includes one man's being a farmer and another's being a banker, includes the nuclear family and well-defined hedgerows. But dividing always runs the risk of turning malignant, in this case dividing Cuthman from the Fipps family and threatening to divide Cuthman from the whole community.

The resolution of the problem with the Fipps family demonstrates how Cuthman is both one with nature—God's providing—and apart from nature—humanity's dividing. God and nature provide a whirlwind which carries Mrs. Fipps five miles away and drops her in a pond; God and nature make clear that Mrs. Fipps is not on the right side. When God defended Cuthman against the mowers through nature, the end result was only that Cuthman and his mother felt better. In the Fipps incident, God and nature not only protect Cuthman but also advance his project.

But Cuthman is also at odds with nature, as any civilized person tends to be. More than ever, he must divide nature: hewing timber, laying brick, being a carpenter. He is also a divider in coping with the rebellious Fipps boys. Cuthman does not wait for another whirlwind to restore the oxen. Since the boys will not surrender the oxen, he works a charm on them which renders them docile as oxen. He puts the yoke on them, and they work for him. Cuthman sees this as of a piece with his charming the sheep to stay within a circle in the first episode.

> One day I took a crook
> And drew a circle in pasture; and to-day
> I draw a circle here to guard the church,
> A circle of a stronger faith than I
> Could ever have mastered then.

His purpose now is far more urgent than an undisturbed lunch break. Before, he was a provider with God without knowing it, back in the meadows; maybe he had even substituted himself in the place of God. But now he is more self-conscious. He knows that he is different from God and that he cannot do very much providing along with God unless he is also willing to do a great deal of very ordinary dividing. To provide for his mother and himself, he must divide himself from other jobs and occupations and be a shepherd; to provide a church for Steyning, he must divide himself from other jobs and occupations and be a carpenter. Now, forcing the hostile Fipps boys under the yoke, Cuthman is also doing the difficult work of division. His charm on the sheep was glib and easy, but this charm on the Fipps boys is as difficult as carpentry. A townsman makes the connection between the charm and carpentry:

It is neither anger nor fun.
It is the same stress that we see
Knotting his forearm and kneading his forehead
To drops of sweat when he wrestles
With timber in the framework of the church.

Dividing is always hard work, and to the extent that Cuthman must still work at dividing, he is not yet thoroughly one with nature or society.

Cuthman is at one with society and not at one with society, at one with nature and not at one with nature. He is not totally comfortable, but he can cope.

EPISODE 7 (pp. 36–39):

God the provider always goes beyond the providing Cuthman does. Cuthman provides withies, but God sends the shower on the mowers. Cuthman yokes the Fipps boys, but God carries Mrs. Fipps off in a whirlwind. And now Cuthman has provided a comfortable place for his mother in the community, but God provides the husband. Old Tawm, the very first person they greeted entering Steyning, proposes marriage. Cuthman provides by dividing—by being a diligent shepherd and a diligent carpenter and by yoking up the Fipps boys when necessary—but he also provides by letting God provide. The projected marriage is the best sign possible that belonging and not belonging in the community is not an insuperable problem.

Nor is belonging and not belonging to nature an insuperable problem. True, gravity and other predictable forces of physical matter make the king-post of the church slip out of place, and that upheaval wrenches the entire building off its foundation. Nature is as impersonally hostile as when it brought death to Cuthman's father or when the ropes broke on the cart to make the mowers laugh. Being at odds with nature in this way puts Cuthman at odds again with society. One by one the laborers give up and leave; they plead inexperience, improper tools, and fatigue. The wrenched king-pin brings about a mutiny greater than the Fipps boys could have envisioned.

Only Cuthman remains behind in the church, facing east in prayer. Then he realizes he is not alone:

I was alone by the unattended pillar,
Mourning the bereaved air that lay so quiet
Between walls; hungry for hammer-blows.
And the momentous hive that once was there.
And when I prayed my voice slid to the ground
Like a crushed pediment.
There was a demolition written over
The walls, and dogs rummaged in the foundations,
And picnic parties laughed on a heap of stone.
But gradually I was aware of some one in
The doorway and turned my eyes that way and saw
Carved out of the sunlight a man who stood
Watching me, so still that there was not
Other such stillness anywhere on the earth,
So still that the air seemed to leap
At his side. He came towards me, and the sun
Flooded its banks and flowed across the shadow.
He asked me why I stood alone. His voice
Hovered on memory with open wings
And drew itself up from a chine of silence
As though it had longtime lain in a vein of gold.
I told him: It is the king-post.
He stretched his hand upon it. At his touch
It lifted to its place. There was no sound.
I cried out, and I cried at last "Who are you?"
I heard him say "I was a carpenter" . . .

Not "I am Jesus the Christ," or "The Son of God," or even "The Man of Sorrows," or any other word that does not show God doing the typically human work of dividing.

A romantic pantheist construes God in the rigid definition of the first part of the prologue: God the provider and the human person the divider. Simply growing up teaches that pantheist that the human person can provide by dividing, that a person can keep a family together by schedules, by a trade or profession, and by specialization. Human sharing in God's work of providing by means of dividing was the burden of the second, third, and fourth parts of the prologue, each of which expressed the need for fuller participation with God than had the one before. The fifth part of the prologue promised something more to be presented in the story of Cuthman.

That something more was slow in coming. From Episode 2 through Episode 6, Cuthman aspires to join in God's work with greater and greater urgency, and does join in it, though never as much as he aspires to. And it is not yet the "working together/Of man and God like root and sky" which the prologue had promised. Even at the end of Episode 6 Cuthman could be called a pantheist, though a restless, unsettled pantheist. He is no longer the pantheist who sees only God as provider and humanity as dividers, all yearning to be providers like God. He has done just enough providing through dividing so that by the end of Episode 6 he is thoroughly compromised as a pantheist. He could easily become Wordsworth at that point, making money from railroad stock while deploring industrialization. Avid pantheism cannot endure life in the everyday world; striving to join God as provider, pantheists find themselves turning into dividers in spite of themselves; and thus they are awkwardly caught in divided and distinguished worlds with all other Platonists, neo-Platonists, idealists, and romantics. The prologue expressed this compromised pantheism, but promised something beyond it in the story of Cuthman. The story of Cuthman progressed through six episodes, and still there was the compromised pantheism, expressed with greater and greater urgency to unite with God, but finding only practical, everyday methods of making progress—by dividing.

The something more that the prologue promised in the story of Cuthman is revealed in Episode 7 to be the Incarnation. Not only do persons learn to provide by dividing, as all mature pantheists know; but God also provides by dividing, not only becoming a human being but specifically becoming a carpenter. All the work of humankind—even railroads—is also the work of the kind of God who becomes a carpenter. It was no figure of speech in the prologue that "with God we work shoulder to shoulder." God has a physical shoulder like our own. The distinction made in the first part of the prologue, God providing and humankind dividing, has vanished.

Pantheists affirm much, but *Boy* affirms more. The carpenter comes, and Cuthman belongs to the community entirely. The rebellious workmen fall to their knees, not now requiring the oxen's yoke but willingly submitting to the carpenter whose yoke is easy and whose burden light. The carpenter comes, the stubborn and unruly timbers become a church again, and Cuthman belongs to nature again. Not belonging to society is death, not belonging to nature is death, and recognizing that one does not satisfactorily belong to either nature or society is spiritual death: alienation. The play is really about the contention of belonging with not belonging, of life with death. While the community kneels before the repaired church towers, Cuthman says:

> There under the bare walls of our labour
> Death and life were knotted in one strength
> Indivisible as root and sky.

An incarnate God renders all distinctions between providing and dividing superfluous, renders pantheism and romanticism limited and hence wrong, and renders a harmonious life in both nature and society a possibility.

The epilogue, like the prologue, deals with providing and dividing but not with the neat distinction of God's providing and humankind's dividing. God does both. He leads "the earth to drink at the sky" as though he were a shepherd leading earth by his "hand." And if a carpenter and a shepherd, why not a postman?

> And still
> The messenger rides into the city of leaves
> Under the gradual fires of September.

And what is the message of the postman?

> The Spring shall hear, the Winter shall be wise
> To warning of aconite and freezing lily,
> And all shall watch the augur of a star
> And learn their stillness from a stiller heaven.

The message of the postman is life (belonging to society, to nature, and to God) and death (not belonging to society, to nature, and to God). In his spring Cuthman had heard about and observed life and death, but he was not wise about them until his winter. For winter is the season of Advent, Christmas, Epiphany, and of a particularly bright star in Bethlehem which augurs for life. Incarnation is what *Boy* is about.

The second part of the epilogue hints for the first time that we of the audience may conceivably be not with Cuthman but with Mrs.

Fipps and the mowers:

> And what of us who upon Cuthman's world
> Have grafted progress without lock or ratchet?
> What of us who have to catch up, always
> To catch up with the high-powered car, or with
> The unbalanced budget, to cope with competition,
> To weather the sudden thunder of the uneasy
> Frontier?

Fry's list includes us all, if not with Mrs. Fipps at least with Cuthman's mother. What rain shower or verbal whirlwind will Fry evoke to carry us off to where all doctrinaire dividers like ourselves deserve to go?

Whatever God did to the mere dividers who crossed Cuthman in his high purposes, whatever hagiographers fabricated into the Cuthman chronicle, Fry uses other methods. Within the play itself he uses the rain shower, the whirlwind, and the yoking of the Fipps brothers more like practical jokes than like grim visitations from God. And now in the epilogue he appeals to us to recognize that we are not merely dividers but providers too, and that God is a divider as well as a provider. If we had to turn abruptly from one to the other, a whirlwind or shower might help; but what we really need is to reconcile both: to become providers without surrendering our capacity for dividing and to worship Christ as provider while accepting him as fellow divider. It is a subtle transition, the providing giving purpose to the dividing, and the dividing making practical the other-worldly providing. "An angle of experience" Fry has called the change elsewhere.[2] The epilogue says it is as subtle as "a moth" brushing "a window with its wing."

Given how subtle the transition is from unbelief to faith,

> Who shall question then
> Why we lean our bicycle against a hedge
> And go into the house of God?

The bicycle is just right, because it is an instrument of division; and leaning it against a hedge suggests an errand not yet completed, interrupted by a church service. The whole play emphasizes the this-worldly and the other-worldly, both of them dividing and providing.

The change from unbelief to faith is so subtle that one can answer only for oneself whether the change has taken place within:

> Who shall question
> That coming out from our doorways
> We have discerned a little, we have known
> More than the gossip that comes to us over our gates.

The similar lines in the prologue were less compelling, for there they represented a romantic, pantheistic scorn for the life of gossip. Here not even the gossip is scorned. Gates and doorways still divide as they did in the prologue, but they are also the entrances by which we can provide one another with our presence. What we say to each other may be only gossip, but any communication with another person, no matter how trivial, is already providing and being provided for at an elementary level. Gossip hardly deserves to be a start, but when the process is finished all things will have become new.

SINGLE, DOUBLE, AND MULTIPLE VISION 3

The Firstborn

Fry's preoccupation with coincidence must have first attracted him to the biblical narrative of Moses. The birth of Moses coincided with the decree of Pharaoh that all Hebrew babies be killed. His mother's putting him afloat in an ark of rushes coincided with Pharaoh's daughter's coming to the river to bathe. Pharaoh's daughter's sending for a nurse for the baby coincided with the scheme springing up in Miriam's mind to offer the services of her mother as the baby's nurse. Later Moses thinks he has not been seen killing an Egyptian, but fellow Israelites happened to see it, making it necessary for Moses to flee to Midian.

Preoccupation with coincidence implies double or multiple vision. The human faculty of common sense always insists stubbornly that chance brings two events together arbitrarily, and common sense makes for single vision. But another human faculty argues just as stubbornly that a controlling consciousness has made these two events occur together with one's self and/or one's cause in mind; the common sense view arguing against this conviction is double vision. Multiple vision is common sense arguing against the conviction that coincidences occur for the ultimate good of *all* individuals and for what is right in *every* cause, contradictory as these individuals and causes may seem among themselves. Double and multiple vision are Fry's trademark as playwright.

A secular account of a coincidence emphasizes chance; a mythical account of the same coincidence emphasizes only divine control. In the Bible, God gives Moses a verbal command to return to

Egypt to lead the Israelites out of the Egyptian bondange, and it is God who sets up all of the coincidences. They begin immediately. No sooner has Moses pleaded slowness of speech than God says that his brother Aaron will be his spokesman, and Aaron is on his way to see Moses.

In the mythical version found in the Bible, God manipulates the coincidences. He orders Moses to predict a plague on the Egyptians if Pharaoh does not let the people go; next, God "hardens Pharaoh's heart" so that he refuses to let the people go; then God finds it necessary to follow through on his threat and sends the threatened plague. And so God, responding to the obstinacy he awakens within the heart of Pharaoh, turns the water bloody and spreads frogs, maggots, flies, lice, one after the other; he then sends hail on the harvest about to be reaped and sends grasshoppers to consume what recovers from the hail. He sends three days of darkness to halt all civilized commerce. Finally, he sends the angel of death to kill all of the firstborn of Egypt. At last Pharaoh begs the Israelites to go. The myth makes a coincidence of each plague with Pharaoh's hardness of heart, because God controls both. It is not "only a coincidence" of common sense reasonableness but is God investing coincidence with meaning.

A myth always begins as a religious corrective to an obviously secular series of events. A myth begins in the interests of double vision. It was not evident to the Egyptians, to the Israelites, or to Moses while they were experiencing it that the season of the natural disasters would be the season of deliverance for Israel. It seemed to be only a purely political struggle between Israel and Egypt. But when it was clear that the Israelites were free, it seemed a miracle too good to be true. The Israelites realized then that they could never have succeeded without God. God must have been *in* the series of natural disasters and *in* the vacillating heart of Pharaoh. God alone, says the myth, made the deliverance possible —but all the while the myth assumes the memory of the literal facts of the secular history as it was lived, very much the way life is always lived. The myth alone is an escape from the world; the literal history alone is the secular escape from God. The literal history and the mythical interpretation together provide the basis for double vision and multiple vision, either vision being necessary if a person is to live a religious life and remain living in the world.

The difficulty comes when the literal history is long forgotten by

Egyptians and Israelites alike and when all that exists is the myth. The stylized myth is then taken for literal history, and the double vision of life, which the myth exists to promote, vanishes. The Christian tradition, which has always looked at the Exodus account as literal history, has lost the double vision assumed by the account. The popular religious belief then holds that in biblical times God sent plagues, hardened hearts, and made seas divide; now, of course, God no longer works that way. Now we have natural disasters; psychological cases like Hitler, Nixon, and Khoumeni; and lucky experiments like walking on the moon. The common religious assumption is that in earlier times God influenced history but that now God leaves us alone. The Bible gives a splendid account of the Exodus, but the newspapers are sufficient for the president's latest budget cut.

Christopher Fry's *The Firstborn* exists to restore the double and multiple vision: the literal and religious together for the benefit of ourselves and our side (the double vision) or for the benefit of all selves and all sides (the multiple vision). The double vision and the multiple vision apply not only to the time of the Exodus but also to our own. The stylized myth is Fry's only source, but he supplies from his imagination the literal world to establish the strong polarity between the literal and the mythic.

In the mythical account, with the triumphant escape from Egypt a recent fact, the Israelites saw Moses as armed in the Spirit and proceeding from strength to strength against Pharaoh. But a person's faith is never as statically complete as the faith of Moses seems to be, from the burning bush through the Exodus. The Freudian debunking of a general like MacArthur follows his victories by at least a decade. In the excitement of victory one is not likely to dwell on a general's setbacks, ambiguities, and crises of confidence.

Oddly, a Christian source, the Epistle to the Hebrews, is at variance with the Exodus account when it dwells on the identity crisis that must have gone on in Moses in overthrowing the Egyptian regime. Not only had the Egyptians spared his life as a baby; they had made him a prince of the realm. The Epistle to the Hebrews makes clear that for Moses in the actual process of leading the revolt of Israel, there were preferences to be determined, refusals to be made, stigmas to be borne as stigmas, without a clear vision of the outcome:

> "By faith Moses, when he was come to years, refused to be called the son of Pharaoh's daughter; choosing rather to suffer affliction with the people of God, than to enjoy the pleasures of sin for a season; esteeming the reproach of Christ greater riches than the treasures in Egypt: for he had respect unto the recompence of the reward. By faith he forsook Egypt, not fearing the wrath of the king: for he endured, as seeing him who is invisible". (*Hebrews 11: 24–27*)

If Moses could without a qualm have destroyed the Egyptians who adopted him, he would have been an insensitive brute to the people who had loved him. How could he then have had the sensitivity to love God? On the day of the Exodus the Israelites remembered the tentativeness of the process, but a victory celebration is not the time to express that tentativeness. In fact, the more one is aware of how tentative the whole process has been the more one is likely to make the victory account an inevitable success from the start. Separating the account of the Exodus from the occasion of its being written makes Moses a super-human hero, makes it impossible to see what really happened, and makes the religious experience different from any religious experience available to people today.

Fry's Moses shows a growing God-consciousness, the process mentioned in the Epistle to the Hebrews. Fry's Moses first confronts Seti, the Pharaoh, in the secular cause of "justice for my people" (23). Not long after, Moses begins to discover both God and the religious awareness of the Israelites: "We have a God who will support the spirit,/And both shall be found" (30). Our need, says Moses, is "To confront ourselves, to create within ourselves/ Existence which cannot fail to be fulfilled" (39).

Revelation in the biblical Exodus account is triumphantly presented as a painless transmission of information and inspiration; for Fry and for the Book of Hebrews, a person must discover, often at great pain, whatever God reveals; whatever a person discovers, no matter how great the individual's effort and pain, God reveals. Celebrating the revelation achieved, one does not dwell on the pain, but that does not nullify the pain.

Fry's Moses comes to understand this process: "My people shall become themselves,/By reason of their own god who speaks within them" (49). As the story is told afterwards, it will seem inevitable that every plague should follow its prediction, but Fry's Moses in the thick of events is frankly surprised that the water is turned to blood:

> We with our five bare fingers
> Have caused the strings of God to sound.
> Creation's mutehead is dissolving, Aaron.
> Our lives are being lived into our lives.
> We are known! (53)

The God-consciousness of Fry's Moses is at once a grace granted and a point-of-view achieved, as it is for any religious person in any age. True, Moses experiences here only the double vision of God's love for Israel in tension with everyday reality; the multiple vision of God's love for all the world comes to Moses later.

Opposite to Moses stands Seti, whom the biblical account depicts as a humorless tyrant. The Israelite victory, of course, made him a tyrant, totally evil, just as the Allied cause and victory of World War II made Hitler totally evil and kept him evil in popular consciousness for four decades. Not until the mid-70's did the home movies of Hitler and Eva Braun show that he was also a vulnerable human being after all; and at the same time a sympathetic movie starring Alec Guinness revealed Hitler as a pitiful psychopath, but also one who brought law and order into a chaotic Germany. One never looks to the winning army in the moment of victory for a fair assessment of the enemy Pharaoh. Not even God's people can be perfectly fair then.

Fry transforms Moses from the static icon of the biblical account into a learning, progressing pilgrim of any time, including our own. Just so, Fry transforms the static villain of the biblical account into a recognizable chief of state. He is not a devil who perversely seeks evil. His is the subtler fault of seeing no good beyond the Egyptian state; any attitude or action is right if it supports the security of the realm. In that respect Seti is no different from any political leaders of any time who get away with much in the name of national security. Seti justifies the slavery of the Israelites because it makes Egypt great: "I have put men to a purpose who otherwise/Would have had not the least meaning" (23). He is the super-patriot, for whom Egypt is the ultimate concern: "My trust is Egypt/And the maturity of the world" (49). With the state his ultimate concern and with a civilized poise his manner, he is incapable of the double vision which allows time and eternity to interact. He insists on the literal view of the plagues, as we today might read about them in the newspaper:

> I'll not be panicked by this chain
> Of black coincidence, which he [Moses] with his genius
> For generalship has taken advantage of.
> He presumes upon the eternal because he has
> No power to strike his bargain. I have not done
> These things to Egypt. I'll not hear it be said. (64)

Seti is exactly what we expect any head of state to be, in our time too. One has only to remember the furor during the 50's when the Queen of the Netherlands consulted a divine healer for her handicapped child. We will allow chiefs of state to make a discreet prayer in an established church, but let them construe coincidences as miracles or see evidence of a divine plan in world events, let them develop a double vision which adjusts human ways to the ways of God, and the secular state has no more use for them. Seti's lack of double vision makes him a particularly excellent chief of state by the standards of our twentieth-century audience.

Heroism on the enemy side is unfashionable for a quarter of a century after victory; it takes even longer to discover the cowardice and duplicity on the winning side. But just as the Germany of Hitler was also the Germany of Adelbert Stifter and Wilhelm Kempff, and just as the Allies led by heroes like Churchill and Roosevelt developed the atomic bomb and leveled Dresden, just so there must have been good on the Egyptian side and evil on the Hebrew side, even though the biblical account, composed in the full flush of victory, simplifies matters. Fry handles this phenomenon by making the person most like Seti an Israelite and by making the person most like Moses an Egyptian.

Rameses is Seti's firstborn son, whose upbringing in the Egyptian palace was identical to that of Moses, and whose earliest hero worship was directed toward Moses. He follows Moses from the palace to the encampment of the Israelites after the first fruitless encounter between Seti and Moses and makes it clear where his identification with the father image lies:

I haven't come
From my father. I used schoolboy's worship, like myrrh
And cassia, to perpetuate you:
The immense and affable god in general's uniform,
Who came and went between wars, who filled the schoolroom;
And I could call him uncle. (31)

As soon as Rameses is convinced of the justice of the Hebrew cause, he takes steps to right matters. He uses his position to protect Shendi, the nephew of Moses, from the law; he uses his influence to get Shendi a good position in the Egyptian army; when his father abdicates and leaves him the throne, Rameses makes it clear that he will free all of the Israelites.

Yet Rameses is the firstborn son and hence is a victim of the angel of death in the tenth plague. As soon as Moses understands the implication of the tenth plague for Rameses, he rushes from the Hebrew ghetto to the Egyptian palace in order to save Rameses. But God's stipulation requires blood over the door, and the stipulation is not met. The destroying angel arrives at the same moment as Phipa, the princess of Syria, who has come to marry Rameses. Phipa comes with the promise of life, but the grim reality is the angel of death.

Rameses identifies both with Moses and Seti, with Israel and Egypt; and these identifications give Rameses the multiple vision lacking not only in Seti but in Moses as well, at least at the start. Seti has the narrow vision of his responsibility to a great civilization. Moses has the double vision of his dual responsibility to God and to Israel. Rameses has the multiple vision of responsibility to God, to Egypt, and to Israel. Rameses is superior to the double-visioned Moses, yet Rameses must die.

The circumstances surrounding the death of Rameses catapult Moses from his double vision into multiple vision. He has argued for God and Israel against Egypt all along; but when he thinks of Rameses as a vulnerable firstborn, he rushes to the aid of Egypt; and at that point he achieves multiple vision: responsibility to God and to all people, whether Egyptian or Hebrew. The pain of living in divided and distinguished worlds is brought home to Rameses by the simultaneous arrival of Phipa and the angel of death; the same kind of pain is brought home to Moses by the simultaneous delivery of Israel and the death of Rameses. Now Moses feels blind and despairing:

> All was right, except this, all, the reason,
> The purpose, the justice, except this culmination.
> Good has turned against itself and become
> Its own enemy. Have we to say that truth
> Is only punishment? What must we say
> To be free of the bewildering mesh of God?
> Where is my hand to go to? Rameses,
> There's no more of me than this. This is all:
> I followed a light into a blindness. (92)

Moses feels blind and despairing, but that feeling is actually progression in his understanding of God. God must be the God of Egypt as well as of Israel if God is to be God:

> Anath—Egypt,
> Why was it I had to be disaster to you?
> I do not know why the necessity of God
> Should feed on grief; but it seems so. And to know it
> Is not to grieve less, but to see grief grow big
> With what has died, and in some spirit differently
> Bear it back to life. (94)

Moses is saying that nothing but the death of Rameses—or something equally devastating—could ever have made him progress from his double vision of God and Israel to his multiple vision of God and everyone, Egypt too.

What the plight of Israel had been to Moses, the plight of everyone becomes. During his double vision of God and Israel, Moses had reasoned his case for activism in response to the Hebrew martyrs under Egyptian oppression:

> Death was their question to us, and our lives
> Become their understanding or perplexity.
> And by living to answer them, we also answer
> Our own impermanence. (29)

As Moses awakens to multiple vision, the death of Rameses is the question of Rameses to Moses, and the life of Moses begins to embody the understanding or perplexity of Rameses. By living to answer Rameses, Moses will answer his own questions about his own purpose in the light of mortality. It is in this sense that Rameses is "here pursuing the ends of the world" (94) even though he is Egyptian and even though he has died.

It is a good bargain, even for Rameses. While Rameses had surpassed Moses at the beginning of the play in the same way that multiple vision surpasses double vision, Moses had surpassed Rameses from the start in translating vision into political action. Rameses promotes Shendi to the rank of officer in the Egyptian army, and immediately the freed slave out-Egyptians the Egyptians in cruelty. Even Rameses' most elementary political efforts backfire, in spite of the rightness of his multiple vision: God, Egypt, and Israel. Rameses is frustrated:

> It's insufferable
> That my voice, without the accompaniment of good fortune,
> Should be so out of key, so faltering,
> So cracking with puberty. —Aunt Anath,
> What's the meaning of my manhood, to be found
> So helpless, to be so helpless: what is there to do
> Which I could do and haven't yet seen? (71)

Paradoxically, by dying Rameses overcomes his own inability to act. His death brings about an action within the mind of Moses, the movement from double vision to multiple vision; and that action within the mind of Moses has political consequences for the good of the whole world.

Thus, at the beginning of the play, Rameses is superior to Moses; he is a more complete visionary, seeing God and all sides of all conflicts related to each other, while Moses saw only God and his own side. But by the play's end, Moses is the superior character, for he is both a multiple visionary and a man of action, while Rameses is only a multiple visionary.

In Fry's own words, "Rameses is the innocence, humanity, vigour and worth which stand on the enemy side, not altering the justice or necessity of Moses' cause, but linking the ways of men and the ways of God with a deep and urgent question-mark" (5). Rameses is Fry's way of cleaning out the propaganda of World War II from his own heart and life.

Parallel to the good on the Egyptian-German side is the evil on the Hebrew-Allied side. Though he is the son of Miriam, the sister of Moses, though he has the miracle of the Exodus going on all around him, though he is given every opportunity to develop a double vision of the ways of God with Israel and even the multiple vision of the ways of God with all people, Shendi remains unimpressed. He can see no further than his own personal advantage. Institutionalize his single vision, put him in authority with sufficient power to enforce it, and you have Seti. What Rameses is to Moses, Shendi is to Seti: a younger version on the opposite side.

We first see Shendi bursting into Miriam's tent under pursuit of two Egyptian overseers. He has been involved in a Hebrew strike against Seti's order to gather straw for the bricks as well as supply the daily quota of bricks. In spite of Moses' being his only hope, he is contemptuous of his uncle:

> Who's that?
> My uncle, is it? The great fellow that was.
> The man who thought he was Egypt. Have you come
> To try again, murderer? Look at your crop of relations
> And how they do in the land you dunged for us.
> Do you hear that? They're whipping the side of the tent.
> You know I can't stand up, they've come for me,
> You know it was the sun—uncle, uncle! (38)

Shendi's only concern is his own hide and, in his better moments, his mother's; but his concern is never Israel.

When Shendi bursts into the Hebrew camp in flight from the Egyptian police, he does not know that Rameses is part of the company. When the police appear, Rameses orders Shendi released. The episode works strongly on Rameses; and home in the palace, he sets the machinery in motion to have the Hebrew Shendi appointed an Egyptian overseer. The move is evidence of the multiple vision of Rameses: God is the God of all nations.

But Rameses also shows his political ineptness in making Shendi the vehicle for bringing the two nations together. Once an overseer, Shendi is more Egyptian than the Egyptians. He and his mother move out of the Hebrew ghetto and into Shendi's new officers' quarters. When Moses pleads with Shendi to renounce his commission for the sake of Israel, Shendi shows that his contempt for Moses and Israel has not abated since his commission:

> Listen to that!
> As my uncle happens, this is no surprise.
> Only one of the family must rise
> And glow in Egypt. The rest of us can keep

> Against the ground, and lose the whole damned world
> Because Moses prefers it. (57)

Worse, Shendi is even more cruel to the Hebrew slaves than the Egyptian overseers have been. Shendi's single vision allows him to be cruel without feeling guilt; like Seti, he considers the cruelty necessary. The multiple-visioned Rameses, on the other hand, sees Shendi's guilt as his own:

> I suggested he should do it. Yes,
> I put the whip in his hand. I raised that arm.
> I struck that Jew. I did it. I did not know
> How the things we do, take their own life after
> They are done, how they can twist themselves
> Into foul shapes. (68)

Both Rameses and Shendi fall victim to the angel of death, but the death of Rameses becomes the occasion for the multiple vision of the later Moses; Shendi's death becomes the occasion for nothing at all.

Shendi's death shows the disintegration of a personality. Shendi has followed Miriam back to the Hebrew community. She has decided that she cannot live among the Egyptians and has come back to be identified with the Israelites. Not Shendi: "Must I tell you that I'm an Egyptian?/An Egyptian! I'm an Egyptian" (81). He has come to fetch his mother back to the officers' quarters. But midnight comes, and so does the angel of death. Blood is over the lintel and the Israelites are to stay inside. Shendi insists on going out, but Aaron and Miriam succeed in holding him down, and he actually escapes the angel:

> The wings were right over me and I was wrenched by a hand
> That came spinning out of them. I'll not be sent into a grave.
> I'll be what I was. I am Shendi, a Jew.
> How can my blood alter and make me Egyptian? (84)

He has escaped, but then perishes out of perversity. Tearing off his Egyptian uniform, he fights his way out of the tent and pursues the angel:

> Let me go. It's a chance! I'll make them see me. Wings,
> Shadows, eagles! I am Shendi, Shendi, the Jew!
> I am Shendi the Jew! Shendi the Jew! (85)

Hebrew identity had been prescribed by God for the night of the passover: remaining inside with blood over the lintel. Shendi will be Jewish but in his own way; he knows nothing of obedience to God or of identification with a community for reasons which transcend personal advantage. In Shendi Fry has given us as clear a metaphor as anywhere for what he conceives the torments of the damned to be: the disintegration of the self.

At the multiple-visioned end of the continuum are Moses and Rameses (the names echo each other); at the single-visioned end are Shendi and Seti (and their names echo each other). Midway between the two polarities are two very similar women: Anath and Miriam, the one Egyptian and the other Hebrew.

Long before the play opens, both women are bitter. Anath defied the royal family of Egypt in order to adopt a Hebrew baby, when all Hebrew babies were under sentence of death:

> "I was ready
> To raise a hornet's nest to keep him; in fact
> I raised one" (12).

For a time she was proud, because Moses became a popular Egyptian prince and a military hero. But then the exile of Moses for killing an Egyptian separated Anath from the person she loved most: "I loved you until I longed to hear/That you were dead" (90). Now Moses returns: neither to save Egypt in the latest domestic crisis nor to be company for Anath's middle-age, but to stir up domestic discord among the Hebrews.

Among the Hebrews, Miriam watched the events of the adoption of Moses by the Egyptian court from her own point of view. From the time of her arranging for her mother to nurse Moses, she has considered Moses to be her success story. Now, returning from exile, Moses does not return to Miriam, but to Israel—not to the family, but to his self-appointed role of leading the revolt against Egypt. From the point of view of Moses, it is a God-appointed task; but to Anath and to Miriam, Moses has appointed himself to the task to spite them. They are bitter women.

Miriam is bitter toward Anath:

> There's a man
> Who should have been my brother. A king's daughter

> Swallowed him and spat out this outlaw. I'll
> Not have any more in the family. (28)

Miriam resents that Anath kept Moses separated from his Hebrew past:

> How she disliked me then! But what a talent
> For condescension she had. I never saw you
> After you were a child except by waiting
> Among the crowd in the streets. (29)

Anath's discrimination against Miriam was part of the general discrimination against Israelites embodied in the words and attitudes of the Egyptian way of life. Miriam resented words like

> Pogrom, for one. And the curses of Egyptian children
> When I ran towards them expecting to play. (30)

Within the play Miriam is bitter against Moses because he judges harshly the happiness that Shendi and she can have together:

> Shendi is to be all
> That he can become—all; and I say so,
> I who made him. Am I to go on holding
> The guilt for his unhappiness when opportunity
> Offers to deliver me from it? (58)

> I mustn't think of Moses. Many things
> I must be sure to keep my thoughts quite away from. (60)

Almost immediately after moving in with him, Miriam quarrels with Shendi and returns to her own tent; but she continues to defend Shendi's new Egyptian life. At the same time she resents it:

> I left him.
> I came away from him. I couldn't watch him
> Live what is now his life. (76)

Disillusioned with the Egyptian way of life, Miriam does not cease to be disillusioned with Moses: "He came back from Midian a madman" (77). Bitterness of all kinds has rendered Miriam incapable of commitment to either side, Egyptian or Hebrew. Hers is not double, but vacillating vision.

Anath is like Miriam. She is bitter with Moses for deserting her and wishes he would stay away, just as Miriam wishes it. She tells Seti:

I tell you
He is better where he is. For you or me
He's better where he is.
We have seen different days without him
And I have done my hair a different way.
Leave him alone to bite his lips. (16)

She is too bitter to participate in Teusret's celebration of the engagement of Rameses:

I?
Sing? With the crack in my voice? Not songs for bridegrooms.
Only songs in the minor, where a false note
Can be taken to be excessive sensibility. (46)

Anath is bitter against Seti for implying that because of her attachment to Moses she has influenced Rameses' liberalism on behalf of the Israelites:

Am I a planet,
To be so influential? No, Seti, it is not.
I would rather infect him with something less dubious
Than the blood of Moses. (44)

Bitterness has made Anath as incapable of commitment as it has Miriam. She too has a vacillating vision of reality. Confronting Moses, she represents Egypt:

Come with me. I came by the old walks.
What have I seen? You shall come with me
And see it and tell me, and see the men and women
Bewildered in the doorways, for the name of their world
Has changed from home to horror. And is this
What you have in your heart for Egypt? Then favour me
And also have it in your eyes. (59)

Confronting Seti, she represents Moses:

You tricked Moses.
And what has come of it I would bring back to you

Until pity came out of you like blood to the knife,
Remembering how disease swept all the cattle,
How we could not sleep for intolerable lowing
Till daylight rounded up the herds of the wolftorn
Death. You tricked him, and that feculent moment
Filthied our blood and made of us a nation
Loathsome with boils. (63)

Confronting Moses, she is the liberated comparative religionist:

Does this god use you
Or do you use this god? What is this divinity
Which with no more dexterity than a man
Rips up good things to make a different kind
Of good? For any god's sake, if you came here
To get justice, also give justice.
In this mood the lot goes headlong. (73)

Confronting Seti, she is the superstitious mystic:

I admit it.
I am superstitious. I have my terrors.
We are born too inexplicably out
Of one night's pleasure, and have too little security.
No more than a beating heart to keep us probable.
There must be other probabilities.
You tricked Moses . . .
and what followed followed. (64)

Anath cannot sustain the double vision of God and Egypt at once; Anath cannot sustain the multiple vision of God, Egypt, and Israel at once; Anath vacillates.

Anath and Miriam have been rendered incapable of full commitment by bitterness with Moses, yet both have some capacity for commitment, and hence for double vision and multiple vision. Under stress, they even opt temporarily for commitment and for double vision. At great risk to herself, Anath responds to the first plague by seeking out Moses among the Israelites and confronting him with the evidence. In her heart she rejects Seti's secular dismissal of threat and plague in relationship. Though she pleads Egypt's case to Moses, she knows that Moses has the power. The crisis of the first plague makes Anath realize that her ultimate loyalties lie with Moses, though the crisis becomes familiar as plague follows plague and Anath is less sure. In the crisis Miriam discovers, just as Anath does, that she is not so hostile as she had thought against Moses and Israel. True, she returns to her tent because of a quarrel with Shendi; she is afraid of the Israelite cause as Aaron explains it (76–78); and her fear makes her contemptuous of Moses. Yet, when Moses predicts the death of the firstborn sons and advises Shendi to stay within the tent, Miriam does her best to obey. Although bitterness has made both Anath and Miriam incapable of voluntary commitment, a crisis makes them opt for the side of the angels.

Made bitter by suffering, both suffer even more. In spite of her efforts Miriam cannot keep Shendi within the tent; he rushes out, pursuing the angel of death. Miriam's only remaining hope had been Shendi's success and happiness, just as Anath's only remaining hope had been Rameses: "If the dynasty is safe/We can at least be partly ourselves" (42). Anath loses Rameses to the same angel of death as Miriam loses Shendi. The death of Rameses is the occasion of a fuller vision on the part of Moses, but Anath is not comforted by that; and the freeing of the Israelites is cold comfort for Miriam in losing Shendi.

The chief difference between Miriam and Anath is their articulateness. Miriam's bitterness has been as intense as Anath's all along, but less articulate; at Shendi's destruction she runs out after him calling his name. Anath grows more and more eloquent as her bitterness increases:

> You have your freedom of the darkness, Moses.
> Why do you wait? Haven't you recognized
> The triumph of your purpose? Your twelve hundred
> Thousand souls, out there in the dungeon of the night,
> Are waiting to hear the long bolts grate back.
> Rameses has died,
> And the air stands ready in the wilderness to take you in.
> Rameses has died. Tomorrow the lizards
> Will be sparkling on the rocks. Why aren't you dancing
> With such liberty for such starving souls? (93–94)

Anath's bitterness is public and articulate because her hopes had been public as well as private: first Moses and then Rameses, whom she loves privately, providing the kingdom with a splendid future. Miriam's only hope is private: Shendi's happiness. Miriam is bludgeoned into submission; Anath refuses ever to submit. Their comparative positions—establishment princess and oppressed slave girl—account for much of the difference.

Teusret, the young sister of Rameses, represents—not innocence, which can be acquired after nocence—but prenocence. At the end of the play she first experiences the kind of catastrophe that has turned Anath and Miriam bitter. Teusret's catastrophe does not come until the very end of the play, but she has been confronting Anath's bitterness from the beginning. Anath's domestic details ("The striped linen/You once cut up for a doll's dress was the dress/Made for me that summer" 11) do not hide the bitterness in her account of what happened between her and Moses: "I held forbidden Israel in my arms/And growled on my stubborn doorstep, till I had my way" (11). Teusret's first confrontation with change, a preparation for the end, is the news of the engagement of Rameses. Teusret can go either way, and does: "Phipa, Phipa, Phipa! The noise a flute makes/When the mouth's too full of saliva" (42). But she ends up turning her temporary disappointment into an occasion for hope:

> Flowers for Rameses
> Then! We must make it an occasion. I'll fetch my lute
> And celebrate. Garlands! I'll make you into
> A nice little afternoon god. Don't go away.
> You have earned a ceremony.
> Would you rather have me in tears? This isn't silliness
> But a proper formality. I need to do it. (43)

The ceremony she provides is her expression of hope and a way of coming to terms with change. Indeed it is not silliness. It requires multiple vision: not only God with me and mine, but God with me and with everyone, even Phipa. Teusret, like most children, has multiple vision and does not know she has it. She does not notice how her flower ceremony resembles a funeral, yet she points it out:

> What *are* flowers?
> What is the bridge to be crossed, I wonder,
> From a petal to being a wing or a hand? (45)

She might as well be saying the "All flesh is grass" from the "Burial of the Dead." She has the double vision of intuiting mystery in human affairs, funerals in weddings, for instance. She also has the multiple vision of perceiving that the mystery means all the world well. That is why she immediately turns her momentary disappointment into a flower ceremony. It is a partly hysterical effort to cover her pain, to let the child protect the woman in her, but her hysteria does not blot out her multiple vision.

The question is whether she will keep the multiple vision when she loses a brother in death rather than in marriage. Fry does not allow us to see what happens to Teusret. At the moment Phipa arrives, Teusret is accompanying Rameses to welcome her. Rameses meets the angel of death and buckles; Teusret goes out to welcome Phipa alone, not understanding that Rameses has died. She is ecstatic:

> I have seen her. O Rameses,
> She has come so gifted for you,
> With pearls like seeds of the moon,
> With metal and strange horns, ebon and ivory,
> Spilling chalcedonyx and male sapphires.
> Doesn't their brightness come to you? Do they glimmer
> Nowhere into the cupboards of your sleep? (94–95)

What will she say when she knows that Rameses is dead? Will she be as adept at turning death to life as she was at turning loss of a brother by marriage into a flower ceremony? Or will she become bitter like Anath and Miriam? Only the bitter reaction is perfectly understandable. To see death and to recognize triumph in it is a miracle: the double vision and multiple vision of grace.

Anath, Miriam, and Teusret are the women of all sides in any war. Their sons, husbands, brothers, and lovers go off to war and some never return. The experience makes most women bitter, but the possibility remains for seeing resurrection in death. The character of Teusret is about that possibility.

Aaron is everyman: he is not a visionary like Moses; he is not devoted to Israel as Seti is to Egypt; he has no cause for bitterness as do Anath and Miriam. Even taking into account the dramatic change of Moses from double to multiple vision at the play's end, the audience sees nobody, not even Moses, change as much as Aaron.

Aaron begins on the Seti-Shendi side of the continuum with single vision. He is the bureaucrat for Israel, as the following dialogue demonstrates:

Aaron: Twelve hundred thousand Israelites are under
Your dominion. Of these two hundred and twenty thousand
Only, are men. The rest are in the proportion
Of four hundred and fifty thousand women
And five hundred and thirty thousand children.

Seti: I have my census-takers.

Aaron: So perhaps
Has Death got his; but I think he has not referred
His undertakings to your dynastic understanding.
Here I have his estimate: between April and July
Six hundred and one deaths suffered in old age
But an old age of forced labour, their backs bent twice,
Under the weight of years and under the mule-whip.
Also thirty-eight deaths of healthy men
Who made some show of reluctance of momentary
Impatience.

Moses: That was a good cure. They are now
Patient for all eternity.

Aaron: Also the deaths
Of a hundred pregnant women, forced to dig
Until they had become their own gravediggers.
Also the deaths of eighty-four children, twelve
Unofficial crucifixions. . .

Seti: This is intolerable
Singsong! (22–23)

In the biblical account Aaron is appointed to help Moses because Moses is slow of speech and wants eloquence. No such limitation hinders Fry's Moses. Aaron is Israel's walking Bureau of Statistics.

Hardly have Moses and Aaron finished their confrontation with Seti, than Aaron is the Intelligence Squad: an Egyptian sergeant has reported that the whole city is buzzing with the return of Moses; a minister's wife was wearing an M made out of small lilies and the minister's daughter ripped the lilies off; Aaron's lists of the Hebrew dead are tidy and complete with names. Aaron simply reports the facts; Moses needs to be his own politician.

As well he may be. Even in the simplest domestic situations, Aaron is no diplomat. Miriam's devotion is to her son: "I'll keep my nights of sleep, and I'll keep/My son." Aaron wisely sees that she needs persuading away from her domestic limitation but foolishly argues that her son is expendable: "In this country of murder?" "I'll keep my son/In whatever country" (28) is Miriam's response, and who can argue with her? Aaron has lost the argument by introducing the red herring of the expendability of sons, the wrong place to start in raising the consciousness of a mother. Aaron understands little about human nature and understands even less about the Exodus. He asks Miriam, "But do you understand him?/In fact, do I understand him?" (29) Aaron begins as a bureaucrat.

Miriam and Anath vacillate between the Hebrew and the Egyptian causes; Aaron moves from being a stolid bureaucrat to vacillator like them. On the one hand he favors compromise with the Egyptians. He argues that Moses ought to accept the terms laid down by Egypt, become the general, and in return get permission for the Hebrews to worship: "My dreams were less; not a third as felicitous" (32). He argues that Shendi should be allowed to become an Egyptian officer: ". . . here surely is a kind of proffered hand" (57). And when the waters turn to blood, he argues against Moses as Seti would:

> Isn't there confusion enough? Confusion I call it!
> A contradiction of what we have always known
> To be conclusive: an ugly and impossible
> Mistake in nature. And you, you of all men
> Accept it, identify yourself with it. It must be
> Denied. What has become of you since yesterday?
> Is it not possible still to be plain men
> Dealing with a plain situation? Must we see
> Visions? You were an unchallengeable leader once.
> That is the man I follow. A plain soldier. (54)

But on the other hand, Aaron is right with Moses the moment

Anath appears in the Hebrew camp and offers to bring Moses and Seti together: "This will be a great day for Israel" and "It has been easier/Than I should have thought possible this morning" (60). It will not be easier, of course; there are nine plagues to go. The implication is that when Pharaoh hardens his heart, Aaron urges compromise with the Egyptians, and when Pharaoh yields, Aaron swings to the side of Moses and Israel.

But bitterness does not make the vacillation permanent in Aaron as it does in Anath and Miriam. Gradually Aaron moves to the side of Moses, difficult as that move is for a bureaucrat. He tries to put a political interpretation on the passover feast:

> [Moses'] way of achieving
> Unity among us, before the event,
> That we should all fill this waiting time by doing
> The same thing, however trivial. (77)

Splashing blood over the doorway is different; it is "quite inexplicable" (77) in Aaron's mind. He is still the bureaucrat, not himself subject to prophet ecstacies but willing to govern his life by the discoveries Moses has made about God:

> His madness seems to be a kind of extended sanity.
> But he tells me nothing, nothing is discussed or planned
> Even with me, his lieutenant. And this closeness
> Has hurt me, I won't try to deny it. And yet
> He has me by the scruff of the heart and I ask
> No questions. I've begun to believe that the reasonable
> Is an invention of man, altogether in opposition
> To the facts of creation, though I wish it hadn't
> Occurred to me. (77)

Aaron is the ordinary Christian, permitting himself "a wonderful hope" (77), though at considerable threat to his reasonable habit of mind. Like Tertullian, he believes to be true what he knows to be impossible. Without the institutional church, nobody is called to believe the impossible, and so Aaron believes with all of the doggedness of a church bureaucrat.

Aaron, of course, is a church bureaucrat. Aaron is to become the high priest after the play ends, and one wonders whether bishopry, archbishopry, and church politics generally have not gone into the formulation of Aaron's character. His pedantry is only one side of him; his eye for bureaucratic implications is very useful to Moses. When Moses expansively explains God's strategy in the passover, Aaron sees immediately that Rameses will be taken. Then Moses is smitten with a guilty awareness; but Aaron sees that the issue is like any war, the young going off to die to resolve the wickedness of the old: "The boy/Pays for the father" (82). Moses is sufficiently beside himself to call off the passover and the deliverance. Now it is Aaron's turn to lead his brother:

> Is this how you fought your other wars?
> There were boys then who put
> Eager toes into fatal stirrups, who were young
> And out of life altogether in the same
> Almighty and unthinkable moment. You learnt
> Then to grieve and advance, uninterrupted.
> And so it has to be now. (82)

In his agitation Moses does not seem to have taken in Aaron's speech. He rushes to the palace to save Rameses but fails; and as Rameses dies, Moses is desolate: "I followed a light into a blindness" (92). In the bleak moment of despair to which the mystic and poet are particularly prone, the remembered hard-headedness of the church bureaucrat pulls Moses through. Moses says that the "necessity of God seems to feed on grief," that grief must bear the dead person back to life in a transfigured form in the lives of the survivors, and that life must not go forward "by guilt and guilt" but by "pursuing the ends of the world" in spite of death (94). In his recovery Moses provides a homily on the text that Aaron provided for him: we must "grieve and advance, uninterrupted" (82).

And so Fry has established a continuum in *Firstborn:* those with multiple vision, like Rameses and the mature Moses, who regard coincidence as part of God's work in all the world; those with double vision, like the earlier Moses, who see coincidence as part of God's dealing only with them and their cause; those like Miriam and Anath, who vacillate between seeing God in coincidence and not seeing him there; and those with single vision, like Seti and Shendi, who write off coincidence as chance, not involving God at all. Any of these options is open to Teusret. Aaron progresses through all of them.

The biblical coincidences for his characters to react to were, as was stated at the outset, a compelling reason for Fry's choosing the Moses narrative. But Fry provides many more coincidences of his own. Anath's telling Teusret about Moses coincides with Seti's deciding to invite Moses back as general, which events coincide with the unexpected arrival of Moses himself. The arrival of Moses also coincides with the arrival of Rameses from hunting. Shendi's flight home from the pursuit of the overseers coincides with the presence of Rameses in Miriam's tent. Miriam and Shendi quarrel, and the aftermath of their quarrel brings them both back to Miriam's tent; their return coincides with preparations for the Exodus and gives them opportunity to participate. The arrival of the bride of Rameses and of the angel of death at the same time is the last coincidence. These coincidences, together with the biblical coincidences, form a texture of coincidence that the audience cannot miss. How the characters respond to coincidence becomes Fry's way of sorting them out.

Another technique for accentuating the importance of coincidence is the recurring image of wheeling birds. When birds are driven up, they fly away and wheel back to the very same spot. It is not mere chance that wheeling birds find the same spot. It is a divinely controlled coincidence, working both inside the birds and outside them, that the take-off place and the landing place are the same.

As the play opens, a Hebrew workman dies in an accident, and Anath and Teusret record the wheeling of the birds:

> Some man is dead. That scream was password to a grave.
> Look there: up go the birds. (9)
> You are right. Nothing. It was something once
> But now it is only a scare of birds in the air
> And a pair of women with their nerves uncovered. (10)
>
> The birds are back on the roof now. (10)

The wheeling of birds is again associated with death in the account Rameses gives of his hunting expedition:

> But I
> Waited for daylight. Until then the marsh was a torpor.
> I clucked and clapped as the sun rose
> And up shot so much whistle and whirr
> I could only hold my spear and laugh.

> All the indignant wings of the marshes
> Flocking to the banner of Tuesday
> To avoid the Prince of Egypt!
> Off they flapped into the mist
> Looking about for Monday
> The day they had lived in peace: and finding nothing
> Back they wheeled to Tuesday. (17)

The birds wheel between past and future in order to escape death. The bird does not escape:

> I had recovered myself by then and killed
> One that had the breast of a chestnut.
> At last he could feel the uninterrupted darkness
> Of an addled egg. I watched his nerves flinching
> As they felt how dark that darkness was.
> I found myself trying to peer into his death.
> It seemed a long way down. The morning and it
> Were oddly separate,
> Though the bird lay in the sun: separate somehow
> Even from contemplation. (17–18)

The wheeling and the absence of wheeling are obviously contrasted. Even apparently purposeless wheeling is to be preferred, as a way of disposing past and future in the present, to not wheeling at all. The wheeling ceases; and past, present, and future cease to matter in death. It is the fear of death and the attempt to escape from death that give the wheeling such urgency.

The wheeling of birds seems to be Fry's metaphor for a person's problem with time: the uncertainty of present and future, the certainty of death, and in the following passage the persistence of an unresolved past. Aaron urges negotiation with Seti; Moses responds:

> What would we talk of, Aaron? What quiet subject?
> They tell me centuries of horror brood
> In this vivid kingdom of fertile mud. Do you think
> If we swung the rattle of conversation
> Those centuries would fly off like so many crows?
> They would wheel above us and come to feed again. (32)

Moses wants a resolved past, but the past can never be resolved so completely that wheeling is unnecessary. One remembers the dead bird of Rameses as the only alternative to the wheeling birds.

True, the past Egyptian bondage will be resolved in the death of Rameses and Seti, but then Moses will have the guilt of having caused their deaths. Wheeling, making peace with time, is the condition of a living person. To want to resolve the past so that wheeling will be unnecessary is to wish for death, one's own or somebody else's. Then life "goes forward by guilt and guilt" (94). The cause of Moses is richer than the narrow patriotism of the Egyptians; but Moses embraces it with unrealistic revolutionary zeal at first, not yet achieving the multiple vision that includes Egypt: ignore the past, render wheeling unnecessary, and utopia will emerge. The revolution, alas, becomes the guilty past for the new future, and the wheeling to resolve the past continues. The rattle of conversation, negotiation, is the only alternative to violence.

The wheeling of a hawk has two aspects: the graceful soaring upward and the predatory dive downward. Rameses wants more than anything to identify with Moses, his hero-uncle:

> I should burn
> Throne and lotus gladly if I could break
> Myself of boyhood, if burning would do it. But you
> Are clear and risen roundly over the hazes.
> You have the formula. I need it. (35)

Moses as the moon, elegant ascending, is the image Rameses chooses. Moses sees himself as a hawk, graceful and predatory:

> Clear?
> Evidence of that! Where in this drouthy
> Overwatered world can you find me clarity?
> What spirit made the hawk? a bird obedient
> To grace, a bright lash on the cheek of the wind
> And drawn and ringed with feathered earth and sun,
> An achievement of eternity's birdsmith. But did he
> Also bleak the glittering charcoal of the eyes
> And sharpen beak and claws on his hone of lust?
> What language is life? Not one I know.
> A quarrel in God's nature. (35)

Both elements—the freeing of the Israelites and the death of Rameses—are part of the necessity of God. Making peace with time includes both elements, requires wheeling: coming to terms with the graceful ascent and the predatory descent.

Sometimes the wheeling is energetic and nervous, as in the case of Teusret: "Put your hand in one place, she is already/Beating her wings in another" (41). Sometimes it is the more leisurely wheeling, like that of Phipa, coming in joy as a bride to conclude a peace negotiation, leaving with the sorrow of a widow, with a war still going. *Phip* itself is a pet name for sparrows, from *Philip,* and suggested to sixteenth-century poets the sparrow's song. *Phipa* is the feminine form. The *sparrow-Phipa* identification makes it seem that the wheeling of sparrows is figured in her pointless round trip.

The last speech of the play, spoken by Moses to console Anath, puts the wheeling of birds and people into the context of the cosmic orbits of the planets. *Wheel* as verb is a strange word to go with *the round of light,* the sun, as subject: strange, because the sun is stationary and only seems to wheel; strange, because the common verb for the circular motion of heavenly bodies is *orbit.*

> Anath: What is left
> To call to me?
>
> Moses: The morning, which still comes
> To Egypt as to Israel, the round of light
> Which will not wheel in vain.
> We must each find our separate meaning
> In the persuasion of our days
> Until we meet in the meaning of the world.
> Until that time. (95)

The sun only seems to wheel, when actually the earth wheels. The psychological reality and the astronomical reality are different from each other. Similarly, the wheeling of birds and of people feels to them to be their own desperate activity. Fry's image insists on the opposite: God, *the round of light,* wheels. The wheeling of birds and of people is a predictable result in a world of an immanent God, who wheels both inside and outside his creatures' wheeling. The pre-Copernican image of a wheeling sun is a better metaphor for Fry's God than the remote and stationary sun would be.

Wheel is an odd verb for planetary motion. Orbits are prescribed and not at all what birds and people do. To say *wheel* instead of *orbit* makes planetary motion seem as arbitrary as a flock of birds wheeling around and settling down. On the other hand, the word makes the wheeling of birds—and the abstract wheeling of people making their peace with time—seem as fixed and predictable as planetary motion.

The summer solstice occurs on 21 or 22 June; sunset times can be calculated for any day of the year, years in advance; eclipses occur just when the newspapers say they will; and yet we never take the correspondence of our scientific predictions to the world of fact as coincidence. It is a secure universe. Scientific, reasonable predictions are one thing and coincidences in human affairs are quite another. Any yokel can tell the difference.

Aaron begins as a reasonable man who can tell the difference between an accurate prediction and a coincidence, but he comes to believe

> "that the reasonable
> Is an invention of man, altogether in opposition
> To the facts of creation" (77).

This is also Fry's opinion.

Of course, Fry does not say that predictable scientific events and coincidences are coterminous. The planet's orbit does not have the predatory half of the hawk's wheeling; the orbit of planets is not to be accelerated by fright as is the wheeling of birds. A star's orbit is perfectly secure in time, accurate to the second. But humankind lacks such staidness, and human wheeling, like that of birds, involves violence: the predatory desire, the risk, the fear, the panic, and, though this does not apply to birds, the guilt.

Since violence will not be eradicated in the foreseeable future, the optimum unified vision—the orbits of planets and wheeling of birds and people being the same thing—remains an impossibility. Three alternatives exist: 1. the single vision of Seti, regarding as mutually exclusive the predictability of scientifically predictable orbits and the wheeling of people; 2. the double vision of the earlier Moses, who sees the predictability of a planet's orbit as related to coincidences in the wheeling of Israel; and 3. the multiple vision of the later Moses, who sees the predictability of a planet's orbit as related to the wheeling of all the human beings in the world.

The relationships that Moses sees but that Seti does not see have nothing to do with the zodiac or with predicting the future.

The zodiac itself is a mechanical contrivance and, more importantly, it lacks an imperative. The imperative as Fry and his Moses see it is the elimination of violence from human affairs—from the self most of all.

That is why Moses cannot simply be dedicated to the freedom of Israel. A free Israel will do no more to eliminate violence than a free Egypt. That is why Moses as politician, though he must continue at play's end to work for recognizable ends like national independence, must always have more ultimate ends in view: elimination of secular mechanistic rationalism; recognition of natural, human, and supernatural reality, even when they seem to contradict each other; adjustment of natural, human, and supernatural reality towards each other; and the elimination of violence. When the ultimate ends have been realized, the kingdoms of this world will have become the kingdom of our Lord and of his Christ, and he shall reign forever and ever.

But the program begins modestly enough: never mistaking a miracle for a coincidence.

FRY'S (Not Barth's) *KURZE ERKLÄRUNG DES ROMERBRIEFES* 4

A Phoenix Too Frequent

"The story was got from Jeremy Taylor who had it from Petronius," Fry informs us of *A Phoenix*.[1] The story is all, however, that the three works have in common. Petronius is cynical: loving until death is a pretty intention that disregards the human need for sex.[2] Taylor is moralistic: immoderate grief leads to other immoderate passions.[3] Fry is ecstatic: the widow's decision to live demands celebrations. The present study will demonstrate that Fry's unique handling of his identified sources is to be explained in part by his work's specifically Christian content. This study will also suggest a probable and hitherto unnamed Christian source.

The presence of Christian influence is most simply to be noted in the setting, the time, and the symbolic tree. Fry's setting is an example of his symbolic use of merely narrative detail provided by Petronius and Taylor. These both place the story in the tomb and have the soldier report on the crucifixions. Fry combines the crosses and the tomb in his setting: "An underground tomb, in darkness except for the light of an oil-lamp. Above ground the starlight shows a line of trees on which hang the bodies of several men." (1). The strong visual image of a tomb and crosses together immediately alerts the audience to expect *Phoenix* to be symbolically Christian.

There is also the clue of time. Taylor says nothing as to how long the lady and her maid mourn in the tomb. Petronius makes it five days. Fry has Doto the maid specify that two days have been spent in the tomb mourning (9); and the play opens after midnight (7) or on the morning of the third day. Like Christ's macrocosmic resurrection, the microcosmic resurrections occur in the play on the third morning.

Finally, the kinds of trees on which the criminals are executed are not specified by Petronius and Taylor. In Fry's play there are "Five plane trees and a holly." (11) It is from the holly tree that relatives steal the body of one of the criminals, and it is on the holly tree that the soldier must die:

> How could I settle to death
> Knowing that you last saw me stripped and strangled
> On a holly tree? (40)

The holly tree is a common Christian symbol of the cross, its red berries construed as drops of Christ's blood.[4]

A work which so consciously employs Christian symbols may well be based on Christian sources. This study takes note of the similarity between the following parable from Paul's Epistle to the Romans and *Phoenix:*

> Know ye not, brethren, (for I speak to them that know the Law,) how that the law hath dominion over a man as long as he liveth? For the woman which hath a husband is bound by the law to her husband so long as he liveth; but if the husband be dead, she is loosed from the law of her husband. So then if, while her husband liveth, she be married to another man, she shall be called an adulteress: but if her husband be dead, she is free from that law; so that she is no adulteress, though she be married to another man. (7:1–3)

This parable opens chapter 7. The closing verse of chapter 6 reads: "The wages of sin is death; but the gift of God is eternal life through Jesus Christ our Lord." The common division of Romans 6 in the King James Bible* is three paragraphs: verses 1–11, 12–22, and 23.[6] Verse 23 constitutes the third paragraph of chapter 6. In

*The King James Version is still Fry's favorite: "I've taken to reading the second lesson in the village church since the Admiral left for Malta, but have put my foot down about reading it from the New English Bible, which is flatter than Bedfordshire." Christopher Fry, letter to SMW, 21 September 1969.

Phoenix, when the soldier returns to the tomb after the body has been stolen, he says:

> It's section six, paragraph
> Three in the Regulations. That's my doom.
> I've read it for myself. (40)

The legal wages for his legal infraction is death, and he has no reason to hope for gifts. The second half of the text ("... but the gift of God is eternal life...") seems to be echoed in the words of the widow: "My darling,/I give you Virilius" (43).

Because Paul's parable and paragraph bear a possible relationship to *Phoenix,* and because the paragraph and the parable are part of a single context in Romans, the whole of the context is worth investigating for similarities to *Phoenix.*

After the parable in chapter 7, Paul begins his famous statement about ambivalence:

> For the good that I would I do not: but the evil that I would not, that I do. Now if I do that I would not, it is no more I that do it, but sin that dwelleth in me. I find then a law, that, when I would do good, evil is present with me. For I delight in the law of God after the inward man: But I see another law in my members, warring against the law of my mind, and bringing me into captivity to the law of sin which is in my members. O wretched man that I am! who shall deliver me from the body of this death? (7:12–24)

There is in Paul's statement the problem of doing evil and omitting good, but there is also the problem of the law of the members warring against the law of the mind; there is a moral ambivalence, but also a psychological one. Each of the characters in Fry's play is also conscious of a moral and/or psychological ambivalence.

Fry's maid has been a jolly and promiscuous girl who, even with death approaching, cannot keep men out of her mind—nor does she really want to. Her problem is not primarily a psychological one of internal conflict as Fry presents it, but one of external behavior. When she admits to her mistress that she should not have allowed the soldier into the tomb, she becomes explicit about her problem:

Maybe I *could* have kept him out
But men are in before I wish they wasn't.
I think quickly enough, but I get behindhand
With what I ought to be saying. It's a kind of stammer
In my way of life, madam. (36)

The maid's ambivalence is moral.

The soldier's ambivalence is primarily psychological. He rejects the sexual allurements of the tipsy maid, but becomes attached to the widow precisely because she is out of reach and pure and dying:

We'll put a moat of tears
Round her bastion of love, and save
The world. (12)

Involvement with a dying woman is really escape, and in single speeches he shows strange shifts in attitude:

Eros, no! No!
. . . .
O Dynamene,
Let me unload something of my lips' longing
On to yours receiving. (30)

Shall he love the lady as a beautiful idea or in the flesh? His problem is primarily psychological.

Dynamene, the most complex character, has an ambivalence approaching the complexity of Paul's: both moral and psychological. Both Petronius and Taylor emphasize the widow's inordinate grief; but to the twentieth-century Fry, inordinate grief, like self-torment of any kind, is a transparent attempt to atone for guilt.[7] The widow's decision to die is an atonement for not having treated the dead husband better. Not aware of her motivation, she condemns the departed even when she thinks she is praising him. "You were the peroration of nature" (5); she intends to say that he was the climax of nature, and implies as well that he was a stuffy moralist. A pedant, he could not abide mystery.

You explained everything to me, even the extremely
Complicated gods. You wrote them down
In seventy columns. Dear curling calligraphy. (5)

Desperate for something to praise, she praises his penmanship and, elsewhere, his punctuality: "he was so punctual, you could regulate/The sun by him" (3). A stolid, sober Roman, her husband was afraid of involvement in love and life, and he saw all of life in terms of his rigid profession, bookkeeping. His voice made "Balance-sheets sound like Homer and Homer sound/Like balance-sheets" (5). Such a husband does not respond to erotic love naturally: "I taught you/In your perceptive moments to appreciate me" (5); no doubt she would have preferred a husband who would need no teaching, because, more than most women, she is by temperament involved in life:

> What a mad blacksmith creation is
> Who blows his furnaces until the stars fly upward
> And iron Time is hot and politicians glow
> And bulbs and roots sizzle into hyacinth
> And orchis, and the sand puts out the lion,
> Roaring yellow, and oceans bud with porpoises,
> Blenny, tunny and the almost unexisting
> Blindfish; throats are cut, the masterpiece
> Looms out of labour; nations and rebellions
> Are spat out to hang on the wind—and all is gone
> In one Virilius, wearing his office tunic,
> Checking the pence column as he went. (6)

The marriage may at best have been congenial, but it was far from ideal. Now that he is dead, she feels guilty for not having made a better marriage of it; she carries her self-punishment to the point of wanting to die. Yet, can such a high-spirited woman really want to die? She has, she confesses, "the constitution of a whirlpool" (31) and is a compass "susceptible to two conflicting norths" (31). She has Paul's problem:

> When the thoughts would die, the instincts will set sail
> For life. And when the thoughts are alert for life
> The instincts will range to be destroyed on the rocks. (18)

Her problem is both moral and psychological.

Petronius and Taylor see only moral ambivalence; they see it only in the widow, and they sit in cynical and holy judgment respectively. Like Paul, Fry accepts moral and/or psychological ambivalence as the inevitable human lot. Unlike Paul, he humors it as well.

Paul's resolution to moral ambivalence is also Fry's: resurrection.

"But if the Spirit of him that raised up Jesus from the dead dwell in you, he that raised up Christ from the dead shall also quicken your mortal bodies by his Spirit that dwelleth in you. Therefore, brethren, we are debtors, not to the flesh, to live after the flesh. For if ye live after the flesh, ye shall die: but if ye through the Spirit do mortify the deeds of the body, ye shall live" (8:11–13). Although Paul emphasizes Christ's resurrection on Easter and the resurrection of all people on Judgment Day, another reiterated emphasis falls on being raised with Christ in the Spirit, now, in time, by inward renewal. Not only does Paul emphasize present resurrection but an abundant, pluralistic one: "Likewise reckon ye also yourselves to be dead indeed unto sin, but alive unto God. . ." (6:11).

Fry's play concerns present and abundant resurrections. The widow's guilt is metamorphosed into love:

> . . . you boy,
> I can't look away from you. You use
> The lamplight and the moon so skilfully,
> So arrestingly, in and around your furrows. (29)

By the time the soldier leaves the widow to inspect the bodies, his ambivalence has disappeared:

> Hush, smile of my soul,
> My sprig, my sovereign: this is to hold your eyes,
> I sign my lips on them both: this is to keep
> Your forehead—do you feel the claim of my kiss
> Falling into your thought? And now your throat
> Is a white branch and my lips two singing birds—
> They are coming to rest. (34)

He has become capable of an unambiguously erotic response. And the maid, in view of her sexual preoccupation and her enforced abstinence, might be expected to claim prior right to the gentleman. When the soldier had said he had found "loyalty, enduring passion,/Unrecking bravery and beauty all in one," the maid, with a prostitute's sense of competition, had responded: "He means you, or you and me; or me, madam" (18). Now she leaves the tomb with playful irony: "Remember me to Cerberus" (38). It is a moral resurrection for her. She sees that love is more important for the grieving wife than for her. She is still preoccupied with sex, but she leaves the grave giving evidence of a more idealistic, romantic attitude: "Ye gods, what a moon" (38). She had opened the play talking about beds.

The phoenix experience is as frequent as there are characters in the play. Like the resurrections in Romans, the resurrections in *Phoenix* are present and abundant. In life too, the phoenix experience is so present and so abundant that the Taylors and Petronii of all ages write it off as a change in mood. It is too frequent.

Continuing the examination of the context of the parable and paragraph in Romans, this investigation now moves backwards into chapter 6 of Romans, which deals with Paul's symbol for spiritual death and spiritual resurrection: baptism.

> Know ye not, that so many of us as were baptized into Jesus Christ were baptized into his death? Therefore we are buried with him by baptism into death: that like as Christ was raised up from the dead by the glory of the Father, even so we also should walk in newness of life. (6:3–4)

All three of the characters undergo baptism. Spiritually dead, they are physically buried in a grave with a physically dead corpse. They leave the grave in newness of life. Even the physically dead corpse, although not physically resurrected, is taken from the grave as a means of life at play's end. Just as baptism is a symbol of death and resurrection, just as the resurrection of baptism confers a new identity on the object of it, and just as Christian practice has always associated baptism with naming, so the three characters of Fry's play undergo burial and resurrection, so each gains a new identity, and so each either has a name change or a change in the name's meaning.

The soldier enters the tomb with the name *Tegeus*, from Latin *tego, tegere*, "to cover," and Greek *τεγος*, "roof." That Fry considers Tegeus to be a covered person is demonstrated by what the widow says of his name: "That's very thin for you,/It hardly covers your bones" (20). A covered person is too tedious to be with, and the British pronunciation of *tedious* and *Tegeus* is identical. The new name that occurs to Dynamene is Chromis from Greek *χρῶμα*, "color." Through the artifical cover of his tedious shyness and escapism, the genuine color of his personality emerges.

Dynamene is from Greek δύναμις, "power." Tegeus senses the danger of tangling with her power. Even after she has rechristened him *Chromis*, he cannot bring himself to call her *Dynamene:*

> It makes you real.
> Forgive me, a terrible thing has happened. Shall I
> Say it and perhaps destroy myself for you? (23–24)

He is right in his tentative fears; admitting her name, her power over him, may mean destruction. She may destroy him by intensifying his problem of shyness; would not anyone despair of keeping up with Dynamene? Or she may go on turning her energy against herself, declare herself unavailable, and hence destroy his hopes and newly emerging self. She may also destroy him by helping him to forget the old shy Tegeus and so substitute the new Chromis in its place. The latter, although constructive, is not altogether pleasant. There is danger in the feminine power of Dynamene.

The change that comes over her is the change from destructive to constructive power. Her new lover has as many limitations as the dead husband. To what extent was she responsible for her dead husband's pedantry? Dynamene's resurrection is in part her **learning how to dispose her feminine power to creative ends.**

The maid's name, *Doto,* from Latin *dos, dotis,* "dowry," has two meanings: by widow's dowry Doto was left by Virilius to Dynamene; by bride's dowry she becomes the property of Chromis. The exchange of masters is a dominant theme in chapters 6 and 7 of Romans: "Know ye not, that to whom ye yield yourselves servants to obey, his servants ye are to whom ye obey; whether of sin unto death, or of obedience unto righteousness? But God be thanked, that ye were the servants of sin, but ye have obeyed from the heart that form of doctrine which was delivered you. Being then made free from sin, ye became the servants of righteousness" (6:16–18). Paul's complete argument concerning the law, sin, and grace is summarized thus: The law makes people aware of sin, for no person can keep the law perfectly. There are two methods of defeat in trying to keep the law: water down the demands of the law or admit inability to keep it. Both are sins; hence, the law is synonymous with sin for Paul. As a servant to the law and sin one can gain no redemption. On the other hand, as a servant to grace one can claim the absolute integrity of the law and one's own integrity too, in spite of not having lived up to it; for the lag between the law and one's observance of it is taken up by God in forgiveness. Doto has been a servant to sin ("men are in before I wish they wasn't" 36) and to the law of the upright but impersonal bookkeeper:

> My master, my poor master, was a man
> Whose nose was as straight as a little buttress,
> And now he has taken it into Elysium
> Where it won't be noticed among all the other straightness. (1–2)

Doto can accept the uprightness of her former master more wholeheartedly when she is the dowry of her second master. At play's end Doto toasts "The master. Both the masters" (43). Fry, through her, has resolved the tension between law and grace.

Virilius, derived from Latin *virilis*, "virile," is the ironic name for the pedantic bookkeeper, now dead, who could only be taught to appreciate Dynamene in his more perceptive moments. But when his body is substituted for the doomed Chromis, Dynamene says:

> And now we can give his death
> The power of life. Not horrible: wonderful!
> Isn't it so? That I should be able to feel
> He moves again in the world, accomplishing
> Our welfare? (43)

The name *Virilius* loses its irony, for by him comes not only pedantry but also the resurrection.

Petronius in his anecdote and Taylor in his exemplum do not assign names to their characters. A drama requires names in the way that a tale does not, but Fry does more than assign names as a dramatic convenience. He has metamorphosed the grave of Petronius and Taylor into a baptismal font.

Continuing to move backwards from Paul's parable and paragraph, this study arrives at chapter 5 of Romans and Paul's discussion of the substitutionary atonement: "For when we were yet without strength, in due time Christ died for the ungodly. For scarcely for a righteous man will one die: yet peradventure for a good man some would even dare to die. But God commendeth his love toward us, in that, while we were yet sinners, Christ died for us" (5:6–8). Christ died *for* us. The common interpretation of the word *for* in this passage is "instead of," allowed by the Greek preposition ὑπερ. Christ is hanged instead of Christians just as the dead husband is hanged instead of the soldier.

Passages similar to those quoted from Romans can be found in all of Paul's epistles, and taken by themselves they constitute no evidence for the influence of Romans. Taken by themselves they serve only as evidence for a broadly Christian interpretation of the play—as do also the setting, the holly tree, and the time.

Taken together, however, all of the passages that show similarity to *Phoenix* are not scattered haphazardly throughout the book but are taken from one clutch of chapters: 5–8. At the very center of that restricted passage stands Paul's parable with its striking parallel to *Phoenix* and the paragraph which gives precise meaning to "Section six paragraph three in the Regulations": "The wages of sin is death, but the gift of God is eternal life . . ." To the extent that one is persuaded to accept the parable and the paragraph as sources for *Phoenix*, to that extent moral ambivalence, and resurrection, and baptism, and law and grace, and atonement all seem (1) more likely to have been derived from Romans than from many scattered New Testament sources and (2) more likely to have been built into the play rather than read into it without warrant.

The influence of Romans 5–8 seems likely enough to warrant the interpretation of the plot of *Phoenix* in the light of Paul's interpretation of his own parable: "Wherefore, my brethren, ye also are become dead to the law by the body of Christ; that ye should be married to another, even to him who is raised from the dead, that we should bring forth fruit unto God" (7:4). The widow in Paul's parable is free from the law when her first husband dies; when Christ died, humankind became free from achieving salvation by the works of the law; when Virilius dies, Dynamene also is free, although she considers herself bound until Tegeus sets her free. The widow in Paul's illustration marries another man when she is free from the law; the Christian aware of the new freedom "marries" the risen Lord; Dynamene marries the renamed Chromis. Alone, of course, Virilius and Tegeus-Chromis are too obviously imperfect to be Christ figures. Together, however, they represent to Dynamene and Doto what the death and resurrection of Christ mean to a Christian. The dying Savior is figured in Virilius; the risen Lord is figured in Chromis. Christ is the dead and the living husband, simultaneously.

At the final curtain Doto is drinking to both masters simultaneously, the one who died under the curse and the living one: "The master. Both the masters" (43). It is the heart of the play, for Virilius and Chromis are complementary eucharistic images, the dying Savior and the risen Lord. Earlier, Dynamene had drunk wine in memory of Virilius: "My husband, and all he stood for." Tegeus had corrected her, "Stands for," and she had corrected herself: "Stands for" (19). She had been drinking to the dying Savior and risen Lord without knowing it. The name *Tegeus* had been changed to *Chromis* because the latter has "a breadlike sound" (22). The whole play centers on the eucharist and its elements.

The play ought not lose comic momentum in being regarded as eucharistic. In drinking to both the masters, Doto has not turned suddenly nun-like. She is in her cups. When Dynamene amends *stood for* to *stands for*, it is the result of erotic awakening on her part. When *Chromis* is said to have "a breadlike sound," the echo is *Hovis*, the trade name for a common English bread.* Fry's eucharist is not the solemn liturgical monstrosity we have made it, but a celebration of Christ in ordinary life: in tipsiness, in eroticism, and even in daily bread like Hovis.

Of course, more is going on in *Phoenix* than can be derived from Paul's Epistle to the Romans, and the preceding two paragraphs demonstrate this fact. There is no doctrine of the eucharist in Romans, and Paul's First Epistle to the Corinthians (11:22–34) must be functioning in *Phoenix* as well as Romans, for the Corinthians passage is Paul's most explicit teaching about the eucharist. To demonstrate that Romans cannot be an exclusive source, this study concludes with a brief discussion of the bowl from which Tegeus and Dynamene drink:

Dynamene: What an exquisite bowl.

Tegeus: Now that it's peacetime we have pottery classes.

Dynamene: You made it yourself?

Tegeus: Yes. Do you see the design?
The corded god, tied also by the rays
Of the sun, and the astonished ship erupting
Into vines and vine-leaves, inverted pyramids
Of grapes, the uplifted hands of the men (the raiders),

*In letters to SMW, 22 August 1966, 5 September 1966, 21 October 1966.

And here the headlong sea, itself almost
Venturing into leaves and tendrils, and Proteus
With his beard braiding the wind, and this
Held by other hands is a drowned sailor—

Dynamene: Always, always.

Doto: Hold the bowl steady, madam. (17)

Any wine goblet in any play about ancient Romans, of course, could be appropriately decorated with a story about the wine god, Bacchus. In the story used here, Bacchus is incarnate as a young lad, being kidnapped by sailors who promise to take him to Naxos but instead set sail for Egypt, where they plan to sell him as a slave. Bacchus causes the ship to erupt into grape vines, and the vines and clusters of grapes so impede the boat that the voyage ceases. The sailors, as punishment for turning kidnappers, are metamorphosed into sea creatures and swim off. Only the sailor opposed to the kidnapping remains a sailor and delivers the god to Naxos as planned.

Fry's deviations from his source[8] are significant. Fry shows the kidnapped Bacchus bound in ropes; Ovid shows no ropes, but has the god confined to one section of the ship. Fry involves the sun god (Apollo) and a sea god (Proteus); neither appears in Ovid. Fry does not show the raiders metamorphosing into sea creatures, but shows them with uplifted hands in terror and supplication. Fry shows one extraneous sailor drowning, held by "other hands." The sea itself, for Fry, almost erupts into vine leaves; in Ovid only the ship metamorphoses.

These changes are all expressive of Tegeus as amateur artist. Leave it to an amateur to clutter the composition with three gods when one will do. He knows he cannot manage a convincing metamorphosis of sailors to fish, so he keeps the sailors at their first moment of surprise—leave it to an amateur to make the piece melodramatic. And how does the amateur show a captive god disguised as a person without inventing cords to indicate captivity? For the amateur a wiggling line is a wiggling line and a straight line a straight line: it is a little hard to tell the wiggling lines Tegeus made for the sea from his wiggling lines for the grape vines, so Tegeus interprets the sea as "almost/Venturing into leaves and tendrils. . ." It is a little hard to tell the straight lines of the sun's rays from the straight lines of the cords which bind the god, so

Tegeus interprets the corded god as "tied also by the rays/Of the sun. . ." Not able to manage the metamorphosis of men to fish, he can manage a drowned sailor touchingly held by unspecified "other hands"; of course, the drowned sailor has nothing to do with the myth depicted, but an amateur's aim is not authenticity but making the bowl as pretty as possible. Dimly aware of bad craftsmanship, Tegeus is putting a good face on it.

But for Fry this awkward goblet about Bacchus is a chalice. Bacchus is bound because Jesus Christ was bound. The "corded god" is tied, not only by the cords of the raiders as efficient cause, but by the will of Apollo the sun god as final cause—just as surely as Jesus Christ was crucifed by a coalition of Jews and Romans but was also crucified by God the Father to provide redemption for the world. If the corded god is a prototype of God the Son, if the sun god is a prototype of god the Father, then Proteus is a prototype of the Holy Ghost, "his beard braiding the wind." Wind is one of the symbols of the Holy Ghost, together with fire and water; Proteus, too, is associated with fire and water as well as wind. The "astonished ship" erupting into vines and grapes is a metaphor for a radical conversion like St. Paul's; though ultimately forward movement, the experience is hardly pleasant at the time. That is why the "uplifted hands" of the raiders indicate shock and outrage, but also prayer; not only the ineptness of Tegeus keeps him from depicting the metamorphosis of the men into fish, but also the design of Fry, who wants the men transformed into better men. In Fry's sacramental view of reality, not only bread and wine are offered to God in the eucharist, but the whole physical universe; not only the water, forced through the green fuse into grapes and fermented into wine, is offered to God, but all water—"the headlong sea, itself almost/Venturing into leaves and tendrils." All reality is undergoing the metamorphosis of grace. Even the "drowned sailor," who comes from the hopeful turning point of T. S. Eliot's *Waste Land* (Movement IV), exemplifies the ambiguity of baptism: "buried with him in baptism, raised with him in newness of life" (Romans 6:4). The "other hands"—other than the outraged praying hands of the raiders—imply a deliverance by someone outside the picture, a summary of the rest of the bowl.

The mention of death by drowning makes Dynamene tremble and almost spill her wine; though Tegeus is apologizing for his bad art, his excitement in describing the bowl is more than vanity of the kind that says, "Pretty good for an amateur, don't you think?" The characters in the play intuit the essence of the Christian gospel without verbalizing it, thus expressing Fry's conviction that "God need not be named to be worshipped."*

Just as primitive Christians took the pagan symbol of the phoenix and turned it into a Christian symbol of the resurrection, and just as Fry took the pagan joke by Petronius and turned it into the world's wittiest commentary on the Epistle of Paul to the Romans, so Tegeus uses the myth of Bacchus kidnapped. What the Bacchus bowl is to Tegeus, *A Phoenix Too Frequent* is to Fry.

POSTSCRIPT:

The part of the preceding essay that deals specifically with the relationship of *Phoenix* to the Epistle of Paul to the Romans appeared earlier in *Modern Drama.*[9]

The theory has met with considerable criticism but not from Mr. Fry. In a letter dated 22 August 1966, Mr. Fry writes:

> Thank you for your letter and for sending me your study of *A Phoenix* which goes right to the root of it. Yes, indeed: Romans." In a letter dated 5 September 1966, Mr. Fry writes: "You need have no doubt about Romans 6:3 being Section 6: paragraph 3 of the Regulations. It is true I had been reading St. Paul at the time I read the Widow of Ephesus story in Jeremy Taylor, and discussing the epistles with friends in my army company towards the end of the war. But I wrote the play out of my general state of mind at the time, without wishing for any precise definition: hoping that what truth was in it would come across to an audience who had no knowledge of Paul's writings or much interest in Christianity. For the truth of Christianity, as we know, is that it is *in* life, that God need not be named.
>
> ....
>
> I tried to let the mystery speak for itself. The Christian content—and indeed the meaning of the incarnation is central to that—comes from breathing, rather than reading, even rather than from believing. I tried to let it arise simply as a fact of life. For that reason I have been against myself attaching to the plays an exposé of what they

*First suggested to me by my colleague at Calvin College, Professor George Graham Harper, later confirmed by Fry: "Yes, of course, Hovis was in my mind, though it's a rather poor joke." Christopher Fry, letter to SMW, Christmas, no specific date, 1973.

meant for me. If there is anything of life or truth in them it is better that I shouldn't tap on it with a latent lecturer's pointer. I might try to prove I had written more than I'd succeeded in doing. (But when commentary comes from you, with such understanding, it is of the greatest help to me.) They are plays and comedies at that, though I can't deny that they're Christian plays or I should be denying that Christianity is a revelation of life.

CREATION'S WELCOME TO LONELY FLESH 5

Thor, with Angels

In *Thor, with Angels*[1] Fry is at pains to express his dissatisfaction with Christianity that is merely institutional, impersonal, and nominal. The play is about the confrontation between Christianity and Germanic paganism at the time of the mission of St. Augustine to England in 596. Again and again Fry equates institutional Christianity of today, not with the Christianity preached by Augustine, but with the paganism of the Jutes, Augustine's first converts. Thus the pagans attend "early rite" (102) at times of national emergency, just as an Anglo-Catholic might attend early mass. The Jutes pride themselves on being "Wodenfearing" (101), just as their descendants pride themselves on being godfearing. They are "decently religious" (109) and "orthodox" (121), just as their counterparts today. Today's Christians are notorious for their contempt toward lesser breeds without the law; these Jutes have the same kind of contempt for "godless Christians" (126) and Christian "heathens" (130), considering it worse being a Christian "than having no god at all" (119). Fry implies that to be a nominal, comfortable Anglican (or Quaker, or Calvinist, or any other kind of establishmentarian Christian) is to be no different from a pagan.

Not only does Fry equate the pagan Jutes with institutional Christianity; he also equates both with the ancient Israelites. Jahweh of the Israelites demanded that all enemies be killed, even women and children, so that Israel would remain racially and religiously pure and Jahweh's honor unblemished (Numbers 31: 1–54; Joshua 6:20–21; Joshua 8:22). Modern Christian states wage war against women and children in Hiroshima, Dachau, and My Lai for the honor of God and country. Jutes live under the same compulsion from Woden and Thor. In war against the Saxons, Cymen the Jute spares a young slave of the Saxons and takes him prisoner. Cymen's fellow Jutes regard saving an enemy as blasphemy:

> The gods relish a knock or two
> Before they lean back and insist on being
> Propitiated. But by no right does this Briton
> Break in and ruffle them beyond all hope. (136)

But the three communities are most alike in their compulsive religious rituals: Jewry produced the Pharisees; Christianity produced ceremonialists, sabbatarians, and compulsory tithers; and Fry's Jutes exhibit a similar formalism:

> I wear myself out securing us to the gods
> With every device that's orthodox, sacrificing
> To the hour, to the split minute of the risen sun.
> But how can I keep them kind if always
> They're being displeased by the rest of you? It isn't
> Easy to keep on the windy side of Woden
> As anyone knows. (121)

Like Jews and Christians, the Jutes deplore blasphemy while they indulge in it:

> Who's blaspheming in the thick of the mist?
> I've got you on my weapon's point.
> (Where the Valhalla is it?) (101)

Equating pagan Jutes, ancient Israelites, and contemporary institutionalized Christians determines the point of view of the play.

Fry implies that the Jewish religion of the Old Testament is as pagan as any other religion, but then the converse is also true: many a pagan religion comes as close to discovering God as does the Jewish religion. Just as Jesus the Christ came to fulfill and transform the Jewish religion into Christianity, so he comes to fulfill and transform all the religions of the world—including formalized Christianity.

Whenever Christianity calcifies into prescribed form and ritual without the experience of God being its essential concern, then it sinks again to the level of Jewry and paganism. This state is better than no religion at all, to be sure. Even the prescribed forms and rituals, dead and calcified though they be, keep alive the memory of God. This awareness of God, no matter how pedantic and doctrinaire, amounts to an elementary hope. But it is not enough. The person of Jesus Christ must revitalize, fulfill, and transform formal establishment Christianity just as certainly as he once revitalized, fulfilled, and transformed the Jewish religion, and as he can revitalize, fulfill, and transform all the religions of the world. That is why Fry makes the pagan community in *Thor* so remarkably similar to our own.

Nothing about *Thor* is more anti-establishmentarian than Fry's ordering of the familiar story. The typical history of Augustine's mission to the Jutes places primary emphasis on Augustine's preaching, secondary emphasis on the response of the Jutes, and tertiary emphasis on the work of God in individual Jutish hearts. Persuasion, not essentially different from Antony swaying the multitude in *Julius Caesar* or a president explaining his tax cuts to a hostile constituency, is the essence of the Christian gospel in the Christian establishment's writing of its own history. The establishment's preoccupation with polemic, apologetic, and dogmatic formulations grows out of its considering the gospel primarily a rhetorical phenomenon. While Fry does not quibble with the necessity of preaching, he gives it only tertiary importance; Augustine's men approach singing in the distance as the play ends. For Fry is convinced that the gospel first arrived in England, not in the preaching of Augustine, but in the direct work of God within human lives, without which no preaching is effective. In Fry's organization of the play, God's work within the heart is of primary importance, the human response to the work of God within the heart is of secondary importance, and preaching is of tertiary importance.

Fry shows God working in human hearts independently from preaching. Fry presents a network of coincidences involving Jutish hearts that are changing even before Augustine has preached. The warlike Cymen turns peaceful by allowing a captive Celt to escape. His daughter, Martina, gives up her hostility to non-Jutes by turning hospitable to the captive Celt. This goes on before Augustine has spoken a word. Only a God who works primarily within human hearts could make such changes happen; only an almighty

God could make these changes—and more—happen all at the same time. If prophetic ecstasies and mystic revelations are beyond their reach, members of the dogma-encrusted establishment still can begin their recovery by tuning their sensibilities to coincidence. Coincidences are for Fry more convincing arguments for the existence of God than any rhetoric.

Two persistent criticisms of Fry are his fondness of coincidence and his episodic plots, in which events follow each other but are not caused by each other. Actually, the two criticisms come down to one, for Fry rarely employs coincidence in its narrowest form, two events going on simultaneously on the stage. Fry makes events happen one after the other, as does any playwright, but Fry's events do not form an inevitable chain of cause and effect. His events form a pattern, but it is not the naturalistic pattern the audience expects. Granted, Fry presses coincidence—related events following each other, though not causing each other—beyond the credibility of the typical audience. But the typical audience is conditioned to thinking of coincidence as mere chance and hence unimportant. Even the decently religious audience thinks of life as natural cause and effect and of God as something one talks about in church. Fry emphasizes coincidences precisely in order to smell out the modern person's offense with meaningful coincidence and with a God who makes coincidences happen, and happen for a recognizable purpose.

Seven coincidental episodes make up *Thor*.

1. The return of Quichelm from battle (101–105) coincides with the return of his mother and the women of the household from sunrise worship, where they have been praying for the safe return of their men from war. The prayer, superstitious and formalistic as it is, coincides with the answer. The characters do not notice the coincidence, but the answered prayer registers on the audience. An orthodox status quo always considers a first-hand experience of God as a threat to its comfort. That is why Quichelm's news from the war is so frightening to the characters. Quichelm tells how his father, Cymen, inexplicably took captive a Celtic slave fighting on the side of the Saxons; in Jutish warfare all captives are killed. Cymen's wife, Clodesuida, could not be more incensed at this news if her husband were an SS trooper who suddenly had qualms about Nazi policy on Jews or if she were a Daughter of the American Revolution whose husband turned

traitor in Viet Nam because he could no longer napalm women and children. Cymen swore, Quichelm reports to Clodesuida, that his sword "broke/Against a staggering light" (104), but Clodesuida knows better. She wonders how his sword really broke and is worried that Cymen blasphemed against Woden: "It's hard enough/ To live well-thought-of by the gods" (105).

2. Cymen returns (105–116), and with him come his younger son, Cheldric; his wife's brothers, the deliberate Tadfrid and the impulsive Osmer; and his prisoner, Hoel—that is, Hell, the most uncomplimentary name the Saxons could think of for a slave taken from the Celts. Clodesuida and Martina could not give Cymen a cooler welcome home if they were comfortable Anglicans who had just heard that he had spoken in tongues. Indeed, he has spoken in terms completely foreign to his Jutish culture. His brother-in-law Osmer, an articulate and glib reporter, clears up the mystery of how the sword broke and repeats Cymen's blasphemy:

> Like a bear-sark blundering
> He hit up our downcoming swords, sprang in
> As white as a water-spout spinning in a full moon,
> Shouting 'The gods can go and beg for blood!
> Let 'em learn of us!' (108)

The ironic coincidence is that just before Osmer reports Cymen's linguistic aberration, the company itself has been speaking in the new tongue:

> Tadfrid: Our guilt be forgiven us.
> Clodesuida: What kind of talk is this?
> Cymen: Tell her, tell her. I'm humble.
> Clodesuida: Do you say that?
> Guilt, forgiveness, humility? What next?
> Are you mad (107)

Though nobody in the play sees the coincidence, the audience cannot escape the fact that the context in which Osmer reports on Cymen's speaking in tongues is itself a context of speaking in tongues. And hard upon it Cymen weeps, though weeping is not legitimate male self-expression in Jutish society. New possibilities for self-expression are opening up.

Even badgering can be God's work; God's work need not be sweet talk. The Germanic warriors drag Hoel into the center of their circle to execute him. After all, Hoel the Celt, fighting for the Saxons, has killed Eccha the Jute. But Cymen wants information from him first and badgers him:

> You can tell me; what flogged away my strength,
> What furtive power in your possession
> Pulled the passion of my sword? Name that devil!
> I'll have our gods harry him between the gaps
> Between the stars, to where not even friends
> Can feed. Name him! (111)

Hoel responds to the threats and badgering: "Who? Who am I to name?/I swear to God I know nothing of what you mean" (111), and later:

> It was my grandfather who knew him well.
> The One God, he's called. But I can't remember
> The details . . . (112)

Hoel remembers when badgered, but he also remembers and speaks because God is breaking through into Jutish society. Stimulus and response, cause and effect do not cease to exist, but they no longer account for everything.

Hoel's remembering the Christian God from his Celtish past is part of the speaking in tongues which precedes it and which follows. Suddenly the sun breaks through the mist. Cymen sees this phenomenon as a symbol of the victory of Thor and Woden over cowardice and sentimentality. Instantly he throws Hoel to the ground and puts a heavy foot on his neck. He extends a glass of mead to the rising sun and expects now to have the courage for the kill. Only, the warlike toast he proposes to drink to the rising sun will not come out right. Instead of the warlike oath, he says, against his will: "Let us love one another" (114), and the goblet drops from his hand. The God to whom Cymen is really drinking a toast is far greater than Thor and Woden, and he considers love greater than courage. This greater God also demands that one should love one's neighbor as oneself and that every fellow human being, even an enemy, should be considered a neighbor. Cymen lunges at Hoel with his sword, but the sword plunges instead with a will of its own toward Cymen's eldest son, Quichelm:

It seems
All one, it seems all one. There's no distinction.
Which is my son? (115)

No distinction, indeed.

Cymen is picking up the gospel before the gospel is preached. God is also at work in Hoel, bringing to mind a God-consciousness he had forgotten. God is renewing the language of the whole tribe without their knowing it.

3. Cymen exits to get some rest for his fevered brain, and his entourage leaves with him. The stage is left to two incongruous couples: Hoel and Martina, Cymen's daughter, who barely begin to be romantically interested in each other; and Colgrin and Anna, married domestics in Cymen's household, who are past romance and trapped in a union that nobody would choose.

As individuals all four have been characterized by incidental appearances in the previous episodes. Colgrin is the lazy servant who cannot find his sword and who is slow in opening the door to the returning warriors. Anna is all business and attention. Episode 3 makes clear that, while affection has replaced romance, Colgrin and Anna have no illusions about each other:

Colgrin: There's my weapon!
There's my dimpled sword! What do you mean, woman,
Hanging wet linen all over it? It's wrong
If it's rusty.

Anna: And a man is, too; and you're
So thick with rust you'd choke if you blew on yourself. (117)

It is time that Colgrin and Anna rediscovered each other romantically.

Colgrin and Anna stand at the opposite polarity from Hoel and Martina, who have a romantic curiosity about each other. While Cymen's threats have brought Hoel to remember God enough to mention him, Martina's curiosity helps him to remember more:

When I was a boy I was only
Allowed to have one [god], though in that One, they said,
There were three. But the altars are broken up. I've tried
To pick away the moss to read the inscriptions
But I've almost forgotten our language. I only know
The god was both father and son and a brooding dove. (119)

He also remembers his Celtic grandfather, whom the Saxons kept as a slave because he worked in metals; the grandfather saw to it that Hoel was baptized. Martina is all attention and encouragement: "It's a pity/You had to be born a Briton. I'm forced to hate you" (120).

The two couples imply a cycle: romantic interest, leading to marriage, leading to disillusionment, leading to the possibility for romance again. The cycle of romance is parallel to the cycle of God-consciousness. Cymen is discovering God; the missionaries from Rome will interpret what he has discovered; this interpretation will fix a theology and establish a religion (like marriage in the erotic cycle); the established religion will harden into a dead orthodoxy not distinguishable from paganism of Clodesuida's sort (like Colgrin and Anna in the erotic cycle); and then will come the process of remembering God again as Hoel does.

While the romance cycle and the discovery-of-God cycle are not identical, neither are they mutually exclusive. That people discover and rediscover each other romantically is not a merely biological phenomenon; the process has a touch of God in it. That people discover and rediscover God is not merely a mystical phenomenon; it is as natural as falling in love, as natural as the cycle of the seasons.

4. The Merlin episode (120–130) is about the cycle of the seasons. Martina describes her discovery of Merlin come back to life as though it were part of gardening in spring:

> I dug him up. He was rather buried,
> I found him in the quarry where it caved in.
> His beard was twisted like mist in the roots of an oak tree,
> Beaded and bright with a slight rain, and he was crying
> Like an old wet leaf. His hands were as brown as a nest
> Of lizards, and his eyes were two pale stones
> Dropping in a dark well. (121)

Christianity, the Celts, and Merlin were eradicated from Britain centuries ago; Merlin describes the silence he has been through as winter:

> This wide harp of winter
> Reverberates. I had stupidly imagined
> The human landscape had left me for ever.
> The face of the foam for me (I told myself)

Until I die. All your expectation
Of friendship, old man (I said to myself)
Is a wink from the eye of a bullfinch
Or the slower solemnities of a tortoise
Or the grudging goodnight from the dark lungs of a toad (123).

And more important, Merlin articulates the mysterious relationship between the seasons and Cymen's discovery of God.

Cymen does not know it is God he is discovering. He asks Merlin, ". . . what cuckoo power/Is it that usurps the nest of my soul?" (127). Merlin answers indirectly. First he asks another question: "You ask an old pagan?" (127). Merlin is a Christian, of course, but Christianity in any time is embodied in a culture, and Christians mistakenly identify their culture with their Christianity, considering whatever is foreign to be also pagan. While the essential Christianity that died with Arthur and the Celts is identical with the new Christianity being reborn in Cymen, the cultural manifestations will differ greatly. Cymen's Christianity will make Merlin look downright pagan, though at bottom they will be fellow Christians. It is a greater mark of Christian maturity to consider oneself a pagan than to consider oneself an impeccably orthodox Christian whose orthodoxy justifies warfare, oppression, and all kinds of unchristian cruelty. Using oneself as the standard for Christianity does damage all around. The old pagan continues:

Old Merlin, old
Eternal suckling, who cannot drag his lips
Away from the breast of earth, even to grow
Into the maturity of heaven. Nothing can wean him
Until his mother puts upon her nipple
The vinegar of death, though, when I walked
Between the dog-rose hedges of my manhood,
It was in a Christian land: in Arthur's land. (127–128)

Merlin does not answer Cymen's question directly ("What power usurps my soul?"), though obliquely he creates an answer: the cycles of life. The images of breast feeding and dog-rose hedges (youth and spring) are at the opposite polarity from the vinegar (ripeness gone sour). The one moves toward the other, just as the land that was Christian under Arthur is not Christian now but will become Christian again:

There I gleamed in the iris of creation's
Eye, and there I laughed as a man should,
Between the pillars of my ribs in the wide
Nave of my chest. A Christian land. (128)

Fry's Merlin considers laughter to be a profoundly religious phenomenon, transforming the human torso into a church. The cycles themselves are comic when viewed at some distance. Tell the chick struggling to get out of the shell that its anxiety is part of normal growth; tell the baby that vinegar on the breast helps it to grow up; tell Cymen that the pacifism he regards as the blemish of cowardice within himself is a normal development in the cycle of forgetting and remembering God. They are comic experiences:

A Christian land. There
It was, and old Joseph's faithful staff
Breaking into scarlet bud in the falling snow.
But, as I said at the time, the miracle
Was commonplace: staves of chestnut wood
And maywood and the like perform it every year. (128)

The Glastonbury thorn, which flowers at Christmas time, believed to have been brought by Joseph of Arimathea, is no more miraculous than the ordinary spring. "What power usurps my soul?"asks Cymen. "The same power that makes it turn spring," answers Merlin in effect.

And men broke their swords in the love of battle,
And broke their hearts in the love of women,
And broke the holy bread in the love of God. (128)

The cycle of kingdoms and civilizations (Celts vs Saxons vs Jutes), the cycle of romance (Hoel and Martina vs Colgrin and Anna), and the cycle of the discovery of God are all as natural as the orbits of planets and the cycle of seasons; and all the cycles are controlled by God. How these cycles belong and do not belong to each other was to be Fry's concern in *Curtmantle*, a decade after *Thor*. Simply recognizing the similarities is at the heart of *Thor*:

I saw them ride away between their loves
Into a circle of the snow-white wind
And so into my head's old yellow world
Of bone. (128)

Merlin is sufficiently abstracted from time and place to have an inkling of how all these cycles form a single pattern. Merlin's chief function in the play is articulating this overview, giving evidence from experience that in the long pull of the centuries all things do work together for good. In addition, of course, Merlin is a patriotic symbol, a nostalgic apparition from King Arthur's court, and a spokesman for the beauty of the English countryside in springtime. But these functions do not detract from his effectiveness as Christian chorus, articulating the ways of God with humankind. Merlin's comments on providence (124), on Hoel's death in baptism (129), and on the centrality of the incarnation in Christianity (129) are just obvious enough for us in the audience to appreciate but just vague enough so as not to rush the process of God-discovery for the Jutes.

The Merlin episode does not deal only with Merlin; it deals also with Martina. Non-Jutes are heathens in Jutish society, and Martina is not above referring to Hoel as a "godless Christian" (126); but even before Hoel arrives, Martina has been showing hospitality to Merlin, a stranger. She has been feeding him in his cave and he has been telling her fortune. This hospitality to strangers, in defiance of her community's—and especially her mother's—hostility to strangers, is parallel to Cymen's pacifism and to Hoel's remembering the God he had lost. It is all part of the pattern that Merlin describes:

Be lost
And then be found. It's an old custom of the earth
From year to year. (124)

5. Suddenly, without the conventional dramatic preparation, wolves attack Cymen's sheep, and all the men rush out to fight them (130–138). The wolves represent what the lion represented to Samson (Judges 14:5–9) and the lion and the bear to David (I Samuel 17: 32–37): a necessary step in a youth's becoming a man.

The wolves
Are beaten off. But the Briton killed the grimmest,
The greatest: with his hands, with his hands as bare
As mine: met and mauled the scavenger, with a grip
Under the blood and froth of the jaws, he shook
And choked the howling out of its fangs
And forced it to a carcase. It was horror
And hope and terror and triumph to see it. (134)

Hoel is suddenly a hero: "What shall we do to reward him?" (134).

In addition to the echoes from the Old Testament which mark the beast-slayer as hero, there are echoes from the New Testament which mark wolves as the embodiment of evil (John 10:12; Acts 20:29). The wolves attacking the sheep give the Jutish community an opportunity to choose between good and evil. We of the audience side automatically with Hoel; our expectations of the theater make us celebrate his triumph as the triumph of right. But we find discerning the right much more difficult in life than in a play. The characters in *Thor* have no reality outside of the play, and their moral complexities are like ours in real life. We who are only clever about ethics in the theater need not scorn Cymen's sons and brothers-in-law for their trouble in discerning the right side.

The sons and brothers come back from the wolf hunt convinced that Hoel must be killed. His influence brought the wolves in the first place, and "who's going to kiss/Future trouble?" (134). He was able to kill the wolf only because the Devil helped him (134).

Clodesuida agrees with her brothers, but she also admires how Hoel killed the grimmest of the wolves. On the one hand she asks, "What shall we do to reward him?" (134); on the other she questions whether her brothers may not be right. She vacillates.

Cymen has a genuine intermediary position. His relatives persuade him that there must be a sacrifice to relieve "the weight of the silence that's on our shoulders now" (135). But Cymen refuses to sacrifice Hoel, who has risked his life to kill the wolves. Cymen wants to sacrifice a goat: "One silence of death is as deep as another/To satisfy the silence" (137). But why any sacrifice at all? In despair and desperation Cymen complains to the gods directly, at the altar:

> The deed of death is done and done and always
> To do, death and death and death; and still
> We cannot come and stand between your knees. (138)

In this mood he throws down the stones of the altar. He overthrows the religious establishment entirely. He is "the outlaw" (139), having broken permanently with orthodoxy. He has progressed from a religion of human sacrifice to vicarious sacrifice of animals, to direct prayer, to agnosticism. As an agnostic he defies the gods:

> Silence me! Come down and silence me!
> Then at least I shall have some kind of part
> With all the rest. (138)

If the gods strike Cymen dead, at least the community will know that the gods exist. If the religious establishment is validated, even Cymen will yield to it again. Cymen and Hoel will both need to die then, but Cymen will die belonging. It is worth the risk.

God answers, but not by striking Cymen dead. While all but Cymen and Hoel cower on the ground waiting for the gods to strike Cymen dead, a messenger appears, coincidentally, inviting Cymen to hear St. Augustine. By answering Cymen on the spot, God demonstrates that he approves the overthrow of the dead orthodoxy. He approves of it as much as he approves of winter turning to spring.

The heart of the wolf episode is coincidence, and at the heart of the coincidence is God. God makes the appearance of wolves coincide with Hoel's being a prisoner. God makes the invitation for Cymen to hear Augustine coincide with Cymen's desperate prayer. True, the play can give only an illusion of God. Fry sets up the coincidences as a test for the audience. Just as the characters in the play group themselves for and against Hoel, so Fry sets up the coincidences so some members of the congregation—it was written for church—will need to call the play bad theater. Such viewers dislike coincidence and prefer to have their plays limited to cause and effect. Members of the congregation who find Fry's use of coincidence convincing will be stimulated to find God in the coincidences of their own lives. Take it or leave it, but Fry's formulation leaves no doubt as to which members of the congregation he considers closed-minded.

Fry weights the scale in favor of meaningful coincidence by means of Merlin, who keeps hysteria controlled while the others go to fight the wolves, and, before settling to sleep, indulges in a long soliloquy. One starts with appreciating coincidences and ends with Merlin's poise. Merlin's near-sightedness seems to confuse the seasons of the year with seasons in human affairs. Actually, what looks like confusion is the profoundest unified view of reality:

> Considerable
> Age makes me nod; I neither agree
> Nor disagree. I'm too near-sighted now

> To be able to distinguish one thing from another,
> The storm-swollen river from the tear-swollen eyes,
> Or the bare cracked earth from the burnt-out face,
> Or the forest soughing from the sighing heart.
> What is in one is in the other. . . (132)

Merlin had expressed the relationship of seasons of the year and human season before in Episode 4, with the emphasis on spring. Now, with the wolf hunt going on off-stage, the emphasis is on winter:

> What is in one is in the other, a mood
> Of rage which turns upon itself to savage
> Its own body, since there's nothing except itself
> On which anger can alight. . . (132)

On one level Merlin is saying that they who live by the sword shall perish by the sword; the Saxons conquer the Celts, and the Jutes try to conquer the Saxons. On another level Merlin is saying that destroyers do damage to themselves when they destroy others; their consciences make life unbearable or they lose conscience, which makes life unbearable in another way; destroyers are burdened like Cymen or like the Jutish establishment. And on another level Merlin is saying that anger produces anger; the anger in A becomes the object of anger in B. From the limited perspective of the characters, of course, the wolves must be fought and killed; even from the perspective of the audience. From Merlin's perspective over the centuries no violence is worth it, for it accomplishes nothing in the long pull. The violence saves only these sheep for these people. On the other hand, winter is the violence in a nature which groans to be delivered. Merlin has developed the poise to accept violence in the human seasons as one accepts winter in the natural. For anger—that is, violence—

> Sinks into time
> Like a sword into snow
> And the roots receive all weathers and subsist,
> And the seasons are reconciled. (132)

The wolves attack the sheep, Hoel attacks the wolves, and the Jutes attack Hoel and the wolves. Merlin has seen it all before:

The Romans fell away from our branching roads
Like brazen leaves, answering
The hopeless windy trumpets from their home,
Your tribes waged winter upon us, till our limbs
Ached with the carving cold. You blackened
The veins of the valleys with our dried blood. And at last
Your lives croaked like crows on a dead bough
And the echoes clanged against you. (132–133)

All violence is waging not war, but winter. If winter comes, can spring be far behind? Fry's Merlin holds that wherever God's liberating word appears, springtime shakes off the restrictions of winter's dead orthodox violence:

But I can hear
Faintly on the twittering sea a sail
Moving greatly where the waves, like harvest-home,
Come hugely on our coast: the men of Rome
Returning, bringing God, winter over, a breath
Of green exhaled from the hedges, the wall of sky
Breached by larksong. Primrose and violet
And all frail privileges of the early ground
Gather like pilgrims in the aisles of the sun.
A ship in full foliage rides in
Over the February foam, and rests
Upon Britain. (133)

Having made his peace with time, Merlin is no longer the victim of any crisis or of his own hysterical reactions as the other characters are. His comment on the wolf attack is that Augustine's men are coming; his consolation in the winter of violence is that Augustine's boat is loaded with flowers and spring; his comment on time is that he cannot distinguish springtime from harvest-home; his comment on progress is that it is a process as natural and slow and inevitable as the seasons, and the only progress which is not illusory is the rediscovery of God.

No wonder Merlin appears scatter-brained to Colgrin: "He's in the clouds, you see; he's away/On his own; he's blowing about like the hairs in his beard" (133).

6. The absence of Cymen to hear Augustine (138–151) makes the establishment turn more orthodox and pagan than ever. In the

minds of the establishment the invitation for Cymen to hear Augustine does not constitute an answer to prayer. "Rigid with reality" (140), the sons and brothers-in-law begin to shore up their ruins by building up the altar. Cymen had said they could ("It will be somewhere to sit when the days are warmer," 141), but they do not rebuild it in Cymen's spirit. The rebuilt altar demands sacrifice to be made on it in order for it to be a real altar again, for to the gods

> The stones are still pitching and blundering
> From juting god to jutting god, down
> The scowling scarp of their everlasting memory (143).

The establishment leaves to screw up its courage for what needs to be done, and to pray.

Martina and Hoel are left together.

> Martina: You're a born heathen. Get some sleep.
> You look too tired to be hated
> And that won't do at all.
>
> Hoel: Do you have to hate me?
>
> Martina: It isn't one of my easiest duties. But how else
> Can we keep our footing or our self-esteem? (144–145)

Martina leaves and soon returns with food, which Hoel eats from her hand. "You have to be/A good enemy and eat" (147). Hoel reflects on their growing love:

> What simple-witted things the affections are,
> That can't perceive whether people are enemies
> Or friends. (148)

Just as Martina places a kiss on Hoel's forehead, Cymen's sons and brothers-in-law return from consultation and prayer: yet another coincidence. Now the relatives have the evidence they are looking for: "Toleration has gone its limit" (149). Martina's protests on Hoel's behalf do not convince the orthodox: "We do what's demanded of us, with solemnity,/Without passion" (149).

As the orthodox crucify Hoel, Martina cries for her father, and Hoel mistakes her cry for a prayer. He answers her "Father!" with "Son and the brooding dove" (150). Hoel has remembered his Christianity, and God has remembered the child offered to him in baptism. "The spirit is very tenacious of such water" (130), Merlin had said when told that Hoel had been baptized.

The murderers justify their act as necessary for religious peace and comfortable orthodoxy:

> Osmer: Woden, we pay your dues
> Of blood.
>
> Tadfrid: Receive it and receive us back
> Into a comfortable security. (151)

It is the same comfortable security that the Pharisees wanted to preserve in crucifying Christ. Whenever religion turns experiential, whenever God breaks through into time, dead orthodoxy is threatened and turns violent.

Violence is wicked, but violence ought not shock Christians who understand their imperfect world. Just as during the wolf hunt Merlin interprets the violence by dwelling on the cycle of the seasons, so, as events move toward the crucifixion just described, Merlin soliloquizes again. It is a convenient break dramatically for Martina to prepare food and suggests the passage of time between morning and late afternoon, dividing the play's action into two halves: killing wolves and killing Hoel. But more. Merlin's second long soliloquy begins just where the previous soliloquy (132–133) leaves off: the seasons.

> Welcome, sleep;
> Welcome into the winter head of the world
> The sleep of Spring, which grows dreams,
> Nodding trumpets, blowing bells,
> A jingle of birds whenever the sun moves,
> Never so lightly; all dreams,
> All dreams out of slumbering rock:
> Lambs in a skittle prance, the hobbling rook
> Like a witch picking sticks,
> And pinnacle-ears the hare
> Ladling himself along in the emerald wheat:
> All dreams out of the slumbering rock,
> Each dream answering to a shape
> Which was in dream before the shapes were shapen;
> Each growing obediently to a form,
> To its own sound, shrill or deep, to a life
> In water or air, in light or night or mould;

> By sense or thread perceiving,
> Eye, tendril, nostril, ear; to the shape of the dream
> In the ancient slumbering rock. (145)

Life is a variety of dreams; death a single dream, a simplification, but continuous with life:

> And above the shapes of life, the shape
> Of death, the singular shape of the dream dissolving,
> Into which all obediently come. (145)

Beyond the dreams of life and the dream of death is the awakening into God's morning:

> And above the shape of death, the shape of the will
> Of the slumbering rock, the end of the throes of sleep
> Where the stream of the dream wakes in the open eyes
> Of the sea of the love of the morning of the God. (145–146)

Life as dream, death as waking figures a Platonic afterlife; life as reality, death as dream figures a secular view. In Fry's view both life and death are dreams, from which one awakens to a physical reality in God's morning. Fry affirms the resurrection of the body.

Life, death, awakening, spring: these were also the images in the soliloquy in Episode 4 when Merlin was assimilating the violence of the wolf hunt; but they are not sufficient for Merlin to assimilate Hoel's impending death. Here young love is being cut off; here death occurs for the sake of perverted worship; here the coincidence of the murder with Cymen's hearing the Christian gospel is too cruel—God's timing seems to be all wrong; here the pity is that Hoel's rediscovered Christianity cannot be practiced; here the similarity to Christ's crucifixion makes the previous consolation incomplete. The metaphor of spring for the perpetual return of the Christian gospel is not enough. Merlin needs something more comprehensive than cycles and seasons, something to show progress in spite of Hoel's crucifixion.

Merlin turns to the metaphor of evolution, redefined in Christian terms: humankind must grow into the reality God prepares for it. Merlin introduces the evolution idea by imagining he is a squirrel looking at himself in the nutmeat he is about to eat, as in a mirror:

However warmly I curl
My tail around my feet and admire myself
Reflected in the nut before I bite. . . (146)

It is Merlin's backward look at himself: man to squirrel to nut. The backward look implies a forward look to follow:

Still I observe the very obdurate pressure
Edging men towards a shape beyond
The shape they know. Now and then, by a spurt
Of light, they manage the clumsy approximation,
Overturn it, turn again, refashion
Nearer the advising of their need. (146)

Merlin understands Cymen's process of overthrowing an orthodoxy and redefining his relationship with God without any tradition getting in the way. The basic human thirst is the thirst for God; the thirst is always short of being satisfied because one's concept of God is never accurate and complete. The progress one makes in discovering God is every bit as arduous as the evolutionary process from worm to human being:

Always the shape lying over the life.
Pattern of worm in the sand was not the shape,
Nor the booming body of enormous beast,
Nor the spread fan of the blue-eyed quivering tail,
Nor the weave of the nest, nor the spun wheel of the web,
Nor the maze and cellarage of honey, nor
The charts and maps of men. (146)

Evolution includes worm, elephant, peacock, oriole, spider, and bee; but none of these—not even technological humankind with charts and maps—can know God, can know the shape lying over the life. Only by language can people learn to know something about God:

The shape shone
Like a faint circle round a moon
Of hazy gods, and age by age

> The gods reformed according to the shape,
> According to the shape that was a word,
> According to Thy Word. (146)

Whatever God reveals, humankind must still discover and articulate. Whatever humankind discovers and articulates, God has already revealed. To the extent that the human word is true, it is also God's word. To the extent that it can be made comprehensible to other people, it is a human word. God's word is incomprehensible except when it coincides with the human word. God's word and the human word exist in tension, which is why "the gods reformed according to the shape/. . . that was a word" (146); that is, ideas about God changed as people articulated their experiences with God better.

God's Incarnate Word adjusts the tension between God's word and human words. The Incarnate Word is Jesus Christ; he is the next step in the evolutionary process, except, unlike mechanistic evolutionists, Fry believes that the next step has already been taken. As we now are, Christ once was, trapped in all of the moral ambiguities of a particular establishment; as Christ now is, having conquered evil and death and living forever, we may become.

"According to thy Word" is an echo from the "Nunc Dimittis," the song sung by the ancient Simeon when Christ as baby was presented in the temple: "Lord, now lettest thou thy servant depart in peace; according to thy word. For mine eyes have seen thy salvation, which thou hast prepared before the face of all people, to be a light to lighten the Gentiles and to be the glory of thy people Israel" (Luke 2:29–32). Merlin and Simeon both see an outworn orthodoxy replaced by Christianity. The coming of Christianity strikes both Simeon and Merlin as a rediscovery of something forgotten. Simeon calls the new Savior "the glory of thy people Israel"—a new Moses, David, Elijah. Merlin remembers Britain as a Christian land under Arthur. Having spoken, both Merlin and Simeon depart. They have found the sum of wisdom.

The "Nunc Dimittis" is still sung (or read) at the conclusion of the lessons, before the creed and prayers, at daily Evensong in the Anglican liturgy. Written to be played in a church, *Thor* reminds the audience at this point that the occasion is Evensong.[2] The traditional Evensong dialogue between narrative or doctrine in the lessons on the one hand and the poetry in the psalms, in the "Magnificat," and in the "Nunc Dimittis" on the other is preserved in *Thor*. At Evensong the brute fact of narrative or the starkness of doctrine is muted by the poetry; in *Thor* Merlin's speeches serve the same function. To say that Merlin's speeches diffuse the tragic effect or mar what could have been a Sophoclean unity is to miss what Fry is about. While not underestimating the horror of Hoel's crucifixion, Fry never lets the audience forget that even the grimmest tragedy is only a tragedy as long as one sees it out of context; *sub specie aeternitatis*, Merlin's view and Simeon's, God succeeds at turning even the pain of tragedy into such joy as no cause-and-effect view would have considered possible. Lest any in the audience expect tragic catharsis from *Thor*, the echo from Evensong reminds them that this is church. *Thor* does what any church service is meant to do: to help the worshipper recognize that in God's incarnate Word is a sufficiently broad context in which to interpret one's own situation, to help one adjust the human word to the ultimate Word, and to help one leave for an everyday situation with new hope, purpose, and joy. Moreover, church services move forward not by plot but by episodes.[3]

Nothing about *Thor* is more deliberate then Fry's placing Merlin's evolution soliloquy just before Hoel's crucifixion. The soliloquy is the lens through which to view Hoel's crucifixion.

7. Cymen returns (151–154) at peace with himself and with the world. After Augustine's good news, he is finished forever with dead orthodoxy.

> I have seen our terrible gods come down
> To beg the crumbs which fall from our sins, their only
> Means of life. (151)

Coming back from Augustine's sermon, Cymen knows that all the necessary violence of the world has been borne by Christ in the crucifixion.

> And never again need we sacrifice, on and on
> And on, greedy of the gods' goodwill
> But always uncertain; for sacrifice
> Can only perfectly be made by God
> And sacrifice has so been made, by God
> To God in the body of God with man,
> On a tree set up at the four crossing roads
> Of earth, heaven, time, and eternity
> Which meets upon that cross. (152)

It is one thing to be persuaded that violence is useless, and quite another to stop it. Will Cymen turn violent again, against his relatives this time, when he discovers the cruelly ironic coincidence? While he was away learning non-violence his relatives were crucifying Hoel. If it is only Augustine's rhetoric that changed Cymen, he will revert to violence as soon as the rhetoric wears off.

Legitimate preaching assumes that God, not the preacher, makes pagans into Christians. Preaching is necessary. Cymen would still be perplexed by the strange changes within his mind and behavior if it were not for Augustine's preaching. Legitimate preaching is not so much eloquent persuasion in Fry's view as sympathetic interpretation of God's work within the heart. As was mentioned above, God's work is of primary importance, Cymen's change of secondary importance, and preaching of tertiary importance. Preaching is necessary, but tertiary.

Since the changes in Cymen occurred by God's direct working within his heart and not by rhetorical eloquence, Cymen remains Christian and non-violent even after he discovers the crucifixion of Hoel. Cymen's confrontation with Hoel's crucifixion prompts him to discover what Merlin has been saying all along, though never to Cymen: God turned Christ's crucifixion to the redemption of the world and he can also turn Hoel's crucifixion to good:

> They say
> The sacrifice of God was brought about
> By the blind anger of men, and yet God made
> Their blindness their own saving and lonely flesh
> Welcome to creation. (153)

Is it Cymen who makes Hoel's murder produce good, is it God, or is it God working within and through Cymen? All three:

> For while I leave one muscle of my strength
> Undisturbed, or hug one coin of ease
> Or private peace while the huge debt of pain
> Mounts over all the earth,
> Or, fearing for myself, take half a stride
> Where I could leap; while any hour remains
> Indifferent, I have no right or reason
> To raise a cry against this blundering cruelty
> Of man. (153)

Cymen's hatred of violence within himself and others, and his simultaneous love of others, even though they may be violent: that complicated attitude—committed to action without self-righteousness—is an early good result of Hoel's murder. Cymen is open to change. The closedness of the Jutes is voiced by Clodesuida in justification of the murder: "We have to live" (152). Cymen has become open: "We have still to learn to live" (153).

Cymen's open-endedness is evident in the refrain which Cymen first states immediately after his return, repeats after he knows Hoel was crucified, and repeats again to end the play as with a benediction: ". . . lonely flesh be welcome to creation" (154). Dead orthodoxy makes flesh lonely. It self-righteously alienates the orthodox from other people, and it puritanically alienates the orthodox from a full enjoyment of the physical world and of the senses. But most important, dead orthodoxy posits a closed world of cause and effect. In Fry's view, God is never finished creating the world; he keeps on creating the world through humanity. The world of dead orthodoxy is a world of violence. It begins with competition; it leads to the exploitation of resources, landscape, and people; it leads to hatred; and it leads to war. Even the most humanitarian urban renewal project and the noblest art are not free from the violence of competition. Violence is the prod to productivity among the dead orthodox. The prod to productivity in the happy Christian society—which society does not exist anywhere—is accepting God's invitation to help him finish creating the world.

Representing a state of mind which does not yet exist is Fry's problem in writing *Thor*. Merlin, abstracted from the specific hostilities of a specific time and place, is essential for Fry's purpose. He has made his "peace with Time" (127); he has seen Saxon conquer Celt and then assimilate the Celtish mythology of Arthur as its own, all hostility ended. Merlin has learned to care and not to care. He has come to see human history as one with the cycle of the seasons and with the long evolutionary process. Merlin is totally welcome to creation. Cymen has barely begun to be.

All of this paper is implied in Fry's title: *Thor, with Angels*. Fry is playing with the famous pun of Pope Gregory I, who, when told that the fair-complexioned slaves in the Roman marketplace were called Angles, replied that they were more like angels and proceeded to send Augustine on his mission. With Pope Gregory's pun in the background, one sees three other titles which Fry might have called his play, or rather, three other plays he might have written.

1. *Christ, with Angels* would show a mature Christianity; the play would present the stability of heaven. Merlin's state of mind comes closest to this, but it is out of reach for ordinary people with one lifetime apiece in which to make progress. The title would be wrong for the play Fry wrote.

2. *Thor, with Angles* (that is, with the English): This play would restrict itself to the nationalistic paganism with which the play begins. This play would approve the pagan status quo which crucifies Hoel.

3. *Christ, with Angles* (that is, with the English): This play would drag Christ down to the level of Thor. This tribal Christ existed in the nineteenth century to hold the British Empire together and ceased to exist as the empire waned. This Christ is the Christ of the establishment, sending armies to battle with the sanctions of King and Archbishop. This Christ is served by citizens of any country who put the concerns of God below the concerns of the state. This paganism is interchangeable with that of the community at the start of *Thor, with Angels.* The only difference is that the Christian truth has been reduced to Christian mythology, and the Christian mythology has replaced the pagan mythology. In this hypothetical play, the pagan community would be convinced of its impeccable Christianity.

4. *Thor, with Angels,* the play Fry did write, is concerned with the moment of the religious experience: Pope Gregory seeing angels in his slaves, Martina and Cymen seeing an angel in Hoel, their enemy. The Jutish theology has not yet changed; their god is still Thor, but Martina and Cymen's religious experience is thoroughly Christian.

It is a fragile state of affairs, of course. The moment Cymen comes home with the Christian theology, the mystery is vulnerable to domestication. As soon as Augustine's men arrive—they approach at the end, singing—coincidences will be less important than straight doctrine. When the Jutes organize themselves into a Christian state, they will be justifying wars and hatred of the heathen just as they had for Thor.

When a society feels totally secure in its Christian orthodoxy, its Christianity turns to paganism again. Prolonging the moment of conversion is the point: prolonging the mystery, the coincidences, the sense of God's leading, the love of enemies, and one's trouble defining God—which never should be easy. Awareness of one's pagan past is necessary in order to remain open; one's pagan past is never twelve centuries away, or twelve years, or even twelve hours. Merlin remains so open because he has the honesty to call himself "an old pagan" (127) and "more than half a pagan" (146). Not to remember one's paganism is to identify Christianity with the status quo of the society in which one lives and to assume that one has grown sophisticated about God. One can be sophisticated in the study of theology, but even theologians cannot risk being sophisticated about God.

Fry is not really against established Christianity, in spite of the fact that it is an Anglican altar that is overturned when Cymen destroys the Jutish altar. In spite of the overturned altar, *Thor* is an Anglican Evensong. The greatest danger for the established Christians at Evensong, however, is a dead orthodoxy as pagan as that of the Jutes. *Thor* and the overturned altar are an elaborate metaphor for saying so.

The naming of God is at the heart of it all, for Fry believes that the moment one names God one is in danger of limiting God and in danger of limiting one's own response to God. *Thor, with Angels*, suggesting a changed concept of God without a change in vocabulary, is the optimum moment.

Fry wrote me the following, 16 January 1967:

> To come to your letter: no, of course we have no quarrel. Though there may very well be, as you say, a difference in emphasis. My preference for no-naming to bad-naming is that so many people who are antagonistic to Christianity are conducting a war against windmills. And windmills are what bad-naming is. I can't follow you when you say that "better a distorted concept of God . . . than none at all." A distortion is a lie. Think of the cruelties, social and domestic, that have been inflicted in the misnomer of God. Surely God acts through character (in its deepest meaning), not through human vocabulary. I can't think that God would be helpless if there were no Church or no word God. But he would be helpless if men ceased to respond to the indwelling presence. Don't

> misunderstanding me. Of course the Church and naming can be a creative strength and much to be guarded and loved. I am only saying that the Word is greater than the letters of the word: and I see more future in a non-Christian Christian than in a Christian non-Christian—but you will begin to think that I'm being facetious!

Merlin, Cymen, Martina, and Hoel are non-Christian Christians.

A MANIFESTO FOR WOMEN 6

Venus Observed

The main plot of *Venus Observed*[1] concerns the autumnal Duke of Altair, who has invited three former mistresses to his observatory to watch an eclipse of the sun. He has instructed his son, Edgar, himself of marriageable age, to award a golden apple to one of the three mistresses. The chosen one will become the duke's duchess and Edgar's stepmother.

Rosabel is the Venus of the piece: temperamental actress, she is quite aware of her own physical attractiveness and impatient with competition. Jessie is the Hera: her passive virtues are practical and wifely. She pretends to be a little more stupid than God made her, but her naivete serves her well, sometimes as a weapon—she can disguise insult as compliment—and sometimes as a benign trick of stopping an argument by changing the subject. Jessie, then, is a shrewdly diplomatic Hera, but unintellectual. Hilda, cast as Athene, is possessed of a wisdom that is clear and uncompromising, yet so much like common sense that it tends toward dullness: "I know," she says, "I have/No particular heights or depths myself;/No one who thought me ordinary or dull/Would be far wrong" (45). "The case of Athene," observes the duke, "is minutely complicated/By a husband" (15). However, Hilda's marriage hardly disqualifies her as a symbol of chastity, for her marriage seems to be curiously sexless, indeed, meaningless. By her own account, Roderic, her husband, is a "level depth of dullness" (45). Here, then, are Athene, Hera, and Venus, the goddesses of the myth of Paris and the golden apple, metamorphosed into recognizable twentieth-century types.

According to the ancient myth, the three goddesses argue about which of them is loveliest. They invite Paris to arbitrate their disagreement. Paris chooses Venus, who has promised him the loveliest mortal for his own; Hera and Athene become jealous and bring about the burning of Troy, Paris' native city, through the instrumentality of the Athenians. Priam, father of Paris and King of Troy, must assume responsibility for conducting the resulting war, even though Priam knows nothing of the choice.

The situation is different in the autumn of Fry's play. The argument as to which of the three goddesses is loveliest takes place not among the goddesses but in the mind of the duke. Paris-Edgar is not elected judge by the goddesses, nor does his choice imply any reward for him; he chooses for his father at his father's request. Fry, in short, has changed the myth from a parable about the absolute categories of women into a parable about a very wrong, though prevalent, male attitude toward women.

To the anonymous pre-Homeric myth makers, to Homer himself perhaps, and certainly to the interpreters of the myth after him, the three goddesses were the absolutes of all womanhood. All women are to be typed as sex object, as wife and mother, or as wise companion. The categories say more about the men who framed them than about the eternal reality of womanly nature. The makers of the myth and its interpreters until the present tend to be "male chauvinists,"—the duke too.

But not Fry. His new attitude toward women is the reason for his removing the conflict from among the goddesses and placing it in the mind of his Priam.

Edgar awards the apple to Rosabel, erotically the most attractive of the three women, but Rosabel, though not understanding that she is elected into wifedom, is very much troubled by the apple and by the duke. After an emotional outburst on her part, Edgar has second thoughts and reclaims the apple. He gives it to his father with the suggestion that he give it to Jessie. But the duke is delayed by the arrival of Perpetua Reedbeck, daughter of the duke's steward. She has just arrived from serving a prison sentence in America for disturbing the peace as a member of the Society for the Desecration of Ancient and Modern Errors. Both Edgar and the duke fall immediately in love with her, and the duke offers her the golden apple, but Perpetua produces a pistol and shoots the apple out of his hand. This unladylike gesture does not at all diminish the desires of Edgar and the duke for her; and while the three ignored goddesses disport themselves individually, the two gentlemen compete for Perpetua's affections. Attracted to Edgar, Perpetua is nevertheless persuaded by her brother, Dominic, to favor the duke because their father, the duke's steward, has systematically embezzled from the duke's exchequer over the years and the duke would not be likely to press charges against his father-in-law. Therefore, when the duke invites Perpetua for an afternoon of archery, she consents, although Edgar intrudes into their afternoon. When Edgar invites Perpetua to a Hallowe'en party and when the duke invites her to spend the night with him in his observatory, she pleads travel fatigue to Edgar but agrees to go along with the duke. She understands the politics of sex. Alone with the duke at night, Perpetua explains the ambiguities of her situation, though she does not complain of them or use them as an argument against making love. She simply cannot love the duke as she loves Edgar.

The addition of Perpetua is Fry's boldest adaptation of the myth of Paris.

> And I am the eight duchesses
> And the three housekeepers and the chambermaid
> Combing their hair. I am any girl: Perpetua
> Perpetual, making no gesture I can call
> My own, engraving theirs one lifetime deeper. (65)

Perpetua is the perpetual renewal of womanhood, the perpetual breaking through prescribed categories, the perpetual refusal to adjust to a world that males establish for females. Perpetua is any girl; she fits all categories at once. Erotically desirable, she attracts the duke and Edgar irresistibly when she first enters, and she also can be irresistibly attracted to Edgar in the magic of love.

But Perpetua is also like Jessie. While the other mistresses are full of agitation, Jessie reacts to the upheavals of the morning by writing her father a letter. He cannot read any longer, but he likes to have the postman stop. Perpetua is indulgent of her father in a similar way: "Let me look at you. Every feature where I left it/Ten years ago! I'd forgotten you were so beautiful" (25). Perpetua is also like Jessie in her skill at diverting a line of thought, about an apple, say.

Perpetua is, finally, also a wise and analytical Athene. Like Hilda, she can recognize what is dull; she can also recognize "the unsightly,/The gimcrack, the tedious, the hideous, the spurious,/ The harmful" (30). Hilda can see herself as ordinary and dull (45); Perpetua says to herself, "Perpetua . . . you're no one, you're everybody's colour" (31). And like Hilda, Perpetua is eminently practical. She knows that prudence and emotions cooler than love may require her to marry the duke; if Perpetua married the duke, their relationship would probably be much like Hilda and Roderic's.

Perpetua is more than a combination of the qualities of the three goddesses of legend, of course. For the golden apple coveted by Venus is shattered by Perpetua on behalf of complete women. The rationalistic, categorizing tradition of Greece and Rome has taught the western world to categorize women along with everything else. The dumb blond is our Venus; the only reason for her to study at a university is to hook a man. The good cook and loving mother is our Hera; we buy her cologne for her birthday but never a bikini. And who considers the erotic needs of a woman scholar? Let her be Athene, content with her intellectual probing. When Perpetua shoots the golden apple to pieces, she is asserting that women will no longer submit passively to the typing which a male-dominated society inflicts on them. In any production of the play, Perpetua must be seen as a committed feminist.

But Perpetua is not rejecting the artificially-imposed roles of Venus, Hera, and Athene only to be trapped in another role. She does not become a Diana: Actaeon-killing, man-castrating, and celibate. What she is seeking is the emergence of her own unique identity, the freedom to be what life reveals her to be. The golden apple was "a threat to my new-come freedom" (31), says Perpetua; the golden apple, an ancient and modern monumental error, is not to come between a person and the mystery of self-discovery.

Yet, while she does not accept the Diana role, still Perpetua shows some likeness to the classical Diana. For example, she fires a pistol at the golden apple; and in the afternoon she and the duke disport themselves with bow and arrows—Diana's traditional hunting equipment. Like Diana, Perpetua is chaste, though in a large and special sense, for she agrees to spend the night with the duke. But she does so with the chaste intention of marrying him, and that with the coolest, most sexless motive: keeping her father out of jail.

Thus Perpetua is a flirtatious Venus, a domestic Hera, a wise

Athene, and a pistol-shooting Diana. In Perpetua, Edgar will find everything that any man needs in a woman: lover, wife, companion, and, yes, opponent too.

Not only is Perpetua a complete woman; she is also the cause of completeness in other women. Rosabel says it for the others: "The girl Perpetua/Has the courage that makes a person come true" (57). Again, Fry's play differs from the classical myth; for though the mythical goddesses appear on the scene in character and on good terms with each other, they leave, after the apple episode, still in character but polarized against one another: Athene, articulate about injustice; Hera, frankly envious; Venus, defensive. They are frozen in their roles forever. In Fry's play, the women abandon their narrow roles.

Immediately after Perpetua demolishes the apple, Rosabel is much interested: "If only I/Could be such a brave one, there might be/Some justification for me" (31). Rosabel becomes brave enough to set fire to the duke's observatory as a demonstration. The observatory is as much a symbol of male chauvinism as the golden apple, for in that observatory the duke observes women and stars with equal detachment. He feels no personal relationship with any of his mistresses; so Rosabel commits arson: ". . . he should be made to feel," she explains (57). Following Perpetua's example, in Diana's aggressive manner, Rosabel desecrates a monumental error. Moreover, she refuses to be indulged as the duke's naughty, darling girl; she insists on going to prison like Perpetua before her. No longer simply a Venus, she is on the way to being a complete woman.

Perpetua is the cause for completeness in Jessie too. Jessie is as excited as anybody by the apple scene and characteristically works off her frustrations by writing a letter to her father. But she also eggs Edgar on into aggressiveness. Edgar, envious of his father's teaching Perpetua archery, says, "From here I think I could send an arrow right past him/Into the target"; and Jessie says, "What you think you can, then do." When he shoots and hits the target, Jessie says, "What did you do? Did I encourage you/To be mischievous? I was thinking about my letter." But Jessie knew all the while what she was thinking about:

> . . . as you didn't kill anybody, I may say
> I think it was splendid, and I think perhaps
> You should do it more often. (49–50)

Characteristically domestic about her aggression, she nevertheless becomes more Diana-like; on the other hand, she also becomes more Venus-like. Jessie, of all people, accompanies the much younger Edgar to the Hallowe'en dance, since Perpetua is unable to go. Thus Jessie too is a more complete woman.

As is Hilda.

> Because of the strange business
> Of the eclipse this morning, and what went on,
> We've been thrown into each other's confidence
> Unexpectedly soon. And for my part
> I think I'm thankful. I've always hidden more
> Than was good for me . . . (44)

Clever women have typically needed to hide more than is good for them in order to survive in the western world, but now Hilda has the courage to admit to herself and to Jessie what her wise and probing mind has long known: her husband Roderic is dull. But she also discovers that there is more to herself than probing intellect, for when word comes that Roderic has been thrown from a horse and injured, Hilda, the Athene, is full of a most Hera-like concern. She urges Jessie to "forget I laughed at him" (48) and rushes to be with him; and when she returns she has blended her intellectual convictions about Roderic's dullness with a new sense of the essential mystery of all human life:

> . . . and I sat
> Beside him and marvelled, and wondered how
> So much could lie there in a human shell,
> The long succession of life that led to him,
> Uninterrupted from the time
> Of time's aching infancy;
> In the beginning was Roderic; and now
> Haunting the same shell, were a childhood
> And a manhood, half a hundred years
> Of sights and sounds which once echoed and shone
> And now may only exist in him. And though
> He tries to be a copy of all his kind
> How can he be? He is Roderic-phenomenon,
> Roderic only, and at present Roderic in pain.

> I felt I must tell you so. This afternoon
> I made a cockshy of him, but this afternoon
> I could no more truly see him than he, poor darling,
> Can truly see half that there is to see. (92)

As intellectually penetrating and honest as before, Hilda is now also full of domestic concern like Hera and even capable of genuine romantic ardor for the uniqueness (in spite of dullness) of Roderic-phenomenon. Roderic's injury alone would not have changed her so drastically. Perpetua's shooting the apple gives Hilda the courage to admit to herself and to Jessie that Roderic is a bore. Without that honest admission, she would have gone home to tend him with Athene's sexless determination, but she would not have been open to discovering anything besides dullness in Roderic.

Fry makes other adaptations. In the classical myth, Troy is burned. The pity, one feels, is that a proud city should burn for selfishness and stupidity. But pity is not the point of the fire in Fry's play. Rosabel's motive in setting the observatory ablaze is to help the duke:

> . . . nothing less than fire will do to open his eyes
> On to the distances that separate him
> From other people. (58)

The fire is meant to be, and proves to be, redemptive.

The necessity for violence is one of Fry's chief preoccupations; for him it is one of two ways people learn. Paradoxically, violence is also immoral for Fry. One feels that Fry considers it no more than right that Rosabel should sit in prison for her act of arson. But when violence occurs, evil though it be, it becomes the occasion for insight and growth. The proper response to the experience of violence is never pity but a creative alertness for how to turn evil into good.

The other way that people learn is pacifism. The classical myth says that the youthful, passionate decision of Paris led to the difficulties; in Fry's rehandling, the passive indecision of an old man is to blame.

The duke cannot choose because he has imprisoned the women in mutually exclusive cells. He, with all society, has made each woman what she is by defining her role too rigorously as either a sex machine, or a domestic servant, or a brain, and the women have been only too happy to fit into the compartments. No wonder the duke shrinks from choosing any one of them. His prescribing the roles—rather than simply observing life and letting it reveal itself to him—has turned the women into one-dimensional monsters to whom he cannot commit himself. The women are the passive victims of male chauvinism, but males are also the passive victims of the women. The women have passively become what the men insisted they should, and they now have some right to say, "Now choose." The sexes are in bondage to each other.

As serious as the duke's bondage to women is the duke's bondage to himself. The duke's chauvinism is less a sign of healthy aggressiveness than of fearful passivity. Observing Venus rather than dictating to her calls for flexibility and versatility the duke is not sure he has. Sexually potent in bed, the duke is nevertheless passively impotent in his relationships with women outside of bed. His suavity is only the cover-up for his inadequacy. His male passivity masking as male strength dictates the acceptable roles for the women and becomes, therefore, covert aggression.

The only effective weapon against unrecognized violence is recognized violence. It is the contemporary meaning of the word *demonstration*. The exposure of the duke's hostile passivity requires the shooting of the apple and the burning of the observatory. *Venus Observed* is Fry's demonstration against the duke's attitudes as they appear in society—in us all.

The choice of Paris leading to the burning of Troy provokes astonished pity that passion could cause such devastation. Fry replaces pity with paradox. For Fry both passivity and violence are hostile and wicked and not be condoned; yet they are both inevitable in an imperfect world and the only effective methods people have of learning. Marriages—like schools, governments, and all civilized institutions—hold together by means of controlled violence and controlled passivity. On that paradox *Venus* rests.

The choice of Paris occurs in a myth about the beginning of things, and the myth itself is one of the oldest treasures of western civilization: nothing but astonished pity to sustain a civilization barely underway. Fry's rehandling occurs at the end of a civilization, and proposes a merry, if paradoxical, future. Why so dismal at the beginning of a civilization and so merry at the end?

Fry's merriment is rooted in the Christian hope, which informs *Venus* throughout. One must immediately add that for Fry hope by definition is not a settled orthodoxy, delivered once and for all. *Venus* is not a propaganda piece for Anglican marriage as prescribed by Canterbury. For Fry, the Christian hope and the Christian gospel are always synonymous with exploration, discovery, and openendedness. For Fry the search for who we are is not furthered much by St. Paul's "Wives, be subject to your husbands as to the Lord," so legalistic, prescribed, and inapplicable to twentieth-century mores; the search for who we are is furthered much more by St. Paul's "There is no such thing as Jew and Greek, slave and freeman, male and female; for you are all one person in Christ Jesus" (Galatians 3:28) and by St. John's "Here and now, dear friends, we are God's children; what we shall be has not yet been disclosed, but we know that when it is disclosed, we shall be like him, because we shall see him as he is" (I John 3:2). In *Venus*, the phrases "no such thing as male and female" and "what we shall be has not yet been disclosed" resonate recognizably.

For if "male and female" are not our genuine and profoundest identities and if "it is not yet disclosed what we shall be," then surely typing a woman as lover, as wife and mother, or as intellect is certainly not compatible with Christianity's best definition of personhood. Indeed, traditional Christian marriages, with their prescribed and inflexible roles for husbands and wives, come closer to the pagan idea of women, as expressed in the myth of Paris, than to the dynamic of the Christian gospel. That is why the golden apple, that ancient and modern monumental error, must be shattered. Christianity has taken many pagan elements into itself, among them the typing of women, and by institutionalizing them has given them a spurious absolute sanction.

Perpetua, the perpetually renewed person, is Fry's model for Christian womanhood: lover and wife and intellectual companion and withal a chaste woman, having at once a casualness toward and a respect for marriage. Suppose she marries the duke for pragmatic reasons; her marriage will not define her totally. On the other hand, she prefers to marry Edgar for love. The whole woman embodies all such contradictions in patterns which change as life changes.

The fire in the observatory is a demonstration against victimizing women by label, but it also suggests the redemptive fire at the end of time, when Christ will return "from heaven with his mighty angels in blazing fire" (II Thessalonians 1:7). And both fires, the protesting and the redemptive, are at once desired and dreaded. They are necessary for growth, yet are fearful, even hateful, in their violence. Further, a closely parallel ambivalence is evoked by the concept of passivity. Waiting on the Lord (Psalm 130:6) can be simple laziness; yet without waiting, patience, and openness, no relationship with God is possible. The duke's passivity, as noted above, is aggressive, for his inability to choose, or even to make encouraging and compassionate gestures, forces the women to make ever more self-abnegating bids for his attentions, for his love. Rosabel must become sexier, Jessie more domestic, Hilda more intellectual and companionable—each more hopelessly confined by the role in which she has been cast. The proper sort of passivity, for the duke, would lead him to observe Venus with love rather than with silent demand. In other words, the duke might better let Venus define herself, become herself. Properly observed, the mistresses might, to adapt T. S. Eliot's phrase, be like flowers that have the look of flowers that are looked at.

The ambivalences that attach to violence and passivity may all be subsumed in the central paradox of Christianity: is God or the human person the agent of human redemption? Fry's play is valuable because it treats this question in its more immediate forms and without dogmatism. The play does not force an unequivocal choice between mutually exclusive alternatives. The very word *paradox* implies a merely logical problem, while Fry presents a human condition to be lived in all its particularities and uncertainties. Fry may suggest a theological problem but his terms are less recondite, less abstract: *passivity* and *activity* carry their resonances of *masculinity* and *feminity* and their associations with violence and pacifism, which in turn imply the conflict, so agonizing in our time, between ideal commitment to truth and justice on the one hand, and the necessary loyalty to institutions on the other. Such dilemmas are appropriately realized in comedy, for comedy deflates the pretensions of humans before such grand theoretical formulations without making light of the real problems themselves.

A playwright less poised than Fry would make main plot and subplots all move in the same direction. If the main plot holds that the traditional idea of women needs to go, then the subplots must say the same. But at that point art becomes propaganda for a cause and the cause becomes idolatry. Necessary as liberating women is, it is not an absolute necessity. Women are not God.

And so Fry uses his subplots to put the liberation of women into a broader context. Any woman's search for her identity is part of a still broader search of every person for identity. The subplots deal with the quest for identity and thus support the main plot, but they do not deal specifically with the quest of women to be free. The contrary motion provided by the subplots is typical of Fry's commitment to a cause like women's liberation, even whole-hearted commitment, but not absolute commitment.

One subplot deals with the duke's decadent staff. The duke is so poor he needs to hire help wherever he can get it. Reddleman, the butler, is a lion tamer who lost his nerve through shell-shock during World War II. In battle he was subjected to violent discipline of the sort that he imposed on the lions before. The war is over, and he cannot bring himself to tame lions. Reddleman feels ambiguous about it. "I lost me nerve . . ." (4) is the only way he can articulate the change in himself. He is frustrated.

Bates, the footman, is an ex-burglar:

> He was caught
> Red-handed with the silver, and his Grace,
> Being short of staff at the time, asked him to stay
> And clean it. (8)

The duke's principle is right: substitute positive action for negative. But the duke has mistaken Bates's fondness for silver as his weakness. Actually, Bates is a more complicated thief. He has a pathological fondness for climbing ladders, and had to "rationalize it when he got/To the top" (8) by going through with the theft. Polishing silver is a way of staying out of jail, but it is not exactly what Bates had in mind.

So both Reddleman and Bates are alienated from themselves, frustrated, and on very bad terms with each other. Says Reddleman:

> I have to tell your Grace, in all decency
> To the footman Bates, who I religiously despise,
> If the fellow comes on duty with a bloody nose
> 'Tis my doing, and long may it bleed. (4)

Says Bates:

> But don't let's say anyfing good about
> Captain Fussing Reddleman, lord of the kitchens.
> He can go tame his lions on some uvver poor bastard's
> mug.
> I prefers to keep mine natural. (49)

The syndrome of frustration leading to violence is as strong in Bates and Reddleman as it is in Rosabel and Perpetua. The fire which Rosabel sets is the salvation for both Bates and Reddleman, for they rescue the duke and Perpetua from the burning observatory. Bates can indulge his passion for ladders, and Reddleman recovers his nerve by fighting the flames as though they were lions. "Relax yourself, as though you was mink," says the former mink thief, carrying Perpetua down the ladder (76). "Tossing your mighty manes, roaring yellow murder!/The Captain's not afraid!" cries the lion tamer to the flames (76). The thief and the coward are restored to themselves.

The plot of the servants reinforces several themes of the main plot. Violence is necessary, for apart from Rosabel's arson, neither Reddleman nor Bates would be put together again. But passivity is also necessary. Bates and Reddleman need to wait; nobody could have rushed the arson. Yet passivity may carry its own built-in aggression. The waiting for they-know-not-what is almost too much for the servants to bear, so they are violent with each other. Their violence is pointless, unredemptive, pathetic, funny—but not profoundly comic. Bates and Reddleman become comic figures only when they are integrated by Rosabel's arson.

The main plot is reinforced also by the subplot of the Reedbecks. Dominic's moralism is in fact a habit of placing people in socially approved categories; hence, his very moralism is a variant of the duke's failing. When Dominic discovers that his father has been stealing from the duke, he accuses his father of "unrelieved, wicked cupidity" (8). But Dominic's righteous indignation is provoked by a rather selfish and a very petty concern for public opinion:

> Of course I go down from Cambridge. I couldn't stay there
> When any morning I might wake up and find
> I'd become the son of a convict. (8–9)

But the duke has known for years of Reedbeck's thefts and has indulged them secretly, since "we were being so happy together" (69). For Dominic's priggishness the duke has a generous and good humored contempt:

> My dear conscience-nudging,
> Parent-pesting, guilt-corroded child,
> If I may address you with so much affection,
> The arrangement was perfect. It embarrassed
> Neither of us. Take a drink to wash
> Your conscience down. (87–88)

In this case, at least, the duke perceives that human relationships have nothing to do with labels or with absolutes, theological, psychological, or moral. A thief is never so ultimately a thief as the label would imply. Dominic must learn this from the duke, just as the duke must learn that women cannot be labeled.

The subplot of the servants and the subplot of the Reedbecks form a context of the search for identity which has nothing specifically to do with women's search for identity. To champion freedom for women, for thieves, and for the shell-shocked is not yet to champion the freedom God has in mind for us. That freedom is not to be confused with any of the lesser freedoms which are parts of it. The arrangement of main plot and subplots is so effective because it shows the duke in the process of becoming: having achieved some freedoms, he must achieve more. In the past he learned to be free toward thieves and shell-shocked cowards; now he is learning how to be free toward women. Who shall say how many freedoms the duke has still to acquire? For he is God's child, ever stretching his perspectives and his sensibility; and it is not yet disclosed what he will be.

The scenes of the play reinforce both the finding and the more-to-be-found. The play alternates between two spots: the duke's observatory and a classical pavilion in his garden, "The Temple of the Ancient Virtues." Among the ancient virtues which the temple celebrates is the acceptance by women of their prescribed roles in society. It is a laughable temple, as Reedbeck explains it:

> Now this, my dear, called sometimes the Temple
> Of the Ancient Virtues, and at other times
> The White Temple, both because it is white

> And because it was designed by Martin White
> In seventeen hundred and ninety-three, was erected
> By the third Duke of Altair for his wife Claire
> For her use when she played the part of the Delphic
> Oracle,
> A way she had of informing the Duke of her pregnancy,
> Which she did on twenty-seven separate occasions. (35–36)

Based on prejudices, on prescribed roles, and on human bondage, the temple nevertheless represents a definite life style. Perhaps it is a life style that deserves to be laughed into a waning, autumnal existence but what will replace it?

The observatory represents a magnificently expanding universe: discovery, open-endedness, and freedom. But the danger of the observatory is remoteness. At the beginning of the play the duke appreciates his women as he appreciates the stars: remotely. His remoteness freezes his women into roles as irrevocable as the "Temple of Ancient Virtues" ever did. The temple is an ancient error, the telescope a modern one; and Perpetua's Society for the Desecration of Ancient and Modern Monumental Errors must desecrate both as models for human relationships.

But some life style is necessary. The duke is finally liberated from his remoteness toward women, but just how will his new insight be lived? Rosabel will not be the type to announce her pregnancy disguised as the Delphic Oracle, but will she announce it with such charm? Will Roderic need to be less compulsive about hunting now that Hilda loves him? Will Jessie enroll in the university now that she is liberated? And granted that thieves are never merely thieves, but how is society to cope with thieves? Are prisons to be obsolete?

Open-endedness ought not to mean vagueness. A definite life style which is to the observatory what the old life style was to the "Temple of Ancient Virtues" needs to be established. Comic aloofness ought not to mean remoteness. Remoteness toward one's own problems allows for genuine comedy; remoteness from other people's problems alienates a person, not only from those people but from oneself. Making the telescope the symbol for remoteness toward self and for involvement with others is necessary if the telescope will be to the new life style what the Georgian pavilion was to the old.

Fry insists as strongly as Germaine Greer that the present life style, with its unjust relationships between men and women, needs to go. For Greer, that is the one thing needful. For Fry, as for St. Augustine of Hippo, our souls will be restless until they rest in God. The restlessness between the sexes is only symptomatic of a more basic restlessness. But restlessness is not the same as hopelessness. An important difference is that restlessness gives endless occasion for laughter. Any laughter is only a temporary respite from the unavoidable restlessness, but laughing with Fry—heartily, with complete awareness, free from bitterness, full of hope—almost makes the restlessness seem worthwhile.

FRY'S WASTE LAND 7

A Sleep of Prisoners

Hamlet:	What have you, my good friends, deserv'd at the hands of Fortune, that she sends you to prison hither?
Guildenstern:	Prison, my lord?
Hamlet:	Denmark's a prison.
Rosenkrantz:	Then is the world one.
Hamlet:	A goodly one, in which there are many confines, wards, and dungeons, Denmark being one o' th' worst.
Rosenkrantz:	We think not so, my lord.
Hamlet:	Why then 'tis none to you; for there is nothing either good or bad, but thinking makes it so. To me it is a prison.
Rosenkrantz:	Why then your ambition makes it one. 'Tis too narrow for your mind.
Hamlet:	O God, I could be bounded in a nutshell, and count myself a king of infinite space—were it not that I have bad dreams.[1]

Substitute *The Church* for *Denmark* in the passage from *Hamlet*, and you have a perfect epigraph for Christopher Fry's *A Sleep of*

Prisoners.[2] The audacious setting of *Sleep* is a church converted into a military prison during wartime. Written to be played in a church,[3] *Sleep* is not quite itself when played in a theater, a church set redone as a prison. Not the theater-going audience, but the church-going audience needs to recognize its imprisonment in status-quo orthodoxy. Not a make-believe church, but the real Church must be shown to be a prison.

Thus, the role of the audience is very different in the scene from *Hamlet* and in *Sleep*. The audience identifies with Hamlet's bad dreams against the deluded Rosenkrantz and Guildenstern, who consider themselves free. The four prisoners in *Sleep* know they are prisoners, all four in Hamlet's position. *Sleep*'s church-going audience is unaware it is in prison, in the position of Rosenkrantz and Guildenstern; church-goers consider themselves the kings and queens of infinite space. Shifting the audience to position of antagonist against the four characters of the play—against the play as a whole, really—eliminates the traditional hero and traditional plot. The audience of *Sleep* must see the thematic and symbolic connections between the six independent episodes—the play as a whole—and identify with the play as a whole or reject it. The audience either sees *Sleep* as a unit or it sees nothing at all. The audience identifies perfectly with Hamlet without having a clear view of *Hamlet* as a whole, if, indeed, such a view of *Hamlet* is possible.

Both *Hamlet* and *Sleep* are called poetic drama, but the strange position of the audience as the antagonist, being given a unified effect to reject or gradually to come to accept, makes *Sleep* more like a lyrical poem than is *Hamlet*. Instructive as it is to put Fry's generic comedies—*Sleep* is not one—next to the comedies of Shaw, or Wilde, or Eliot, it is more instructive to put *Sleep* with Eliot's *Waste Land* and *Four Quartets*. The purpose of this essay is to provide a rationale for future criticism to compare *Sleep* with the pieces that most resemble it. As Northrop Frye says, "The purpose of criticism by genres is not so much to classify as to clarify such traditions and affinities, thereby bringing out a large number of literary relationships that would not be noticed as long as there were no context established for them."[4] The chief vexation of past *Sleep* criticism is not outright disagreement, but disappointment that the various pieces of criticism fail to add up.[5] That *Sleep* criticism has turned so fragmentary is because its point of view has been neglected and hence its genre misinterpreted. *Sleep*, it will be argued here, is a lyric.

The lyric, according to Northrop Frye, is "a literary genre characterized by the assumed concealment of the audience from the poet and by the predominance of an associational rhythm distinguishable both from recurrent metre and from semantic or prose rhythm."[6] The concealment of the audience from the poet, so that the audience "overhears" what is too personal for the poet to confront the audience with directly, occurs in *Sleep* behind a bewildering smokescreen of forms and hints of forms. To that hiddenness of the audience from the poet this study now turns, leaving the "associational rhythm" of the definition until later.

At its simplest level *Sleep* can be seen as four mystery plays: Cain and Abel, David and Absalom, Abraham and Isaac, and Daniel's three friends in the fiery furnace. Fry had written a three-act mystery play before, *The Firstborn* (1945), about the life of Moses; but an evening-length mystery play is an anomaly, since medieval Corpus Christi plays were performed in succession on pageant wagons or simultaneously on various stages arranged around the edges of the town square. On Corpus Christi Day a spectator was invited to witness the history of the world from the Garden of Eden to the Last Judgment. Northrop Frye calls this teleological structure of the Bible, reflected in the mystery cycles, "encyclopaedic form,"[7] and, with a minor exception, *Sleep* is in this form. The exception: the Abraham-Isaac story should precede the David-Absalom story to make the cycle chronological. More important than the exception, however, is the theme which *Sleep* embodies: the overcoming of violence. The theme is present in the texts of Christianity, though not often emphasized, and totally ignored in the tradition of the mystery cycles. Thus, *Sleep* carries the tradition of the mysteries forward. The Cain-Abel episode concerns Eden, violence as the outlet for personal anger. The David-Absalom episode concerns violence for the good of the state. The Abraham-Isaac episode concerns violence for the sake of God, with echoes of Calvary and resurrection. The fiery-furnace episode concerns apocalyptic violence, endured patiently for the sake of the peace of God within. Thus, *Sleep*, in spite of its truncation and its chronological adjustment, presents a complete teleology: Eden to apocalypse, with the chosen-people syndrome and soteriology of the sacrifice of an only-begotten son between. *Sleep* is a mystery cycle, an example of encyclopaedic form.

Sleep is also a morality play, the form originally having grown out of the mystery cycles, solving the problem of how to achieve the teleological-apocalyptic effect of a day's cycle in two hours. The solution: avoid individual stories and present the abstract pattern of a mystery cycle in allegorical form. Let Everyman or Mankind be the protagonist, Death and the Devil his antagonist, Good Deeds his defender, each of the deadly sins his accusers, and let the protagonist at last arrive at heaven. Since only four actors play all of *Sleep*, it has a built-in continuity from episode to episode, so that the characters become the abstractions of a morality play. Cain, full of personal vindictiveness, metamorphoses into David, doing violence for the state, becomes Abraham, doing violence for the sake of God. Abel, passive-aggressive and annoying in the extreme, metamorphoses into the willful, father-taunting, decadent Absalom, and then into the perplexed but remarkably self-sacrificial Isaac. Adam, backer of Cain, metamorphoses into Joab, who actually kills Absalom on military authority of David, and again into the Angel of the Lord who comes with new orders for Abraham to release Isaac. In the last episode all three have metamorphosed into the children in the fiery furnace: Cain has learned how to be passive enough to suffer, Abel how to be active enough to suffer, and Adam how to take responsibility in suffering. The three together make a kind of Mankind composite, the redemption of Mankind redefined as the overcoming of violence.

In addition to these human biblical characters, Tim Meadows plays God, cursing Cain for the murder of Abel in the first episode and disappearing from view during the second episode, almost as though the king's state as the supreme good in the David-Absalom episode has displaced God entirely. The god-figure returns in the third episode as a donkeyman, giving Isaac a ride down the mountain after the escape; God must take whatever place he can, no matter how lowly, after his displacement. This incarnational moment of *Sleep* coincides with sacrifice and deliverance moments in the third episode, like Christmas, Palm Sunday, Good Friday, and Easter happening all at once. In the fiery furnace the god-figure gives the other three advice on how to endure apocalypse; in the biblical story of Daniel the fourth figure is called the "Son of God," traditionally taken by Christian theologians as an Old Testament manifestation of Jesus Christ.[8] A composite Mankind, made up of allegorical figures like Activity, Passivity, and Irresponsible Authority, overcomes the moral problem of violence with the help of God the Father (in the first episode), God the Son in his humiliation as lowly donkeyman (in the third episode), and God the Son in his glorification (in the fourth episode). *Sleep* is a morality play.

Sleep is also a saint's play, a miracle play. The god-figure ("the image of God," in both a religious and a dramatic sense) is different from the other characters, whose names parallel the names of the Bible characters they play: David King, Peter Able, and Joe Adams. Tim Meadows is different from the others in having no biblical parallel for his name. *Timothy* means "fearing God"; *Meadows* suggests the pastoral paradise which was lost and the paradise which will be regained as a reward, "mead." No identifiable saint, he has the stylized characteristics of sainthood: a stigma, a wound that makes him limp; the moral flaw of pride to be overcome—having played God before his peers in judging Cain, he drops out of the play until he has learned humility and reappears as the donkeyman; a miracle, that he helps the three men to withstand the apocalyptic fire. *Sleep* conforms to the pattern of a saint's play even better than Fry's *A Boy with a Cart* (1939), about the life of St. Cuthman, because, while *Boy* presents miracles, it emphasizes the domesticity of sainthood, not typically an emphasis of the genre.

The simultaneity of these medieval modes of drama prevents any one of them from being *Sleep*'s most encompassing form. *Sleep* is a kaleidoscope. Regard the Cain-Abel episode as a mystery play and God is God the Father, who else? Regard *Sleep* as a cycle of mysteries, and the character who plays God in the first episode plays Christ as the donkeyman of Palm Sunday in the Abraham-Isaac episode and plays the Christ of the apocalypse in the fiery furnace. Regard the play as a morality play, and God drops out of the David-Absalom episode because the state, not God, is there defined as the supreme good; regard *Sleep* as a saint's play and the saint drops out of that episode as a penalty for thinking himself God in the first. Regard *Sleep* as a mystery cycle, and the David-Absalom episode about violence for the sake of the state is a necessary step between raw violence and violence for the sake of God; regard *Sleep* as a saint's play and that episode becomes a choric interlude, an illustration of what happens when sainthood withdraws. As a mere actor is "the image of God" in the mystery play of Cain and Abel, so any saint is the "image of God" in life off the stage, which is what the god-figure projects when *Sleep* is regarded as a saint's play. Criticism has not done justice to this kaleidoscopic quality of *Sleep*—only the medieval half of which has been described here. For *Sleep* also embodies several Renaissance forms of drama: comedy, history, *débat*, and satire.

As comedy, four ordinary soldiers are imprisoned in a church by their enemies, the Towzers. Peter Able, the pacifist, annoys David King, the militarist, by picking out melodies on the organ, reading the Bible, and delivering a mock sermon. David attacks Peter in the pulpit, and Joe Adams, the corporal in charge, is unable to stop the fight between these two privates. Tim Meadows, an older, wounded private, stops the fight. Then the men retire for the night, and each man dreams the events of the fight as reinterpreted through the religious myths: Tim Meadows dreams the Cain-Abel story, David King the David-Absalom story, Peter Able the Abraham-Isaac story, and Joe Adams the apocalyptic fiery furnace. Each character dreams the others as he considers them to be, except that at the end of the last dream all the characters are dreaming the same dream.[9] Dreaming his own dream helps each of the characters to understand the violence in himself and in the others, allowing all of them to endure the violence of the apocalyptic furnace together. The society emerging at the conclusion of *Sleep* represents a peaceful, free society like that at the end of *The Tempest*. Is it, however, an ironic understatement of such a society:

> Adams: Well, sleep, I suppose.
>
> David: Yeh. God Bless.
>
> Peter: Rest you merry.
>
> Meadows: Hope so. Hope so. (211)

Fry himself said of the play that it "could not end in a glorious suffering, or even the indication of victory—we have too far to travel for that—but certainly, in hope."[10] But Fry also said of it, "I wanted to move from division to unity," thus showing that he intended to write what the other Frye calls comedy.[11] Intentions aside, even, there is no mistaking the comedy, as William Spanos has demonstrated.[12]

Two problems need discussion here in order to show how the irony of *Sleep* qualifies its comedy: the first to distinguish the irony in *Sleep* from the bitter irony of Browning's *Ring and the Book* and the Japanese movie *Rashomon*; the second to describe a double-edged irony in the relationship of the low-mimetic characters of comedy to the epic-proportioned characters of the mysteries.

Sleep looks superficially like Browning's *Ring* and the movie *Rashomon*. In both *Ring* and *Rashomon* a series of witnesses give an account of a murder. The similarity in the accounts is sufficient to recognize the event, but not enough to allocate the guilt. Is it possible to find the accurate truth about any event, *Ring* and *Rashomon* ask, given the divergence of human perceptions? Unlike these works, *Sleep* begins with what really happened, followed by mythic interpretations of it. *Ring* and *Rashomon* prod the audience to sort out the unadorned prose facts from the embroidered accounts and then to give up and say the plain truth is unknowable; the motion of the mind is centripetal. The motion of the mind of the audience of *Sleep* is centrifugal; knowing the unadorned facts, the audience must look for the broader mythic meanings in them. The irony in *Ring* and *Rashomon* is bitter; nobody, including the audience, knows the truth. The irony in *Sleep* is comically incongruous; the mythic meanings of the event seem too epically grand for the commonplace event itself.

This comic irony in *Sleep* goes beyond Northrop Frye's theory of displacement, the telling of a supernatural myth in the low-mimetic, everyday mode.[13] Chrisopher Fry's play *The Firstborn* had been an exercise is displacement; gone are the infallibility of Moses and the total evil of Pharaoh as found in Exodus. It will not do to say Pharaoh was a devil for not listening to Moses and at the same time to have doubts about a modern chief executive's pressures from the Pope or from Southern Baptist dogma. To make a cleft between "Bible times," when miracles were possible and moral distinctions were absolute, and the present time, when a non-mythological, scientific-pragmatic reality prevails, is to be non-incarnational, is to be trapped in a Platonic dichotomy of believing one thing with our hearts and knowing the opposite with our heads. A wavering Moses, a just and reasonable Pharaoh, and an Israel involved as much in doubt as in faith was *Firstborn's* way of showing the continuity between the world of Moses and our own. *Firstborn* prods us to mythologize our own reality, yet the net impact is that it simply demythologizes the story of Moses. To that extent the form of *Firstborn* works against itself.

But the form of *Sleep* displaces in two directions. The epic heroes of the Bible are dreamed and acted by low-mimetic characters, soldiers, in their own terms; and the ordinary soldiers are elevated in dream to epic level. Cain and Abel do not compete at sacrifice but at dice, as soldiers would; God, as Meadows, is as attentive to the dice game as Ares and Poseidon to events in Troy. David's instructions to Joab about Absalom are both everyday-military ("Make a soldier of him") and epic ("Make him fit/For conflict, as the stars and stags are," 183) in a single speech. David's anxiety for Absalom is like Jove's for Sarpedon:

> Where is he going now? He carries
> No light with him. Does he know
> The river's unbound: it's up above
> Every known flood-mark, and still rising. (184)

As though he were a bourgeois runaway, Absalom sends a taunting picture postcard:

> Staying with friends, whoever they are.
> Showery still, but I manage to get out,
> I manage to get out.
> The window marked with a cross is where I sleep.
> Just off to a picnic with your enemies.
> They're not bad fellows, once you get to know them. (184)

Hard upon the sombre, heroic issue of human sacrifice, Isaac rides down the hill on a donkey to whom Meadows, the donkeyman, calls, "Home, old girl,/Home from the sea, old Millie-edwinium" (195), recalling the donkey rides at seashore resorts.[14] And in the fiery furnace, the mythical heroes, Shadrach, Meschech, and Abednego, are soldiers:

> Adams: Get into the ranks.
>
> Peter: What's worrying you? We're not
> On active service now. Maybe it's what
> They call in our paybooks 'disembodied service':
> So drill my spirit, Corporal, till it weeps
> For mercy everywhere. (200)

The mundane military terms like *disembodied service*, service with a military unit other than the unit to which one is legally assigned, take on metaphysical meanings appropriate for epic. The double vision of *Sleep*, the displacement in both directions,[15] demands that we demythologize biblical narrative and simultaneously mythologize our own everyday reality, each reality affording an ironic perspective on the other. Until the two realities are one, there will be occasion for ironic comedy.

In addition to being a comedy, *Sleep* is a history play as truly as *Curtmantle*. On one level the history seems to be World War II, with English soldiers held captive in a German church; a bomber flies overhead (195) and the army lingo is WW II vintage. Simultaneously regard David as the Axis, Peter as the Allies, Corporal Adams as the ineffective authority of the League of Nations, Tim Meadows as the goodness of ordinary people enlisting to do their duty and objecting to war, and one sees the history of WW II. Yet, the enemies are not Germans, but Towzers, and *Sleep* is the archetype for all the wars of history. The violence of the Cain-Abel episode is the raw hatred within people, always ready for a war effort. Get the propaganda machinery to harness that hostility for the state, and you have the David-Absalom episode. Get organized religion to support the war effort and you have the Abraham-Isaac episode: violence for the sake of God. The end result in all wars is the same: the apocalyptic fiery furnace for all sides, in which all sides could, if hearts were purer, find the basis for community. Northrop Frye finds that a history play commonly ends with a sense of nationalistic community.[16] *Sleep* does not celebrate a nationalistic community at the end, but a Christian community without bounds.

Like comedy and the history play, the *débat* is a form which came into English drama during the early Renaissance, either giving shape to the whole play (*Wit and Science*), being an element in a broader structure (love vs. friendship in Lyly's *Endymion*), or making an elaborate, many-sided examination of a subject (like honor in Shakespeare's history plays). Flesh vs. spirit is the *débat* in *Sleep*.

In the waking episode before the dreams, David is angry that captivity should be a mystery for Peter (164), but not angry enough to murder until Peter taunts him with fleshliness: "We have here on my left/An example of the bestial passions that beset mankind" (165). The first dream presents the *débat* form most closely; Peter and David consider the assumptions of the other close enough to make persuasion a possibility, and so they argue heatedly about flesh and spirit (172–177). In the second dream the *débat* between Peter and David is all managed through Adams, so far has communication degenerated; David complains of Peter to Adams, who tries to make a soldier of Peter, who flees to the pulpit and taunts David in a form too sarcastic to be answered directly. The third dream, the moment of the atonement-deliverance, shows both Peter and David changing their respective stances toward the flesh. As Abraham, David brings God into his attitude toward the flesh:

> Come up, son, and see the world.
> God dips his hand in death to wash the wound,
> Takes evil to inoculate our lives
> Against infectious evil. (191)

When Meadows as the donkeyman gives Peter a ride down the hill of sacrifice on Edwina the donkey, the episode calls up one of David's lines as Cain, when he was complaining that he, David, was not going to be

> . . . pestered and wondering down hill
> Like a half-wit angel strapped to the back of a mule.
> Thanks! I'll be as the body was first presumed. (176)

Now Peter is going downhill on the back of a donkey—the donkey being, since St. Francis of Assisi called his body "brother ass," the symbol of the flesh—the flesh David derogatorily describes as mule when it is in tension with spirit.[17] Peter is dreaming himself as at heart he sees himself, flesh too. His platonic denial of the flesh masquerades as innocence, but he is actually more sophisticated and earthy than he admits even to himself. His new affirmation of the flesh is childlike, which is why Meadows is the kind of donkeyman who gives children rides at seashore resorts: "Across the sands and into the sea," says Peter (195); "Donkey ride is over," says Meadows (195). To inherit the flesh means also to accept in a childlike way the limitations of time: death. That is why Edwina the donkey—that is the flesh—becomes "old millenium" and "Millie-edwinium," why she goes at the steady pace of time ("Jog, jog,/Jog, jog"), and why her stable is so much like a grave: "In under/The salty planks and corrugated iron./Stable for mangy mokes" (194–195). Thus Peter becomes more physical in the third dream, David more spiritual, and Meadows suggests the unity of the two when he says of Edwina, that is, of the flesh: "Where else/Would you find such a satisfactory soul?" (194)

This identity of flesh and spirit is what the final dream moves toward for Peter and David. David instructs Peter "To feed what you've been riding pick-a-back" (201), the flesh, which Peter sees as "the monster" (201). David objects to the physical indignity of confronting the flames with his feet tied; Peter is on more pitying terms with the flesh than before: "Hobbled,/Poor asses" (203). In this circumstance Adams gives the one order he can: "Fall on your knees" (203), with the result that the restraining cords burn off. In prayer, the physical posture and the spiritual intent merge: flesh and spirit are the same.

Peter's attitude is as much in need of correction as David's. Given the working beliefs of Christians, one would expect David to be the villain and Peter the hero; but that is more the Greek notion of the primacy and immortality of the soul—an idea which has influenced Christianity and sometimes distorted it beyond recognition—than it is an essential tenet of Christianity. Christianity professes not the immortality of the soul, but the resurrection of the body; not imprisonment of the soul in vile flesh, but the affirmation of the flesh which God declared good and which Jesus Christ became; not the dualism of Plato, but the wholeness of Moses and Jesus Christ. So Platonic has Western Christianity become that *Sleep*, which returns to a more physical Christianity than is common, was roundly condemned in Australia and elsewhere for its blasphemy.[18] *Sleep* is as orthodox as Christianity's oldest creeds, and its "orthodox" opponents not as orthodox as they believe themselves to be.

This is how the name *Peter* works in *Sleep*. St. Peter is not only the rock on which the church is built but also the denying disciple who professes not to know Jesus at his trial. To St. Peter, Jesus says, "Before the cock crow thou shalt deny me thrice" (Luke 22:34). In the play Peter's pale spirituality, his "absent-fistedness," is a denial of the flesh which the Incarnation hallows.

The common gloss of theologians is that the fourth man in the fiery furnace is an Old Testament appearance of Christ; Meadows, as *figura Christi*, signals his appearance in the last dream by crowing like a cock. Peter, shrugging off this reminder of his three denials, says, "A lunatic" (205). How Peter stays in the stage picture during the dialogue between Meadows, Adams, and David during the next moments is the only way to document his transformation to insight. When Meadows tells Adams that "patience and love" are necessary to be safe in the fire, Peter must look superior to the others, considering himself a specialist. David, on the other hand, must be devastated; he knows he can have no patience or love in the fire of the human condition. Short of patience and love, Meadows recommends honesty:

> Not to say we do
> A thing for all men's sake when we do it only
> For our own. And quick eyes to see
> Where evil is. While any is our own
> We sound fine words unsoundly. (206)

David, of course, has been sounding fine patriotic words unsoundly, and his previous rages have been a sign that he feels guilty. But Peter has been self-satisfied, sounding his patience and love, unaware of his own more passive use of hostility. Meadows must direct his reprimanding speech to Peter as much as to David, and Peter must show he feels the sting of the words. Peter's insight into his own evil hostility motivates him to recognize the fire as the human condition, both active and passive hostility causing the pain:

> Look how intense
> The place is now, with swaying and troubled figures.
> The flames are men: all human. There's no fire!
> Breath and blood chokes and burns us. This
> Surely is unquenchable? It can only transform.
> There's no way out. We can only stay and alter. (208)

Peter's new awareness of his own responsibility for evil, both as its cause and for its cure, alters him from Peter the Denier to Peter the Rock, on which the Church is built.

Peter's denial of the flesh is *Sleep*'s satire on the *de facto* position of the Church. Peter's learning to accept the flesh is *Sleep*'s celebration of the Incarnation, manifest not only in Christ's physical body, but, in the elaborate metaphor of St. Paul, Christ's metaphorical body, the Church (I Corinthians 12:14–26). Northrop Frye says of satire that "its moral norms are relatively clear, and it assumes standards against which the grotesque and absurd are measured."[19] Sometimes satire attacks what does not conform to the status quo; sometimes it attacks the status quo. The anti-church satire in *Sleep* attacks the status quo, while it celebrates what the Church ought to be. The church of the god whose chief task is to save the queen or to make America great is the church of common sense and decency that *Sleep* satirizes. *Sleep*'s satire, though the comparison is decidedly odd, is like that of Petronius, "which plunges through to the final victory over common sense."[20] No wonder *Sleep* had trouble with the ecclesiastical hierarchy in Australia.

At this level it becomes clear that the players in *Sleep* are in the position of Hamlet, the audience in the position of Rosenkrantz and Guildenstern in the epigraph to this essay. Hans Itschert has alerted Fry criticism to the difference between simply bringing a prison set into a church and revealing the church to be a prison.[21] The church is imprisoned in its Greek notions of immortality. Emphasizing the immortality of the soul, the church traditionally condones any degree of violence to the body: wars, police brutalities, oppressive social structures, poverty, and white-collar crimes. Generally, the church exhorts the faithful poor to be content with physical oppression in hope of heaven's bliss.

This state of arrested development is described by Meadows in his summing up:

> Figures of wisdom back in the old sorrow.
> Hold and wait forever. We see, admire
> But never suffer them: suffer instead
> A stubborn aberration.
> O God, the fabulous wings unused,
> Folded in the heart. (207)

Cain, David, Abraham, Abel, Adam, Absalom, Joab, and Isaac are the "figures of wisdom" because, even in the "old sorrow," that is the old dispensation before Christ brought peace and blessed the flesh by assuming it, these figures of wisdom discovered something about the violence within themselves. What they learned they "hold"—"forever," if necessary, until humanity catches on to what they learned. "We" of the congregation "see" these heroes, "admire" them, but "never suffer them," that is, do not allow their hard-won truth to affect our conduct. And so we suffer violence instead, the "stubborn aberration," which is much more painful—both to inflict and to endure—than the discipline of overcoming it would be. In captivity to the social structures and to a Platonized theology, we will never make progress in faith and conduct: "O God, the fabulous wings unused. . . ."

Satire and celebration merge most intricately in the dialogue at play's end:

Adams: Where's this place? How did I get here?

Meadows: You are born here, chum. It's the same for all of us. (209)

Is the *here* prison? Is *here* the flesh, in which our souls are imprisoned according to Platonic doctrine? Is *here* the church, imprisoned in the social structures and in Platonic doctrines? Again the question is asked:

Peter: I wish I knew where I was.

Meadows: I can only give you a rough idea myself.
In a sort of a universe and a bit of a fix.
It's what they call flesh we're in.
And a fine old dance it is. (210)

Again, *flesh* can be seen as the prison for our immortal souls, though this Platonism does not square with flesh as "a fine old dance." Regard flesh as the Body of Christ in St. Paul's elaborate metaphor for the Church, with the members being hands, ears, eyes, and feet then the Church at its best is that "fine old dance." Or take *flesh* as referring to the flesh that Jesus Christ assumed in becoming incarnate. That our flesh is like Christ's makes our flesh participate in the "fine old dance"; that Christ's flesh was tortured on a cross—the shape, incidentally, of Gothic churches—makes such flesh only "a sort of a universe and a bit of a fix." Taken any way at all "a sort of a universe and a bit of a fix" is a bitter qualifier of the "fine old dance" which might be, and a satiric comment on what is.

Sleep is an effective stage piece because it incorporates techniques and conventions from many dramatic genres: mystery, morality, and miracle play; low-mimetic comedy, history, *débat*, and satire. *Sleep* is so effectively disguised as a play that it must be produced as a play, but its principle of unity is that of a lyric poem. A lyric's necessary "assumed concealment of the audience from the poet" happens in *Sleep* through the kaleidoscopic welter of dramatic techniques and conventions, so that the audience must "overhear" what the poet is saying.

What Fry the poet is saying in this play has been most comprehensively and accurately summarized by John Woodfield as the idea of "exchange," also held by Fry's friend Charles Williams.[22] All personal relationships, the theory goes, involve a sacrifice of part of the personality of both participants: an exchange. The sacrifice of Christ for humanity in the incarnation and the atonement, and humanity's response to Christ in love and obedience is not only the best example of this exchange but the very archetype for all exchanges, for all relationships, and for all improvements in relationships. Thus, that David turns more passive and Peter more aggressive, that Corporal Adams can finally give a military order that is appropriate and heeded ("Fall on your knees," 203), and that Meadows, the wounded private too old to be a private, should become the spiritual authority for the others: all these are examples of exchange. Yet, as Woodward has demonstrated, all Fry's plays make use of the idea of exchange. *Sleep* makes the idea of exchange so private that the audience cannot confront it directly in a straightforward plot.

Sleep is the most autobiographical of Fry's plays. Peter Able is Fry, his Quaker sensibility committing him to non-violence. David King is also Fry, a member of the Church of England and a loyal subject of the crown. At the time he composed *Sleep*, Fry had been both a husband and a father for more than a decade; what father of a decade does not say with Adams: "I am a father unequipped to save" (178)? And Fry replaced his name *Arthur* with *Christopher*, that is, "Christ bearer," being at once identified with Christ and distinct from him, just as Meadows or any Christian is. The fire of the last dream is like the fires of the Liverpool docks, where Christopher Fry spent World War II fighting fires with the Pioneer Corps: supporting the war effort like David King, avoiding overt violence like Peter Able, accepting the responsibilities of fatherhood and citizenship like Adams, and withal being identified with Christ like Meadows. The prison is reminiscent of the army hospital where, toward the end of the war, Fry was confined, the victim of his contradictory selves. The patient in the bed next to his sat up whenever a plane passed overhead, just as Peter does (195).[23]

> Peter: It is one of ours?
>
> Meadows: No question: one of ours.
> Or one of theirs. (195–196)

In his dedicatory letter to Robert Gittings, Fry writes that "progress is the growth of vision: the increased perception of what makes for life and what makes for death" (157). What makes for life is the progressive integration of contradictory selves as shown in *Sleep*. Meadows states the problem, the solution to which is overheard in *Sleep*: ". . . there's strange divisions in us,/And in every man, one side or the other" (169).

This study has demonstrated the "assumed concealment of the audience from the poet" behind the welter of dramatic forms, none of which encompasses the whole of *Sleep*. This study now proceeds to Northrop Frye's other qualification for lyric listed earlier: "the predominance of an associational rhythm distinguishable both from recurrent metre and from semantic or prose rhythm."[24]

"The traditional associations of lyric are essentially with music," says Northrop Frye.[25] As truly as the fourth movement of Beethoven's *Eroica Symphony* or the second movement of Haydn's *Emperor Quartet*, *Sleep* is written in a theme-and-variations form.[26] The theme is the opening episode before the dreams, the mood both more agitated than the third variation and less agitated than the first; *moderato* is an appropriate tempo marking and movement title. The first variation, the Cain-Able episode, is an *allegro* movement; the debate between Peter and David is more fiery here than elsewhere. *Marcato*, in the manner of a military march, is the tempo for the second variation; the only genuine communication between David and Peter occurs through the military chain of command; to the extent that any communication takes place directly, it is mockery: sarcasm from Absalom and retaliatory, military repression from David. The third variaton is an *adagio*, neither Abraham nor Isaac understanding the command of the Lord that Isaac be sacrificed; together both David and Peter prod at the mystery of God's necessity. Peter phrases questions thoughtfully, David's answers are deliberate, and the pauses between speeches must be long enough to indicate reflection. The fourth variation is another *allegro*, but different from the first *allegro*, where the staccato outbursts were between Peter and David, the scrappy energy arising from personal disagreement; the energy in the fourth variation arises from the torment of the furnace for David, Peter, and Joe. Put the first variation as *allegro con spirito*, and the last must be *allegro furioso*. The waking coda is another *moderato*, returning to the mood of the theme, but in a simplified form, dissonance removed. Like Haydn's *Emperor* variations, the theme—that is, the dream—passes to each of the players in the quartet. As one variation blends into the next by means of bridge passages in Beethoven's *Eroica* variations, so *Sleep* joins variation to variation, without Haydn's full cadences between variations. Haydn's *Emperor* variations are an *adagio* throughout, but the theme has been adapted most incongruously to the *marcato* "Deutschland, Deutschland über alles," so much in the auditory consciousness during World War II. Beethoven's *Eroica* was first dedicated to Napoleon, but Beethoven destroyed that title-page when Napoleon had himself crowned emperor; the revised dedication read: "Heroic Symphony, composed to celebrate the memory of a great man." The theme-and-variations form has associations with violence thoroughly appropriate for *Sleep*.

Throughout, *Sleep* calls attention to itself as a musical form. "Now the Day Is Over" and "Three Blind Mice" appear in the statement of the theme as the songs Peter plays on the organ. In the first variation Peter fingers "Now the Day Is Over" on the organ as he did in the theme, but "Three Blind Mice" undergoes profound change. It becomes the dicing song of David and Peter, each in his own way responding to his own blindness before God. David begins the song:

Numbers, be true to nature. Deal me high, Six dark stars Come into my sky.

Peter finishes it:

Deal me high, deal me low. Make my deeds My nameless needs. I know I do not know.

(175)*

*On 11 April 1973, Fry paraphrased the lines "Make my deeds/My nameless needs./I know I do not know" thus: "Peter has an intuition of 'In God's will is our peace.' In that sense, 'Make my deeds accord both with your will, God, and with my own needs, which I think I know, about which I may not know.'"

In the second variation, David's dream, the music all but disappears in David's military paranoia and in the military discipline of Joab-Adams:

> Adams: Get on parade.
>
> Peter: What's the music?
>
> Adams: I'll sing you, Absalom, if you don't get moving.
> And I'll see you singing where you never meant. (183)

In the third variation Peter Able, as Isaac, whistles in his own dream: "I whistle for myself/And anyone who likes it" (190); Abraham-David's knife (191–192) is in dream logic the knife of "Three Blind Mice," going after a head instead of tails. David's line "Shadows of our history/Steal across the sky" (191) echoes "Shadows of the evening/Steal across the sky" from "Now the Day Is Over."[27] Between the third and fourth variations Meadows says, "A man must be let to have a soul to himself/Or souls will go the way of tails" (196). It is Meadows' comment on the reverse process of evolution, but it is also *Sleep* ringing yet another change on the tails of the mice. In the fourth variation David is annoyed by Peter Able and says, "God drown you for a rat" (200); David had spoken of rats in his own dream. Peter calls himself and the other two men "Three Blind Mice of Gotham" (200). The coda replaces "Three Blind Mice" and "Now the Day Is Over" with "God Rest You Merry, Gentlemen," though as all good codas, the theme has been prepared for: "but nothing you dismay" (174) in the very first variation and other, more general references to Christmas: "peace on earth" (190) and its parody "police on earth" (203). The preparation is just subtle enough to keep the reference to the Christmas carol at play's end from being too vigorously hopeful:

> David: God bless.
>
> Peter: Rest you merry.
>
> Meadows: Hope so. Hope so. (211)

Even to the bugle call that ends the play, *Sleep* is a musical form.

"The most natural unit of the lyric is the discontinuous unit of the stanza," says Northrop Frye.[28] It is useful to think of *Sleep* as composed of six stanzas: the theme, the four variations, and the coda. To restrict *Sleep* to its linear plot involves one in the absurdity of changes occurring in David because of his being dreamed by Peter. The ordering of the dreams arises not out of the inner necessity of character or the inexorable forward thrust of the plot, but from the design of the argument constructed by the author. Part of what the theme-and-variations metaphor conveys is that *Sleep* is composed of discontinuous stanzas, each stanza interpreting the event of the first stanza in the framework of a myth, the myths arranged in an order of increasing abstraction.

Another part of what the theme-and-variations metaphor conveys is the repetition of a pattern—that is, "a rhythm which is poetic but not necessarily metrical," as Northrop Frye describes it.[29] Frye objects to calling all long poems epics and all short poems lyrics.[30] In a long lyric the rhythm demands longer intervals between the repetitions, very much like the repetitions in a theme-and-variations form.

The argument between David and Peter and how it occurs with differing mood in each of the variations has been discussed in assigning tempo designations to the variations: the *moderato* theme, followed by the *allegro con spirito, marcato, adagio,* and *allegro furioso* repetitions of the theme, and concluded by a *moderato* coda. But the opening theme on which the variations are based has more than just the argument between Peter and David; it has the "crossing over," the "killing," "the deliverance," and the conclusion. How each variation changes each of these elements, thereby establishing a dependable rhythm in a long lyric without being monotonously repetitious, is where this study turns.

The "crossover" is a religious ritual, the crossing from the epistle side of the altar to the gospel side where the pulpit is, at which moment in the mass (or at any liturgical service in the Christian church) the priest genuflects as he passes before the altar and crucifix, and the congregation rises for the gospel. The readings from the epistle side are not false and from the gospel side true; the contrast is more like prophecy vs. fulfillment, knowing vs. understanding, intellectual appreciation vs. total commitment.

The crossover occurs in the mock service in the theme after Peter has read the genealogy from the lectern on the epistle side (163) and before his sermon from the pulpit on the gospel side (165).[31] The congregation used to worshipping in the church would find his lack of genuflection decidedly odd, empty though the ritual often is. Should the actor playing Peter decide on a broad, flamboyant genuflection, the effect would again point to the emptiness of the ritual. In the first variation David begins at the lectern and Peter also begins on the epistle side in the organ loft. Peter comes down to play dice, still at the epistle side. When Cain loses, he fights Peter back to his bed (177); Cain forces Abel to cross over, making the congregation aware of the crucifix as archetype of such violence. In the second variation Peter starts on the gospel side in the pulpit and David is again on the epistle side. David gets Joab-Adams to train Peter for the military and marches him to the epistle side in the process, but Peter escapes back to the gospel side and the crossing back is made to seem like going through a river:

> David: Does he know
> The river's unbound: it's up above
> Every known flood-mark, and still rising.
>
> Peter: I'm on the other side of the river
> Staying with friends. . . (184)

The aisle from rear of the church to the altar does become a stream of people at the communion, each Sunday renewing the flow forward. Some such association lingers when the point of cross-over so explicitly becomes a stream, with an ironic implication: the stream of the faithful to communion does not protect the hunted from the hunter, the stream of the faithful having compromised with violence. In the third variation David walks toward the pulpit from the epistle side while Peter lies in bed; David does not command Peter to keep up with him, but invites him: "Keep close to me" (190). At the point of crossover, in line with the crucifix, Abraham says:

> "Come up, son, and see the world.
> God dips his hand in death to wash the wound,
> Takes evil to innoculate our lives against infectious evil" (191).

The fiery furnace in the fourth variation is on the epistle side, at the lectern (199). The three men's feet are tied, and they fall on their knees on a desperate order from Adams, thus giving point to the perfunctory genuflection which the congregation is used to seeing and which it has missed in the four previous crossovers.

When Adams asks, "May we come through?" (206), the effect is the same as if he asked whether the men are allowed to cross over to the gospel side, the *through* being a dream memory of the river of the second variation except it is a river of fire now. When Meadows says, "The human heart can go to the lengths of God" (209), he is saying that crossing to the gospel side is possible; but the men wake up before they get to cross, lest *Sleep* turn the crossover glib again, but that is under another rubric.

Important here is the repeated ritual of the crossing over. "Drama," says Northrop Frye, "has a peculiarly intimate connection with ritual, and lyric with dream or vision, the individual communing with himself."[32] That the common ritual of crossing from the epistle side to the gospel side of the altar should occur in a play at all is dramatic; that it should occur five times in one play at regularly spaced intervals in a dreamlike rhythm—that is lyrical. Effective theatre, *Sleep* nevertheless hangs together as a particularly hypnotic lyric.

How predictability and unpredictability work together in the rhythm of *Sleep* is also evident in the mode of "killing": in the theme, strangling in personal anger, hardly prevented by the community; in the first variation, strangling in anger in defense of a world view, not prevented by the community; in the second variation, gunning down impersonally for the state, the community approving; in the third variation, a ritual knifing for God prevented by God; and in the fourth variation, the community enduring the flames caused by the community as a sacrifice to God. The predictability is sufficient to establish a rhythm and the unpredictability sufficient to provide interest and forward movement.

Unpredictability alone determines what follows the "killing" in the theme and each of the variations. Dramatically, what concludes each variation suits what came before it, but musically, each variation changes abruptly to an ironic scherzo-like codetta after each "killing." In the theme, the "killing" past, Adams converses with Peter, David, and Meadows in turn, the corporal asserting himself with calm competence now that the crisis is over; observe that David and Peter dominated the dialogue in their quarrel before the "killing" and Adams stood helplessly by. After the killing in the first variation, Meadows as God judges Cain, curses him, and brands him; the mood of conflict, totally unlike the scrappy *allegro* of the first part of the variation, is that of an ultimate superior dictating to a cowering, whining inferior. The second variation suddenly turns non-military after the killing; the military David, who thought only in military assumptions before the murder, now broods to an uncomprehending Joab, the *marcato* replaced by *grave*:

> Are you sure it is the victory, Joab?
> Are we ever sure it's the victory.
> So many times you've come back, Joab,
> With something else. I want to be sure at last.
> I want to know what you mean by victory.
> Is it something else to me? (186)

In the third variation, after his deliverance, Peter rides down the hill on Edwina the donkey—a completely unexpected comic interlude. A corollary to deliverance is being at home in the flesh, the "brother ass" of St. Francis of Assisi; and one cannot be at home in the flesh without a comic attitude. Christopher Fry explains this in his great essay "Comedy": the "body, with its functions and accidents and frustrations, is endlessly quaint and remarkable . . . and though comedy accepts our position in time, it barely accepts our posture in space."[33] The deliverance in the fourth dream comes when the men can stand in the fire because they have knelt and the cords have burned off, their kneeling and standing happening in line with the crucifix; yet they cannot escape the furnace, cannot cross to the gospel side. The appearance of Meadows in variation four is similar to his appearance in variation three; in both he is a comic figure. The donkeyman in three, Meadows appears crowing like a rooster in four. The appearance of Meadows marks the change of the dream of Adam into "a state of thought entered into by all the sleeping men, as though sharing their prison life, they shared for a few moments of the night their sleeping life also," as Fry says in his dedicatory letter to Gittings (157). Seeing the appearance of Meadows in variations three and four as parallel to each other and seeing both as the beginning of the post-"killing" codetta solves the problem of where the personal dream of Adams changes into the common state of thought, though other critics, notably Hans Itschert, have considered the appearance of Nebuchadnezzar as the point of change.[34]

The difference between the last variation and the rest of *Sleep* is clear against the pattern made by the theme and the other three variations: conflict, "crossover," "killing," and the scherzo-like codetta for each. In the theme and first three variations the conflict is always between David (whether as Cain, King David, or Abraham) and Peter (whether as Abel, Absalom, or Isaac), with Joe Adams taking either side (as Adam and Joab for Cain and King David, as the delivering angel for Isaac). In the fourth variation the conflict is between Nebuchadnezzar, not visible to the audience, and the three men who before were in conflict with each other. Nebuchadnezzar has absorbed the distilled essence of the evil of the three men. Nebuchadnezzar stands on his rank like Corporal Adams (Private Meadows, who does not demand rank, is the real leader), appearing here as the commanding general calling his troops for a severe inspection; even the military Adams admits "he hates his guts" (202). Nebuchadnezzar takes Peter's love of the sound of his own voice, his flair for oratory, his playfulness with language—all of which so annoyed David King—Nebuchadnezzar takes these and turns them into political demogoguery; even Peter is annoyed:

> What bastard language
> Is he talking? Are we supposed to guess?
> Police on earth. Aggression is the better
> Part of Allah. Liberating very high
> The dying and the dead. Freedoom, freedoom.
> Will he never clear his throat. (203)

Nebuchadnezzar carries the active violence of David to such a degree that he hobbles the men and throws them into the furnace. The conflict is not now between the men, but between their increasingly paradoxical view of reality on one side and Nebuchadnezzar "with one eye" (202)—with a non-paradoxical and non-religious view of reality—on the other.[35]

In the theme and the first three variations, the "crossover" occurs before the "killing"; immediately after the "killing," the mood changes abruptly. That concluding codetta is never fully satisfying: a frightening judgment, a father protesting against an unjust military establishment, and a farcical donkey-ride downhill. Even being on good terms with the flesh is not yet a full gospel. The "crossover" has always been too glib, the gospel considered to be there for the taking. The order of the fourth variation is the same as the others, except that the "crossover" does not happen and it is referred to last. The order for the last variation is as follows: conflict, between Nebuchadnezzar and the men; "killing," the three men are thrown into the fire, hobbled; partial deliverance, the men genuflect in attempting to cross to the gospel side with the result that their hobbles burn away and they can stand; codetta, Meadows appears as the comic rooster (the ironic sign that the men are betrayers of the gospel, as well as a sign of morning and hope), who gives advice on how the "crossover" may be managed with patience and love and honesty, assuring the men that "the human heart can go to the lengths of God" (209). In urging them to wake up to the opportunity for "crossover" into a full gospel without violence, Meadows wakens them from sleep instead, and the "crossover" never happens. Since nobody knows what the state of a full gospel would be like—violence eliminated within and without—*Sleep* cannot present it but can only prod the audience toward it.

To demonstrate in *Sleep* "the predominance of an associational rhythm distinguishable from recurrent metre and from semantic or prose rhythm" has been the burden of the second part of this essay. For rhythm is repetition and an "associational rhythm" is a repetition to which clusters of meaning adhere. The gradually clarifying meaning of *Sleep* is embodied in repetition. In this regard, as well as in the other essential quality of the hiddenness of the author, *Sleep* is a lyric.

Having demonstrated that *Sleep* is a lyric, this study turns to a cluster of images within it which suggest the kind of lyric it is. To be sure, the images of church, prison, and army and the ironic interplay between them has been the concern of this study throughout—exemplifying what Northrop Frye calls "ironic and anti-allegorical imagery." But there is in addition a cluster of images which Northrop Frye calls "archetypal," "associative clusters" of images: the four elements of Heraclitus.[36]

Earth is the image of David King. The song that he knows and likes is about the beauty of the earth ("All things bright and beautiful" 161); he eats an earthy beet in the first dream (171); before the murder he predicts "Momentous doings/Over the hill for the earth and us" (173); and the first word spoken to King by Adams after the murder is "How ceaseless the earth is" (177), for

Cain-King goes on like the earth. King trembles "like an earthquake" (183) at Absalom's insolence in the second dream. Even when in the third dream he grows reflective, it is an earthy poetry he grows toward:

> The singing birds
> Drop down and down to the bed of the trees,
> To the hay-silver evening, O
> Lying gentleness, a thin veil over
> The long scars from the nails of the warring hearts. (190)

Air is the image of Peter Able. Even when he speaks of fire and water, he is defining air:

> David: . . . pain prefers us.
> Draws us up.
>
> Peter: Water into the sun:
> All the brooding clouds of us! (174)

David-Cain explicitly links Peter with air to explain how God unfairly favors Peter-Abel: "I saw the smiles that went between/ You and the top air" (176). Between the second and third dreams Peter identifies himself with air:

> They say I'm in a prison. Morning comes
> To a prison like a nurse:
> A rustling presence, as though a small breeze came,
> And presently a voice. I think
> We're going to live. The dark pain has gone,
> The relief of daylight
> Flows over me, as though beginning is
> Beginning. The hills roll in and make their homes,
> And gradually unfold the plains. Breath
> And light are cool together now.
> The earth is all transparent, but too deep
> To see down to its bed. (188–189)

The images begin to blend together, earth rolling in like water, breath cooling fire to produce light, the sea of air covering the seabed of earth. But Peter's dominant image is air.

Early in the play, in the first dream, Adam identifies David and Peter with their elements and himself with water:

Look, sir, my sons are playing.
How silent the spectators are,
World, air, and water.
Eyes bright, tension, halt.
Still as a bone from here to the sea. (174)

After the murder Adams speaks of the "drift of agony" (177). When Abraham offers to undo the cords of Isaac, Adams, the intervening angel, says, yes,

These particular. But never all.
There's no loosening, since men with men
Are like the knotted sea. (193)

Adams' own dream begins with water:

Fish, fish, fish in the sea, you flash
Through your clouds of water like the war in heaven:
Angel-fish and swordfish, the silver troops. . .
And I am salt and sick on a raft above you,
Wondering for land, but there's no homeward
I can see.

Up and down are confounded: clouds and the war in heaven are in the water below; then Adams turns on his back, and he who was man before to the fish below, now becomes fish to God:

God, have mercy
On our sick shoals, darting and dying.
We're strange fish to you. How long
Can you drift over our sea, and not give up
The ghost of hope? The air is bright between us.
The flying fish make occasional rainbows,
But land, your land and mine, is nowhere yet. (197)

Just as up and down are confounded, so air, earth, and water are confounded. Adams remembers the thirty-mile march to their captivity, but the physical medium remains vague: "You can seem to walk:/But presently you drown" (198); when Peter falls out from the march, David cries out: "Man half-seas overboard" (198); Adams sees them as walking on a log boom in a river: "These logs we're on/Are slimy and keep moving apart" (199). Air, earth, and predominantly water vacillate erratically in Adams' dream, for

Adams senses the need for him to be the effective authority which he cannot be: "How can a man learn navigation/When there's no rudder?" (198). The vacillation of air, earth, and water in Adams' dream calls attention to the absent fourth element which can synthesize these: fire.

Fire is the element of Meadows, who helps the men endure the furnace and interprets it for them as "the human shambles" (206). Fire is indistinguishable from the fourth dream and from Meadows, and thus has been treated in the progression of the dreams and in the development of the characters. Fire only needs placing into *Sleep*'s pattern of archetypal images here: the elements of Heraclitus.

The elements of Heraclitus are struggling for unity amongst themselves, just as the characters they are identified with are struggling for unity. When Meadows says in the coda, "It's what they call flesh we're in" (210), it is the fusion of air, earth, fire, and water that he yearns for.

The end of an essay is not the place to begin an exhaustive comparison between *Sleep* and the long poems of Eliot. But not to suggest the possibility would leave the essay incomplete, for—as was noted before—the purpose of genre criticism is "not so much to classify as to clarify . . . traditions and affinities" without which many literary relationships might be missed.[37]

The elements of Heraclitus are a good point of contact between *Sleep* and the Eliot poems. In the *Four Quartets*, "Burnt Norton" exploits the imagery of air; "East Coker," of earth; "The Dry Salvages," of water; and "Little Gidding," of fire. All but one of the titles to the movements of *The Waste Land* suggest the four elements as well: "The Burial of the Dead" implies earth; "The Fire Sermon" and "Death by Water" speak for themselves. The title "A Game of Chess" does not suggest air, but the first rhetorical section of the movement deals with scents in the air; the second and third sections are spoken by personae, in dialogue, speech being the articulation of air. The pointlessness of their speeches is as empty as air. The last title, "What the Thunder Said," implies all of the elements. Thunder accompanies lightning and rain, that is, fire and water; it occurs in the air; rain implies an earth to fall on. Like the last variation in *Sleep*, the last movement of *The Waste Land* points toward the possible reintegration of all things.

Tiresias, the voice for *The Waste Land*, the mythological prophet who cannot die, is trapped in the low-mimetic world of fortune tellers, of pub life, of bored secretaries, and of bawdy songs about Mrs. Porter; and trapped as well in the high-mimetic world of Wagnerian opera, of name-dropping about the archduke, of a boudoir that has the "Rape of Philomel" depicted over the mantel, and of going south in the winter. The displacement of Tiresias is like the displacement of King David, Abraham, Absalom, Isaac, and Adam, not to mention God: displaced first from the myths into the bourgeois high-mimetic mode of twentieth century realism, and displaced again into the low-mimetic context of the prison.

Tiresias speaks all of *The Waste Land*; his one voice is a composite of the many voices. The unnamed persona of *Sleep*—the composite of David, Peter, Joe, and Tim—is parallel to Tiresias in *The Waste Land*. *Sleep* is sometimes criticized as a play because all of the voices in it are so obviously modifications of one voice. But provided that the voices can be distinguished sufficiently for dramatic production (which they can be), the similarity in voice is a positive strength for establishing the persona to bear the weight of *Sleep* as lyric, the one voice hidden behind the dramatic disguise.

Just as *The Waste Land* is a catalogue of lyric forms, from the prothalamion to the opera libretto, so *Sleep* is a catalogue of dramatic forms, from the mystery to the satire. Just as Eliot's wasteland is cursed with every species of infertility, so the wasteland in *Sleep* is cursed with every species of violence. Just as the quest in *The Waste Land* ends in an ambiguously empty Chapel Perilous ("only the wind's home"[38]), so the church in *Sleep* is a prison, in which the prisoners do not have the strength to cross over meaningfully from the epistle to the gospel side. Just as the rooster's crowing at the Chapel Perilous is an ambiguous sign of human betrayal and human hope, so is the crowing of Meadows at his entrance in the last variation. And just as the *Four Quartets* were modeled on the late quartets of Beethoven—and perhaps even *The Waste Land* was, since its five-movement structure is so similar to that of each quartet[39]—just so *Sleep* is modeled on the theme-and-variation form. This tentative comparison is meant only to suggest where a definitive comparison of *Sleep* and the long poems of Eliot could begin. The advantages of association would not all be in *Sleep*'s direction. Criticism about *The Waste Land* in relation to other works usually involves Eliot's use of sources. Certainly *The Waste Land* has more in common with *Sleep* than with *Ulysses* and *The*

Sound and the Fury, the non-sources most often compared with it.

Having demonstrated that *Sleep* is a lyric and subject to fruitful comparison with Eliot's longer poems, this study concludes by saying where *Sleep* does not belong: with closet dramas like Byron's *Manfred,* the more read for its lyrical loveliness, the better—and the less produced—the better, because of its theatrical dullness. *Sleep* abounds in dramatic interest and in theatrical devices that beg for realization, the most notable theatrical device approaching what Northrop Frye calls "the symbol as monad,"[40] by which he means roughly what Joyce meant by *epiphany.* That most notable device is the repeated crossover in front of the crucifix: mockingly, glibly, militarily, reflectively, only to become an impossibility. Unless these crossovers are played, and played in church, and played in a church with a crucifix in place, *Sleep*'s revelation of what the church is and what the Church could become will not be realized. The ecclesiastical hierarchy of Australia did not object to Fry's thinking the thoughts he did or even to his writing them down; they did not ban the publication of *Sleep* and did not question Fry's right to be an Anglican. They objected only to producing *Sleep* in church; in the production lay the offense—and lies the power. Only produced as a play does *Sleep* become the poem it is.

THE COMPLETE PACIFIST 8

The Dark is Light Enough

In their own hearts all people consider themselves to be pacifists. Even those who live by the sword take up the sword in the cause of peace, which cause they call "*Lebensraum*," or "making the world safe for democracy," or "the five-year plan," or which they call "peace," though usually with a qualification: "peace in our time," "peace in Northern Ireland," or "peace with honor." Peace is the only cause a soldier ever fights for.

Pacifists are as blind to their real condition as soldiers. It is the rare pacifist who carries policies on the international scene into private life. Conscientious objectors to war have been known to quarrel belligerently with their wives, to strike their children in unjustified anger, and to turn non-violent demonstrations objecting to a war into violence against the police. The outbreak of violence is a common signal that the non-violent demonstration is over. One applauds the sincerity and deplores the superficiality of the pacifist who urges nations to live at peace, while unable to resolve much simpler personal problems without violence. For what are the crimes of the warmonger but the daily crimes of all of us writ large? Scratch the skin of warmonger and pacifist, and find the same humanity.

Any mature understanding of violence and pacifism must begin with an acknowledgement of the violence in one's own heart, and in *A Sleep of Prisoners* (1951) Fry had defined the progression from the recognition of violence within to a complete pacifism. That play begins with the personal violence of Cain and Abel, moves through the political assassination of Absalom by Joab but condoned by David, progresses to the sacrificial offering of Isaac by Abraham, and concludes with Daniel's friends in the fiery furnace, the flames being the inescapable violence of the human condition, which the pacifist must learn to endure without being violent in return.[1]

Although *The Dark is Light Enough*[2] is three years later than *Sleep*, no other play intervened, and this paper assumes that Fry's perceptions of violence and pacifism remained constant during the interim. The chief difference between the plays is the surrealistic, lyrical organization of *Sleep*, in the writing of which Fry was still discovering his own position on violence and pacifism, and the cause-and-effect plot of *Dark*, in which Fry is expressing what he had discovered earlier.

Though the literary form of the two pieces is very different, the intellectual content is much the same: violence as self-assertion, violence as loyalty to the state, violence as loyalty to God, and, finally, violence to be endured but not to be inflicted.

First, then, the plot of *Dark* embodies violence as self-assertion. As the play opens, one of the Thursday "at homes" of the Countess Rosmarin Ostenburg is in progress, but the atmosphere is discontented. The Countess lives in her Austrian country house while the Hungarian-Austrian war is in progress during the winter of 1848–49. She lives at the boundary between the two nations, and the atmosphere is restless because, with war going on all around, the Countess is strangely absent from her "at home." Unknown to friends or servants, she has left by horse and sleigh in a blinding snowstorm to find Richard Gettner, the former husband of her daughter Gelda. Gettner is an Austrian who has joined the Hungarian army and has now deserted. Held in contempt by Hungarians, Austrians, and all of the guests, Gettner arrives at the "at home" with the Countess, and their arrival coincides with the arrival of Gelda, who has been sent for from Vienna because of the disappearance of her mother. Into the party breaks Janik, a civilian geologist turned colonel in the Hungarian revolt. He and a troop of Hungarian soldiers have observed the Countess bringing Gettner to her house; they have also arrested Count Peter Zichy (Gelda's present husband, a moderate Hungarian who serves in the Austrian cabinet, who has followed his wife to the home of the Countess); and the Hungarians demand that the Countess surrender Gettner (his death will be certain as a deserter) as a condition for the release of Peter. All the guests advise the surrender of Gettner, whom they consider worthless, but the Countess stands firm in protecting Gettner, and Peter remains a prisoner of the Hungarians and Janik.

Before Act II opens, the Hungarians have left, encountered the Austrians, returned from battle to the house, and occupied it as headquarters. The family and the guests of the "at home," stranded by the war, are in process of moving into the stables as the act opens. The atmosphere is as hostile as ever. Gettner has escaped from the house to the stable with a supply of liquor. On his way to the stable loft he meets Gelda alone, they discover that their marriage is not as dead as they had thought it was, and they kiss. As the others arrive, Gettner makes his way into the loft. Colonel Janik, a civilian friend of the Countess, is in the awkward position of dispossessing her to the stable. Eager to compensate for the crude necessity of war, he makes the concession of allowing Peter to join the company, though only in the presence of two Hungarian guards. No sooner is the company complete than Gettner, fortified by drink, makes his way down from the loft. The Countess persuades the guards not to arrest Gettner, and Gettner, expansively successful, announces before Peter that Gelda still loves him. To prove it, he kisses her, much to the disgust of everyone present. To lighten the atmosphere, the Countess suggests that the guards provide music. The guards take off their pistol belts to dance; and Stefan, the Countess's son, disgusted by Gettner's reviving the feelings of the defunct marriage, steals the pistols and, unnoticed by the others preoccupied with the dance, forces Gettner to step outside to fight a duel. When the shots are fired, the dancing stops abruptly; the embarrassed guards miss their weapons; everyone but the Countess rushes outside; and they return to inform the Countess that Gettner has shot her son. Even so, she refuses to be judgmental against Gettner.

Act III opens with the Hungarians defeated, Stefan recovering from a gunshot wound, and the Countess in bed with acute exhaustion. Peter, released as a Hungarian prisoner, stops in at the house of the Countess just long enough to establish a good relationship with Gelda again, but he must hurry off to Austria to persuade the victorious government to stop their wholesale slaughter of Hungarian officers. Gettner is not in immediate jeopardy from the Hungarians as a deserter; he is, however, still in Hungarian uniform and in jeopardy from the Austrians. So Gettner steals a horse from the stable and rides toward Hungary, but he hears rumors along the way that the Countess is dying and arrives at her house during a Thursday "at home." The Countess, ill as she is, manages to attend. Janik, who formerly pursued Gettner as a deserter, is now being pursued by the victorious Austrians. He arrives at the "at home" just before Gettner, and the Countess now grants Janik the same impartial asylum that she granted Gettner earlier. When Gettner arrives, he and the Countess have a long talk together, and Gettner proposes marriage to her; the Countess is pleased but declines, and Gettner leaves, only to find the house surrounded by Austrians in pursuit of Janik. He returns to the Countess, but she has died during the few moments that he was gone. He calmly requests the servant to admit the Austrians, and for the first time in his life he does not run or hide.

From beginning to end, in spite of counteracting influences from the Countess, *Dark* is full of a hostile atmosphere, all the more ironic because the Countess intends the atmosphere to be "at-home" coziness.

Even Cain's anger with Abel disguised itself as moral outrage in *Sleep*. Jakob, a guest responsible for much of the hostility at the "at homes," disguises his antipathy toward the other guests as loyalty to the Countess. When Dr. Kassel deplores not only the absence of the Countess during a snowstorm but also her absence from the "at home" on a Thursday, Jakob suspects the good doctor of mocking the Countess (4); when Belmann refers to the Countess as inscrutable, Jakob suspects him of inventing "crackpot blasphemies" (4); when Belmann criticizes the Countess for having married her young daughter to Gettner, Jakob promptly challenges Belmann to a duel two days hence; when Belmann disapproves aesthetically of one of the paintings of the Countess, Jakob defends it on the basis of "the creative value of the fault" (57). Jakob's restlessness is always on the verge of breaking into violence. When the Countess is absent, Jakob laments: "No, no; we must be anxious. I should have/No peace for a moment if I thought I lacked anxiety" (4). His restlessness needs only a cause to justify violence, and defending the Countess against imaginary insult is his cause. Jakob thinks Kassel's respect for the Countess is too familiar and Belmann's worship of the Countess ought to keep him from commenting on her flaws. A worry that Jakob might be sending Belmann to hell is his excuse for not fighting a duel on behalf of the Countess—not the loftiest argument for pacifism, but sufficient in Jakob's case to prevent his shedding blood.

If Belmann and Kassel are the good-natured, light-hearted Abels against Jakob's Cain, Belmann, Kassel, and Jakob are united as Cains against Gettner's Abel. Bellman calls him "that rag of hell,"

> that invertebrate,
> That self-drunk, drunken, shiftless, heartless
> Lying malingerer. . . (6)

It is so strange that Belmann should accuse Gettner of restlessness, when his accusations are in themselves a symptom of his own restlessness.

> Whoever hates his race,
> His Emperor, his culture, or his mother
> Wins — well, not his heart, which is apparently
> Only locomotor,
> But all the enthusiasm of his spleen. (10)

The speech says as much about Belmann's spleen as it does about Gettner's. It seems as though all the restlessness that the men feel because of the unexpected absence of the Countess, rather than dissipating upon her return, focuses instead on Richard Gettner. Dr. Kassel, Belmann, and Jakob all agree that the Countess should not give Count Peter Zichy as a hostage in exchange for Gettner. Each remains in character: Dr. Kassel doing his best to weigh all alternatives carefully, Belmann deciding on the most humane course with a decidedly secular flavor, and Jakob arguing for the honor of the Countess. Each is unaware of his own violence:

> Belmann: If ever there was a bad exchange, we've seen it now.
> I feel indignant and aggrieved.
>
> Kassel: And I seriously wonder
> Whether the drive you took so far in the snow,
> Rosmarin, is finished even yet.
>
> Belmann: No good can come of it.
>
> Jakob: No good will ever come of Gettner.
>
> Countess: That may be true. (37)

The violent person unaware of one's own violence is never uncertain. Only the Countess is not so sure.

The certain certainties of Kassel, Belmann, and Jakob have a particular attraction for young people not yet sure within themselves. Stefan is never entirely sure of his own judgment and ability to cope. His mother's absence makes him send for his brother-in-law, Peter:

> My first thought, as it always is,
> Was to tell my brother-in-law the trouble.
> To me Peter treads the earth more surely
> And reassures more instantly
> Than any other man. (5)

Stefan is not weak, but dangerously open to influences; not wicked, but very impressionable; not characteristically violent, but able to contract the violence of others. At the beginning of Act II, Stefan is doing his best, not altogether successfully, to understand Gettner's position:

> You just have to show me
> Where you keep your sympathy
> For the people I've most affection for,
> And I'll understand if I can. (39)

But two things happen to change Stefan's mood. First, he is amazed to hear about the duel to which Jakob has challenged Belmann to defend the honor of the Countess (58); and next, the drunken Gettner kisses Stefan's sister, Gelda. Stefan challenges Gettner to a duel, and when Gettner is unwilling, he provokes him into it, all to defend the honor of Peter and Gelda.

The theme of the duel is fascinating to trace through the play. Just at the point that Jakob is using Belmann's hell-bound agnosticism as his pretext for not fighting the duel, Stefan takes up the duel with Gettner. Both Jakob and Stefan are sure that they are issuing challenges in the cause of honor. Still, whether duels are fought or not has less to do with the moral necessities of honor than with the murkier necessities of violence. Violence is like an infection with its own irrational necessities. The violence in the situation and within the people is moving toward a duel; who fights it or against whom or why is beside the point.

The hostile attitude of Jakob, Belmann, and Kassel toward

Gettner, the hostile attitude of Jakob toward the other guests, and Stefan's vacillating attitude toward Gettner suddenly fixing itself on violence are all like the hostilities of the war between Austria and Hungary raging outside. Wherever hostility exists, each side considers itself as essentially non-violent, considers its case as rationally based on a defense of honor.

Like *Sleep*, *Dark* embodies violence as self assertion; both plays also embody the idea of violence as loyalty to the state. The permissive violence of David and the active violence of Joab against Absalom in *Sleep* are justified in the minds of the instigators because they are intended for the good of the state.

Likewise Janik in *Dark* also justifies his violence because it promotes the justice of the Hungarian claims against the Austrian tyranny. Janik first enters the house without being admitted or announced (26); he demands Gettner's release; he keeps Count Peter prisoner when the Countess refuses to release Gettner; he occupies the house as his headquarters next day, sending the Countess to the stables; and he, the erstwhile geologist and civilian friend of the Countess, does this all not out of contempt for her, but on behalf of the "downtrodden men,/The overlong injustice" (51).

As a private person Janik is fond of the Countess. He does not in fact search her house for Gettner; he is willing to discuss the issues of war with the Countess; he kisses her hand; and he allows his prisoner, Peter, to join his family. The civilized private person in Janik always runs counter to the military public person in him, as it must in any soldier.

This includes the soldiers sent to guard Peter. Are the guards military "by nature or misfortune?" (60) the Countess wants to know, and the non-military response of Rusti and the military response of Beppi are amusing. Rusti is soon showing around letters from his wife. When Gettner appears, Beppi knows exactly what he should do; but when the Countess invites them both to undo their collars and sit down (64), both guards oblige. Before long Beppi is playing the harmonica and Rusti is dancing, weapons and uniforms laid aside. When shots ring out and the duel is exposed, both guards turn suddenly military; but when the Countess pleads with them not to make her son's injury the occasion for Gettner's execution, they turn non-military again. For military identity is always an identity imposed from without; a military identity always runs counter to what is within. Military identity proves an outlet for the violence within people, but nothing more.

The inadequacy of a strictly military identity is evident when Janik, who before as a soldier condemned the Countess for sheltering Gettner from the Hungarians, returns to the Countess, at the play's end and after his defeat, as a private person, expecting the same kind of treatment as she gave Gettner before.

A military self is never enough, not even on the just side of a war. For even just wars are fought by military establishments which institutionalize violence, justify violence as the only means to freedom, and measure patriotism by the energy of the violence. Violence for the honor of Hungary or Austria is only a little less selfish, a little less narcissistic, than violence for personal honor.

In addition to violence as self-assertion for honor and violence as loyalty to the state, *Sleep* and *Dark* embody violence for God's sake. The honor of God is the motivation for Abraham's willingness to sacrifice Isaac in *Sleep;* his willingness to sacrifice Isaac is a combination of performing violence and enduring it, of activity and passivity.

The honor of God is at once Peter's consolation and his cause. When the Hungarians are completely broken, Peter consoles himself with the fact of the Incarnation:

> Peter: The Hungarians are completely broken.
>
> Gelda: It was what you were afraid of.
>
> Peter: I was afraid
> They'd lose the liberties they were beginning to gain
> Lately; not that we should lose the humanity
> We took of God two thousand years ago. (79)

The Incarnation is for Peter a redefinition of the concepts *God* and *man,* which cannot be altered by any circumstances, a sure basis for confidence. But the Incarnation is also a process: a learning to become both a son of man and a son of God, along with Jesus Christ. Whatever else being a son of man means, it certainly means taking pains choosing the most Christlike alternative in a muddled situation. Whatever else being a son of God involves, it involves being permanently conditioned against disillusionment in failure.

Thus, Peter's chief concern is never his personal honor. When the Countess chooses to have the Hungarians keep Peter rather than surrender Gettner to certain death, Peter understands perfectly her reasons, though he is honest enough to confess conceit: "I wish there were no conceit in me/To let me bid myself against another man" (35). When Gettner kisses Gelda and Gelda accepts the kiss, Peter is not pleased, to be sure, but neither does he stand on his honor: "It could be. I can see it could be" (67). And when he makes up with Gelda afterwards, he is neither hurt (the barometer of private honor) nor angry (the barometer of public honor). Gelda says she thought she had "almost brought our world to an end,/ But you didn't greatly notice it" (82). Personal honor, private or public, does not drive Peter.

Nor does loyalty to the state drive Peter, for he is loyal to two states: Austria and Hungary. He is Hungarian by birth but serves on the Austrian cabinet, urging moderation towards the Hungarian rebels. As a captive to Janik's troops, who are surprised by a troop of Austrian dragoons, Peter suddenly finds himself fighting for the Hungarian cause:

> In the fight with the Austrian dragoons this morning
> I became the very passion I opposed, and was glad to be.
> I borrowed a sword out of someone's useless hand,
> And as long as the fighting lasted
> I was, heart and soul, the revolution.
> Janik thought he had won me over,
> But on the way back I convinced him otherwise.

Peter's only explanation:

> I suppose
> There's no balance without the possibility
> Of overbalancing. (59)

Peter is free from the tyranny of personal glory and patriotism, both.

But Peter never reaches serenity, for at heart he remains an overbalanced activist. Stefan sends for him and he rushes to Rosmarin's house "the first moment/He could manage to get away" (12). Taken captive by the Hungarians, he fights valiantly on their side. Making up with Gelda in Act III, he can stay only briefly; he must rush off to Austria because the victorious government is "shooting and hanging/Every Hungarian of note who fought in the war":

What torments me
Is whether I might not have prevented it
If I'd never left Vienna: whether that ride here,
Whether Stefan's message of alarm for Rosmarin,
Wasn't one cause of these deaths and the endless consequences.
I'm too late, but I have to go there.
And, though I'm too late, every moment here
Makes me feel I'm betraying someone. (80)

The concept of betrayal keeps coming up, for Peter is never sure he has done the right thing:

You make me think
I shall betray something either way,
Staying or going. If I stay, I think
Of nothing but getting to Vienna. If I go,
I think of nothing but what you have said to me. (81)

Peter lacks a single workable criterion by which he can make moral choices and then, for good or ill, rest in them. Peter is that humanly understandable but logically contradictory phenomenon: the militant pacifist. He fights for peace the way Jakob fights for the honor of the Countess and the way Janik fights for Hungary, but in the cause of peace one should not fight at all. Is Peter not driven, at least to some extent, by violence? Is he not as unaware of the violence within him as Jakob and Janik?

All three learn something about the violence within themselves. Jakob sees it is not an isolated instance of outraged honor which drives him:

One always thinks if only
One particular unpleasantness
Could be cleared up, life would become as promising
As always it was promising to be.
But in fact we merely change anxieties. (84)

The military Janik returns defeated, he for whom the Hungarian cause had become everything. He must be coaxed by the Countess to sing a bawdy song of the soldiers. Only after he sings does the Countess comfort him:

Child,
I know your cause is lost, but in the heart
Of all right causes is a cause which cannot lose. (90)

The unselfishness in Janik's devotion to Hungary must grow into Peter's devotion to God; God is the only cause which cannot lose, though Janik will need to become a child to know that. Peter overcomes some of the snobbery inherent in any pacifist's scorn for the military, when he fights with Janik against the Austrians:

> I'm no less convinced
> Than I always was, they're doing themselves a wrong,
> And doing as great a damage to Hungary
> As to Austria. But I know it now
> In a different sense. I can taste it
> Like a fault of my own, which is not the same
> Flavour as the fault of some other man. (60)

Jakob, Janik, and Peter all acquire insight into the violence which drives them, although they do not change significantly within the play. But their insight into the violence which drives them is essential if they are going to overcome the problem of violence, if not in the play then outside of it, if not in time then outside of it.

Two characters, Gelda and Gettner, change significantly within the play, but a discussion of them must wait for a discussion of the Countess.

The plots of *Sleep* and *Dark* embody the ideas of willingness to endure violence and unwillingness to inflict it. In the last dream in *Sleep* Daniel's three friends in the fiery furnace of life are joined by the son of man under God's command, a *figura Christi*. None of the four are naively shocked at the violence that comes with living, all of them are willing to endure it, and none of them will inflict it. It is the position of the Countess in *Dark*.

She too is a *figura Christi*, surrounded as she is by her rock-like Peter, who

> treads the earth more surely
> And reassures more instantly
> Than any other man. (5)

her James (Jakob = Jacobus = James), and her John (Janik): the three characters who acquire insight into their own violence, although they do not change within the scope of the play. Besides, the Thursday "at homes" are reminiscent of Maundy Thursday, the Thursday of the footwashing, the Lord's Supper, and the new commandment "that ye love one another." That the Countess leaves her nine guests in order to hunt up Gettner in spite of a blinding snowstorm and at great risk to herself is reminiscent of Christ's parable of the good shepherd, in which ninety-nine sheep are left for the sake of one. For readers unconvinced by these implications, Fry has Belmann make the point explicitly, again and again:

> The goddess of it [our Thursday world], in her Godlike way,
> Is God knows where. We can only hope
> She will condescend to appear in her own time. (4)

> You know the Countess has the qualities of true divinity.
> For instance: how apparently undemandingly
> She moves among us; and yet
> Lives make and unmake themselves in her neighbourhood
> As nowhere else. There are many names I could name
> Who would have been remarkably otherwise
> Except for her divine non-interference. (4-5)

> She has a touching way
> Of backing a man up against eternity
> Until he hardly has the nerve to remain mortal. (5)

> One man the Countess will never change
> By her divine non-interference:
> Ten kronen against Gettner's chances. (61)

But simply to label the Countess a *figura Christi* is to make her into a static icon, just as Belmann, that clever but not particularly wise agnostic, does. To freeze the Countess into a *figura Christi* is to make the play into a static allegory and is to ignore the dynamic interplay between human and divine: the humanity we took from God two thousands years ago in the Incarnation. As the human person now is, Christ once was: as Christ is now, we may become. In this state of affairs, how is one to distinguish between a *figura Christi* and a Christian struggling to become more Christlike? The Countess is a believable person and inhabits a world we recognize as our own. Her penmanship is illegible—"Three words, apparently/Entirely composed of E's" (4); she can be genuinely giddy when Janik kisses her hand or Gettner proposes marriage; and she is curiously preoccupied with a bawdy song. The Countess is no icon.

In many ways the Countess is like Peter. When Gettner calls to her to save him, she puts her own world down and takes his up, just as Peter responds to Stefan's call. Just as Peter is a Hungarian in the Austrian cabinet, so the Countess is an Austrian but lives next to the Hungarian border and has Hungarian friends, like the geologist Janik. Just as Peter, a member of the Austrian cabinet, fights temporarily on the Hungarian side, so the Countess protects Gettner from Janik and his Hungarians and protects Janik from the Austrians. Just as Peter refuses to feel threatened when Stefan, Janik, Gelda, and Gettner use him for their own purposes, so the Countess refuses to feel threatened when Gettner and Janik use her.

One great difference between Peter and the Countess is that the Countess is not at all militant about her pacifism. She has learned long ago that violence cannot be organized or fought out of existence. The only effective locus for effecting the victory of peace over violence is the individual human heart: one's own. She has learned that "there is nothing on the earth/Which doesn't happen in your own hearts" (74) and in her own heart too. Peter pursues too militantly the situations where peace is to be made, and then feels he is "betraying" (81) the other causes when he concentrates on one. The Countess waits for situations to come to her. Then she makes perfect her will when she deals with them.

The Countess completely bypasses the intricacies of politics in pursuing peace. She never asks who started it, or what the issues are, or what are the circumstances surrounding the violent situation:

> The arithmetic
> Of cause and effect I've never understood.
> How many beans make five is an immense
> Question, depending on how many
> Preliminary beans preceded them. (97)

In the darkness of the human condition, where degrees of comparative guilt and the causes for a particular act of violence are impossible to discern, only one criterion functions: the least violent alternative is always best, no matter how unreasonable and unjust it may appear. Better that she die in a snowstorm than that Gettner be murdered when he is caught as a traitor. Better that her son-in-law, Peter, whom she loves, should be a Hungarian prisoner than that Gettner, whom she does not love, should be shot. Better that Gelda should enter a bad marriage with Gettner by her own will than that the Countess should violently interfere with the course of life. Better that Gettner should go off free for wounding Stefan than that the Hungarian's punishment of Gettner should be added to Gettner's wounding of Stefan. Better that she should grant refuge to both Janik and Gettner at the same time than that she should decide which one to sacrifice. She is, from the perspective of the audience and reader, an amazingly complete pacifist.

She herself is aware of the incompleteness of her own pacifism, and remains preoccupied with the violence remaining within her. She questions her own motives in not interfering with Gelda's marrying Gettner:

> I let you
> Marry Richard, though I knew you would find
> Happiness only by a fine shade,
> Or in some special sense of happiness,
> Or not at all. (55–56)

With so much risk involved, should not a little interference early have solved the necessity of greater violence later? All wars use a similar rationale, and though the Countess does not follow that rationale, she is human enough to entertain it as a possibility. Accepting as she is of Gettner—"Life has a hope of him/Or he would never have lived" (54)—she confesses that she has not been accepting enough:

> Richard, Richard,
> What virtue I've missed!
> . . . .
> I'm a fool to deny
> What you so beautifully praise me for,
> But truth leaps in me, and I have to confess
> I haven't loved you. (99)

All she did for Richard was done for "what any life may mean" (100), but she is not satisfied with such impersonality. She promises, "I'll not/Leave you until I can love you, Richard," though she does not "mean/Necessarily here" (101). Outside of time she will be able to love all people, even the unloveliest. Her present inadequacy in love—her awareness of the violence remaining within her—is her continuing impetus for growth.

Hence, the Countess has none of the moral superiority which the others demonstrate. Quite secure in their own virtue, Belmann sees Gettner as a "rag of hell" (6), Jakob sees "no/Faith in Gettner" (35), and Kassel agrees with the other two that the gulf separating Peter and Gettner is unfathomable. Janik's opinion of Gettner is no better: the Hungarians are right, Gettner has forsaken the right cause, therefore Gettner is wrong. To the extent that Peter speaks for the Hungarians in the Austrian government, he considers himself better than Gettner; he wishes "there were no conceit in me/To let me bid myself against another man" (35). Belmann, Jakob, Kassel, and Janik attack ethical problems like sixth-graders doing true-false exams. Only the Countess understands:

> Pray for him [Stefan],
> Not because I love him, but because
> You are the life you pray for. And because
> Richard Gettner is the life you pray for.
> And because there is nothing on the earth
> Which doesn't happen in your own hearts. (74)

The stance of the Countess is the stance of the play. When Peter as a Hungarian on the Austrian side temporarily is taken with the Hungarian cause and fights against Austria, we applaud his high spirits and his impartiality. But then we begin to ask whether he is so different from Gettner, the Austrian who enlists on the Hungarian side and then deserts. Not judging by the results but by the condition of heart that produced them, is the denial of Peter very different from the betrayal of Judas? In fact, Fry has Peter use the Judas word *betrayal* about his own moral dilemma in another situation (80–81). Untangling good from evil is next to impossible, given the complexity of the human heart. Judging the violence in others is a venting of our own violence. Seeing the violence in other people as our own makes self-righteous condescension disappear. Then the best and worst seem not very different from each other. "Let us," says the Countess, "say"

> We are all confused, incomprehensible,
> Dangerous, contemptible, corrupt,
> And in that condition pass the evening
> Thankfully and well. In our plain defects
> We already know the brotherhood of man. (21)

For the moral ambiguity which the Countess and the play recognize, the blinding snowstorm is the symbol. The snow is white, yet produces a darkness as effectively as any blackness. The white snow is dark enough to make the journey difficult. But the dark produced by the snow is also light enough, given the divination of the Countess, for her to reach her destination:

> I have been as clever as an ostler,
> And driven alone, one human and two horses,
> Into a redeemed land, uncrossed by any soul
> Or sound, and always the falling perfection
> Covering where we came, so that the land
> Lay perfect behind us, as though we were perpetually
> Forgiven the journey. And moreover
> A strange prescience possessed me.
> One must have talent to go from a place to a place,
> But divination to go so deviously
> That north, south, east, and west
> Are lost in admiration, and *yet* to arrive,
> After a short experience of eternity,
> At the place and people one set out to reach . . . (16–17)

She is describing her journey in the snowstorm, but she might as well be describing her way through the blinding moral situations she confronts. The darkness of the moral situation is always light enough with the one absolute moral principle of the Countess: the least violent alternative is always best.

Her argument against Janik, in which she exploits his commitment to freedom, is a good example:

> Your faith is, your country has been refused
> Its good rights, for many years too long.
> So be certain, whatever the temptation,
> No man is made a slave by you.
> To you Austria is a tyranny.
> Then, to the number of those men who die,
> And far beyond that number infinitely,
> Surely you will show
> One man over another has no kingdom.
> Otherwise, how shall I understand your war?
> Because I have respect for Richard Gettner's
> Wandering and uncertain will, *therefore*
> I have respect for your sheer purpose

> And for those many men I cannot
> Know by name who are waiting in the snow.
> But if you tell me Richard Gettner
> Has thrown away his claim to freedom
> By claiming that a man is free, then you
> And those in the snow, may as well march
> Against your guns and swords. They are tyrannous, too.
> Is it not a quaint freedom, that lets us
> Make up our minds and not be free to change them?
> Poor hope for me! I change my mind
> For pure relaxation, two or three times a day,
> As I get wiser or sillier, whichever it is I do.
> Must I save your cause for you, Colonel?
> If so, then not in my name or Richard Gettner's
> But in the name of all your nameless fellows
> Who trust their suffering is righteous
> I forbid you to invade the liberties of this house. (30)

Janik is not persuaded by this definition of freedom; he calls it anarchy. So from one point of view the Countess loses. But the Countess has won what was her intention of winning. Before her speech Janik had said, "bring him [Gettner] out. Otherwise, I regret, we shall come in and find him" (29); after her speech he considers searching the house "a dangerous delay" (31) and puts forward the plan of keeping Peter hostage. Now the Countess must find new ways to deal with that situation. Nevertheless, without Janik's knowing it, she has won the argument. Janik does not search the house as he had threatened.

Sometimes situations are so complex that no argument, oblique or direct, can avert the violence. Irrational means are needed to avert violence. When the Countess is annoyed with Belmann's sniping at Gettner behind his back and with Jakob's sniping at Belmann to his face, she proposes a nonargumentative solution:

> We're continually coming together, as though to live
> Pleasantly in one another's conversation,
> And each time we find ourselves distracted
> By what is happening to us. Do let us
> For a short while abandon incident
> And charm ourselves with something quite immaterial. (61)

The diversion is provided by the Hungarian guard, who produces a recent letter from his wife, and the Countess is thoroughly absorbed in it. The Countess can also recognize in other people under great stress the need for something immaterial. When in Act III Janik appears, defeated, he cannot trust himself, for tears, to speak. The Countess then urges him to "First of all say any trivial thing;/We shall come presently to the other" (90).

Usually the trivial, quite immaterial thing that averts the feelings of panic and violence is music. When in Act II Gettner appears before the Hungarian guards who are in duty bound to arrest him as a traitor, when Gettner kisses Gelda in front of the imprisoned Peter, and when Gelda confesses she feels something for Gettner too, then music is all that will serve:

> How shall we manage, with time at a standstill?
> We can't go back to where nothing has been said;
> And no heart is served, caught in a moment
> Which has frozen. Since no words will set us free —
> Not at least now, until we can persuade
> Our thoughts to move —
> Music would unground us best,
> As a tide in the dark comes to boats at anchor
> And they begin to dance. (67)

As Janik leaves in Act III for a hiding place in the turret, the Countess insists that he put her in mind of a bawdy song the soldiers sing; it is as much to alleviate Janik's hysteria as to satisfy her own curiosity. She herself needs the bawdy song as she contemplates how she will need to defend Janik against the Austrians, and needs it again as she dies, alone. Music allays the violence and panic within when words no longer work. Janik must stoop to folk music, just as the Countess directs Janik to a door "not much bigger than a child" (92) to get to his hiding place, requiring stooping, too. As the Countess dies, she sings the bawdy song Janik taught her, stooping graciously to death.

Whether by argument or by non-rational means like music, the Countess arrives at her destination—the least violent alternative—as surely as she drives her horse and sleigh to Richard Gettner in a blinding snowstorm. She is like the butterfly in the epigraph to the play:

> The weather was stormy; the sky heavily clouded; the darkness . . . profound. . . . It was across this maze of leafage, and in absolute darkness, that the butterflies had to find their way in

> order to attain the end of their pilgrimage.
>
> Under such conditions the screech-owl would not dare to forsake its olive-tree. The butterfly . . . goes forward without hesitation. . . . So well it directs its tortuous flight that, in spite of all the obstacles to be evaded, it arrives in a state of perfect freshness, its great wings intact. . . . The darkness is light enough. . . .
>
> J. H. Fabre

Like the butterfly, the Countess finds the darkness light enough, which is to say that she finds warmth enough in the winter of our discontent, goodness enough in a wicked world, life enough in death.

That the darkness is light enough for the Countess to pursue her non-violent way non-violently is one important difference between the Countess and Peter. The other difference is that only in her presence do "Lives make and unmake themselves . . . /As nowhere else" (5). There are two people particularly who "would have been remarkably otherwise/Except for her divine non-interference" (5): Gelda and Richard Gettner.

Gelda's problem is pride, the root of all other sin and violence. Violence increases in proportion to one's blindness to the violence within oneself, which blindness is pride.

Gelda begins with pride in thinking herself capable of doing the impossible: marrying Gettner. Even the Countess, who did not oppose the marriage, saw that "loving Richard/Might be a heavy devotion and a long/Experience of daring" (56). Gelda was sure she was equal to it; her pride is parallel to Jakob's unrecognized violence and to Belmann's certain certainties. Just as Jakob and Belmann's personal violence is of less worth than Janik's violence on behalf of society, so Gelda's personal pride progresses to institutional pride: a conventional, normal, society-approved marriage to "Count Peter the sturdy" (8). Gelda's pride is a trifle complacent:

> I am Peter's wife, and everything
> Is so well with us, our marriage vows
> Go on like dancers, with no thought in the world to carry,
> Only to be as easy and loving as we are. (36)

But Gelda is overconfident, for before long she is promising love to Gettner and kissing him both in public and in private, in spite of her perfect marriage to Peter. Her neutrality is like Peter's own, his loyalty at once to Hungary and Austria. Just as the complete pacifism of the Countess supersedes the incomplete pacifism of Peter, so Gelda achieves a new willingness to look inside herself for pride and violence, and hence she becomes more humble and nonviolent. "It may have been right," she says to Peter,

> That first instinct, to put out with a lifeboat
> For Richard, but on to it scrambled
> Such a crew of pirates, my curiosity,
> My pride, my ambition to succeed
> Where I failed before, my longing to discover
> What conversions could be made by love,
> We all began to sink. (81)

The pirates have been there all along, but only now does she recognize them as pirates. The Countess is shown only in full bloom, but before the play begins she must have gone through a series of experiences similar to Gelda's. Gelda's condition at the end of the play approaches humility.

But though one have the humility of Gelda and the passivity of the Countess and have not love, it profiteth nothing. Gettner begins hostile and humble, hostile and passive, which is to say indifferent. He must progress toward a loving pride, which is to say self-respect, and toward a loving activity. His progress throughout the play runs counter to that of the other characters. The reason he is so disliked by the others is not only his hostility, but also his pilgrimage toward wholeness running so incomprehensibly counter to theirs.

And yet the four stages from violence to passivity, abstracted from *Sleep* and applied to *Dark*, have a certain applicability to Gettner's progress from passivity to activity, from hostility to love. Before the play opens Gettner has been personally passive, personally hostile in his marriage, for he has never consummated his marriage with Gelda. His reason is humility, for he knows he would be "The disappointer of expectations" (45); he does not realize that he has been hostile toward Gelda, who means to love and be loved. He is not so different from Jakob, Belmann, and Kassel; they do not recognize the hostility in their activity, just as he does not recognize the hostility in his passivity.

Gettner the anti-Jakob becomes Gettner the anti-Janik. Just

before the play opens he deserts from the Hungarian army; in this situation, too, he is unaware of the hostility in his non-performance: "There's a dreariness in dedicated spirits/That makes the promised land seem older than the fish" (18). No wonder the Countess taunts his passivity:

> Richard sometimes reminds me of an unhappy
> Gentleman, who comes to the shore
> Of a January sea, heroically
> Strips to swim, and and then seems powerless
> To advance or retire, either to take the shock
> Of the water or to immerse himself again
> In his warm clothes, and so stands cursing
> The sea, the air, the season, anything
> Except himself, as blue as a plucked goose.
> It would be very well if he would one day
> Plunge, or dress himself again. (56)

He is as detached from causes as Janik is attached to Hungary.

In response to the taunt above, Gettner kisses Gelda in front of Peter: a clumsy and hostile action, but at least an action. But the action is not satisfying to Gettner:

> They tell you to be a man of decision,
> To take the cold sea in a courageous plunge,
> And when you do they squint at you for a fool. (65)

The action is not satisfying to Gettner because he is as paradoxically impacted between activity and passivity at this point as Peter is between the cause he is "betraying" and the cause he is devoting himself to at any moment, to say nothing of how impacted both Gettner and Peter are between Austria and Hungary. Gettner is an anti-Peter.

The audience shares the surprise of the Countess when Gettner makes a decision, acts on it, and there is nary a trace of hostility in it. After years of passive postponement, Gettner finally proposes marriage to the Countess. No other character in the play could have cheered the deathbed of the Countess with anything so affectionate. Unconventional and indecorous by conventional standards, the proposal is just right for a Countess who at one point is afraid that Gettner is "trying to find words appropriate/ To visiting the sick" (97). Gettner manages to raise a song of hope within her:

You, Richard!
You, of all men on the earth,
To be the one to say to dying things
'Be a beginning.'
And indeed, please God, to the last moment
I will begin . . . (98)

Gettner has become capable of an act of whimsical creativity worthy of the Countess herself. And the change in Gettner is permanent. He tells the maid to admit the Austrians after the Countess is dead. He does not run. Gettner, by a route opposite to that of anyone else in the play, "arrives in a state of perfect freshness" (epigraph) at his selfhood. The dark is light enough.

The change in Gettner is the conversion of Judas. For you are the life you pray for when you pray for Judas—or Hitler. A pacifism which makes an exception of Judas and Hitler is not complete. The conversion of Judas makes the play aesthetically as satisfying as it is satisfying intellectually and religiously, for it provides a motion contrary to the rest of the play; and yet the contrary motion is curiously appropriate to the rest of the play since it can all be analyzed by the same categories. It is a complete play.

The changes in Gelda and Gettner belong in this study to demonstrate how the pacifism of the Countess supersedes Peter's. Not only does the Countess pursue non-violence non-violently, but the result of her non-violence is that in her presence "Lives make and unmake themselves . . . /As nowhere else" (5). But making that point, one admires the aesthetic wholeness of *Dark*. Even the servants reinforce the theme. Bella's concern for the honor of the Countess justifies her lying and justifies her belittling Willi; Willi cannot lie, understands perfectly why Bella lies and forgives her for it, and does not mind being made the fool for the sake of the honor of the Countess (8–11). Bella tends toward Jakob and Janik's end of the violence continuum, and Willi toward Peter and the Countess's end. *Dark*, even to the incidental characters, is organized by theme.

That idea, the progressive stages toward peace, is the same idea as *Sleep*. Are the two plays the same?

The scope of *Sleep* is narrower than, and the scope of *Dark* broader than, the following passage from "Little Gidding," the fourth of T. S. Eliot's *Four Quartets:*

> There are three conditions which often look alike
> Yet differ completely, flourish in the same hedgerow:
> Attachment to self and to things and to persons, detachment
> From self and from things and from persons; and, growing
> between them indifference
> Which resembles the others as death resembles life,
> Being between two lives — unflowering, between
> The live and the dead nettle. This is the use of memory:
> For liberation — not less of love but expanding
> Of love beyond desire, and so liberation
> From the future as well as the past. Thus, love of a country
> Begins as attachment to our own field of action
> And comes to find that action of little importance
> Though never indifferent. History may be servitude,
> History may be freedom. See, now they vanish,
> The faces and places, with the self which, as it could,
> loved them,
> To become renewed, transfigured, in another pattern.

Both plays agree with the poem that one cannot be attached to God unless one has been attached to lesser things first. To be progressively attached to God means that one is progressively detached from self, and from things, and from persons; but to be detached assumes an attachment to begin with. Never to have been attached at all is indifference. When one is satisfied in God, one does not turn with puritanical condemnation toward those objects which have taught one to love previously. They are "transfigured in another pattern." The need for sex, for instance, is the disguised hunger for God; sex arouses hungers stronger than it can satisfy; no sexual encounter can be ultimately satisfying. The saint does not condemn sex or patriotism. The puritanical condemnation of sex or patriotism is indifference, not learning to love at all. The Fry plays agree with the Eliot poem and with each other here.

But the scope of *Sleep* is narrower than the Eliot poem, for *Sleep* makes nothing of the possibility of indifference. The scope of *Dark* is broader than the Eliot poem, for *Dark* not only brings up the possibility of indifference in the person of Gettner, but also shows the path by which indifference too can become attachment to God.

The absence of indifference in *Sleep* and its presence and redemption in *Dark* is only one way in which the scope of *Sleep* is narrower than *Dark*. Already in *Sleep* Fry had distinguished the stages in the ascent through the creatures, but these stages are juxtaposed without transition; the stages are barely discernible in *Dark* because of how one stage folds into another, in Gelda's case for instance. It is part of the flow of life. In *Sleep* all four characters progress to the next stage simultaneously; in *Dark* all the characters are at different stages from each other. Gelda goes through all four stages, Gettner travels all four stages by a contrary route, and the Countess has well-nigh arrived at the beginning of the play.[5] For all its brilliant surrealism, the dream form of *Sleep* remains abstracted from life. No viewer would ever think that four soldiers would really dream these four dreams in such eloquent succession. The illusion of reality is not even attempted in *Sleep*. The evocation of life during wartime in the court of the Countess in *Dark* provides, if not an everyday setting, at least a recognizable one, in which recognizable people hanker after God while they are awake —even though not all of them realize what they are hankering after. Fry knew a great deal about overcoming violence in writing *Sleep*, but he had not yet experienced it sufficiently; or if he had experienced it, he had not had time to assimilate and articulate the experience. In *Dark* Fry knows what he knew in *Sleep*, but he knows it better and he knows more. The form of *Dark* is less splendidly experimental than the form of *Sleep*, but it does not need to be. In *Dark* the human soul thirsts for God in the very world we live in, which Fry evokes rather conventionally; what is unconventional here is Fry's evocation of the experience of that thirst. *Sleep* communicates the idea of the ascent to God through the creatures, *Dark* communicates the experience.

Sleep has "become renewed, transfigured, in another pattern" (Eliot, above). *Sleep* and *Dark* are and are not the same play.

POSTSCRIPT:

"Gettner for most of the play inhabits the limbo. He is 'open' enough to be tortured by the Ego (that psychological double-glazing against the winter of our condition) but can't find his way to what Jung (for, want, I suppose, of a more palatable word) calls 'individuation'—wholeness. Peter has the virtues admirable for immediate practical purposes and shows signs of increasing in them. In the early stages of evolution his spirit would certainly have got us as far as that beautiful creature the giraffe (my favorite animal)." Christopher Fry to SMW, 4 February 1972

"You are really saying what I am saying when you say 'But simply to label the Countess a *figura Christi* is to make her into a static icon'—

except that I would leave out the word *simply*. The divine non-interference is something less explicit. Could equally be an adumbration of the Mother Goddess ('God's a woman')." Christopher Fry to SMW, 12 March 1973

"Luke 15 is behind it [*Dark*] all" (Christopher Fry to SMW, 9 September 1981). Luke 15 is made up of three parables about lostness: "The Good Shepherd," who leaves the flock to seek the single stray; "The Lost Coin," to find which the lady of the house goes into a major cleaning expedition and then gives a party to celebrate finding it; and the very familiar "Prodigal Son." All kinds of parallels occur: "God *is* a woman" in "Coin"; leaving the flock to seek the lost sheep is like Rosmarin's ride into the blizzard to find Gettner; the resistance to the prodigal's return on the part of the elder son is like the resistance to Gettner's return. But the greatest similarity between *Dark* and Luke 15 is the irrational impracticality of the seekers. In this sense *Dark* becomes a noteworthy gloss on the scriptural passage. Familiarity with the parables has domesticated our response to them, so that we look on the seekers as typical, as what we ourselves might do. *Dark* makes us see that the love in Luke 15 is unconditional, reckless, impractical, and at the farthest possible remove from ordinary, decent relationships. Risking the flock for the sake of one sheep is foolhardy; celebrating the discovery of one coin with a party that costs more than the coin is worth is impractical; and when a runaway son returns, we welcome him warmly, but we have the party after a decent interval of probation, to see whether he intends to stay home this time. God's love, Jesus seems to be saying in the three parables, is unconditional, reckless, and impractical—like the love of the Countess in *Dark*. Just as *Phoenix* is the world's wittiest commentary on Romans 5–7, so *Dark* is the most careful exegesis available of Luke 15, especially suited for our time, so dulled by these parables.

LAW, LAWS, AND THE LAW 9

Curtmantle

Though critics of Eliot's *Murder in the Catheral* and of Anouilh's *Becket* seldom refer to Fry's *Curtmantle*, critics of *Curtmantle* commonly compare it to the other two. Discussing Fry's respect for historical fact, W. Moelwyn Merchant asserts that, by contrast, "Eliot was essentially concerned with timeless matter of martyrdom, while Anouilh ignored the tensions of law for those of a relationship which could be set up in any age."[1] According to Emil Roy, "Eliot's construction is focused and ritualistic, Fry's is panoramic and historical, and Anouilh's is musical and choreographic."[2] J. Woodfield explains the function of Marshal, Fry's narrator, thus:

> to manipulate the response of the audience in favour of Henry, a role which is an important corrective to history, especially as recorded in the dramatic interpretations of Tennyson, Eliot and even Anouilh, where the dramatic focus, and inevitably sympathy, lie with Becket rather than Henry.[3]

Gerald Parker, however, sees *Curtmantle* as more like Anouilh's play than like Eliot's, both the Fry and Anouilh plays being about "a confrontation of power."[4] Perceptive and useful as these observations are, they are more tentative than they ought to be, for Fry's concept of law makes *Curtmantle* startlingly different from the other plays. It deserves better than the secondary, dependent existence that critics accord it.

To be sure, the critics mentioned all deal with Fry's concept of law and can hardly avoid doing so in view of Fry's own statement of the themes of *Curtmantle*:

> The play has two themes: one a progression toward a portrait of Henry, a search for his reality, moving through versions of 'Where is the King?' to the unresolved close of 'He was dead when they came to him.' The other theme is Law, or rather the interplay of different laws: civil, canon, moral, aesthetic, and the Laws of God; and how they belong and do not belong to each other.[5]

An understandable error in explicating Fry's statement of theme has lead all critics to misread the play and to make incomplete comparisons of it to *Murder* and *Becket*. This study assumes that a writer of Fry's fastidiousness would not include *canon law* and the *Laws of God* in a single list if he intended them to be synonyms. The laws of God are imperfectly known by people, even the saints. All lesser laws—civil, canon, moral, aesthetic—are imperfect human attempts, usually in conflict with each other, to embody the laws of God. In Fry's scheme, Henry's establishing the common law of England is as much God's work as Becket's urging the claims of the church on the basis of canon law. Neither Henry's common law nor Becket's canon law takes priority over Eleanor's aesthetic law. All are part of the human struggle to discover the laws of God.

Merchant, uncommonly perceptive about the play's religious meaning otherwise, equates canon law with God's law:

> Here [in *Curtmantle*] a central tragic irony points the whole process of thought of which this play is the culmination: that Henry II works for due process of law which is ultimately an expression of God's order, and that Becket, subdued to God's will which is precisely the law towards which Henry's ambitions are directed, finds himself in personal opposition to Henry.[6]

The irony that the two antagonists have a common goal is shrewdly perceived, but Merchant is wrong in asserting that Henry is struggling for what Becket has already attained.

Woodfield, generally sound concerning the play's structure, quotes Merchant with approval and adds that "Henry's affirmative way clashes with the negative way of Becket."[7] One wonders whether Woodfield is not remembering the negative way of Eliot's Becket rather than discovering Fry's Becket, who vigorously asserts the claims of the church and canon law, and gives no evidence of ascetic self-renunciation. Gerald Parker's assumption, that the play is essentially a confrontation of two kinds of power, human and divine, leads him to assert that Fry's rhetoric is all wrong for such confrontation.[8] Actually, Fry's rhetoric could hardly be better suited for open-ended exploration. Identifying Henry with the state against God, and Thomas with the church for God, is the common error of *Curtmantle* critics.

Of Roy too, who describes Becket as "forced to choose between the state to which he owes love and honor and his devotion to a religious ideal."[9] Or again, "Thomas characteristically identifies himself completely with divine power."[10] True, Eliot's Becket identifies himself completely with divine power and with the church, God and the church being nearly synonymous in *Murder;* whatever works against the church in *Murder*—like Henry, who never appears but whose influence is present—is against God.

In fact, Roy admits that he sees Fry's Becket as Eliot's: "Aside from minor idiosyncracies, he closely resembles Eliot's protagonist."[11] One wonders whether this misreading is not responsible for Roy's condescending tone toward Fry's Becket: "Almost from the moment he is appointed Archbishop, Fry's Becket has chosen to identify his life so completely with the Church that he is little more than an instrument, its 'tongue' to be 'used in argument' between the State and Church."[12] Because Roy expects the psychological-spiritual complexity of Eliot's Becket in Fry's Becket, he assesses Fry's Becket as the-same-only-not-as-good. Though Fry's Becket is completely identified with the church, he recognizes that the mystery of God is beyond both himself and the church. Politically, Fry's church must protect its interests precisely so that it can keep alive its explorations into the mystery of God. Fry's Becket is identified with the church and both are under God; Eliot's Becket is identified with the church and God. Fry's Becket makes clear the relationship between himself, the church, and God:

> How, then, without rich form of ritual
> And ceremony, shall we convey
> The majesty of eternal government,
> Or give a shape to the mystery revealed
> Yet as a mystery. (33)

Of this speech Roy asserts that Fry's Becket "does deliver a somewhat abstract assertion of the church's mystery," thereby revealing that Roy himself has failed to grasp what Fry was saying about

God's mystery transcending the church's political-educational function. Church's mystery, indeed!

Becket represents canon law politically, though personally he realizes that God's unknowable law far transcends canon law. Henry represents civil law politically, but personally regards it too exclusively as the complete law of God. Eleanor represents aesthetic law and sees how canon law and civil law can be made into a unity by depolarization. Henry's civil law and Eleanor's aesthetic law are as much God's work as Becket's canon law. Henry is a martyr as well as Becket, and Eleanor is as much a saint as either one. Aligning God, church, and Becket against all the rest of the secular world is a mind-set borrowed from *Murder* by the Fry critics; that mind-set precludes the five sentences which precede this one; that mind-set does not allow *Curtmantle* to be itself.

The categories of sacred and secular fall away in *Curtmantle* and in all of Fry's plays—at least if *sacred* means "churchly." All the world is sacred in the context of *Curtmantle*, and Roy, in comparing the Becket playwrights, does Fry a disservice by saying, "However, Eliot and Fry are both Christians," as though what makes Eliot different from Anouilh is exactly what makes Fry different from Anouilh. Fry is as Christian as Eliot and as secular as Anouilh. All his life an Anglican, Fry is a Quaker by temperament. "Inner light" experiences are life-giving and necessary in his view, but the only proper response to such experiences is an active life in the everyday world, transforming—yea, revolutionizing—the imperfect structures of society until God's kingdom comes. God's church and God's kingdom are identical in *Murder*. Becket represents God's church in *Curtmantle*; Becket, Henry, and Eleanor together represent God's kingdom (not to be identified with Henry's kingdom); and Becket, like Fry, understands the difference between God's church and God's kingdom. God's church is under the jurisdiction of canon law only; God's kingdom is under the jurisdiction of all the laws of God: civil, canon, moral, aesthetic, and whatever other laws and institutions press their just claims on human conscience.

Since *Curtmantle*'s critics have hitherto missed the play's distinctive angle, this study intends to show how the themes designated by Fry work. It begins with the law theme, proceeds to the character of Henry, and concludes with the dominant theme of all of Fry's plays, moral-spiritual evolution, which subsumes the other two themes under it and makes the play a satisfying unity.

The Prologue already shows how inadequate common law is. Henry's barber, the barber's wife, a juggler, a huckster, a prostitute, and Richard Anesty, who has a grievance to present at court, are all camping at the fringes of Henry's entourage. The king is on a whirlwind tour of the country, inspecting courts and establishing justice. The loyal barber says "law and order" will be outcome of the king's frantic efforts:

> Find out the true state of the courts of law and the administration of his kingdom, is what he is after; so come up on them unawares is what he does. Thursday at Nottingham, says the itinerary. So the judges at Nottingham keep sober Monday, Tuesday, Wednesday, put off accepting any bribes until Friday, rub the dirt off their hands, and sit down to business as punctual as the light. And where is the king's majesty? The king's majesty is in Sheffield. (6)

The barber holds a possible view of Henry, seconded outside the play by Winston Churchill: ". . . he had laid the foundations of the English Common Law, upon which succeeding generations would build. Changes in the design would arise, but its main outlines would not be altered" (vii). But Henry's salutary contribution to English society is only part of the truth, as the other characters in the Prologue demonstrate. The king's frantic pace and his makeshift accommodations give him and the nobles a farmhouse for sleeping, the lesser nobility a barn; the still lesser sleep with the cows, the lesser still with the pigs, and the characters of the Prologue have no accommodation at all. The juggler has been wounded in a brawl, attempting to establish precedence for sleeping with the pigs. The prostitute knows rather too much about the king's schedule. Anesty, who has been trying to see the king for two months about a genuine grievance, is persuaded to get some sleep, only to be awakened soon to the news that the king is gone. The king's good motive does not alter the injustice to Anesty or the lawlessness of the royal progress. Civil law is not enough; there are laws outside of civil law which even the huckster understands: "If a man can't have his lawful sleep, to hell with the law" (8).

One of the laws which Henry does not understand is canon law. He names his chancellor, Becket, to be Archbishop of Canterbury, for, says Henry, "Tom loves the law" (15). What he means is that Becket, representing the church, will support without qualification Henry's project for establishing "Order, protection, and justice/For the man who has a shirt or the man who has not" (23). True, Henry has an awareness of the church, but not an awareness of the realities which the rituals of the church express externally. When Henry receives Becket's resignation as Chancellor, Henry scandalizes a priest standing by with his blasphemies; and Henry summons Foliot, his confessor, to absolve him. But all the while he is confessing and being absolved, he is uttering blasphemies more spicy than the one he is being absolved for (28–29). When he offers his own back to be flogged by the Canterbury monks in atonement for Becket's murder, Henry's contrition is less than perfect:

> It was never my guilt, only in the rage of words.
> But, if I think so, I diminish nothing.
> I accept it all, if I can be rid of it all. (78)

He tries to muster a guilt he does not feel so that he can improve his image in the world and stop feeling sorry for himself as a victim:

> They're welcome to take their toll on my flesh
> If I can be free of the world's loathing, and my
> Self-sorrow. (78)

But flogging, and all the ceremonies of penance, were devised to resolve the problem of guilt within the genuinely troubled heart, not to improve public image. When monks from Canterbury confront the dying Henry for a grant of their rights, Henry brushes them off and one of the monks curses him in the name of St. Thomas Becket. A moment later Henry is sending for that very monk to administer extreme unction:

> Go and call back that monk who cursed me with such pleasure that it made him tremble. Now he can absolve me and bless me for his trouble. The formalities of allegiance. I believe in the law. (97)

The person who does not experience the realities behind the rituals of the church is in a poor sort to appreciate the claims of the church against the state.

In one way Becket is as shrewdly political for the church as Henry is for the state. Becket resigns as Chancellor upon becoming Archbishop; he refuses to allow Henry to try clerics in the secular courts even for crimes like rape and murder; he agrees to sign the approval of the church to English common law and then refuses; he makes political hay in France on behalf of the church and against Henry; and he behaves generally as though, in spite of the eternal purposes of the church, he means it to succeed in time and space. The church is as surely a human institution as the state.

And yet, in another way, Becket recognizes a difference between canon law and God's law, a difference Henry never recognizes between civil law and God's law. Becket sees "a true and living/Dialectic between the Church and the state/Which has to be argued for ever in good part" (21). The dialectic lies deep within human nature:

> It can't be broken off or turned
> Into a clear issue to be lost or won.
> It's the nature of man that argues;
> The deep roots of disputation
> Which dug in the dust, and formed Adam's body. (21)

Which is to say, since God made humankind in his own image, that the disputation lies deep within the nature of God. Perhaps as the polarities exist in God they reach an equilibrium, but humanity can never discover the will of God without a dialectic between church and state and among as many other God-given institutions as press a legitimate claim on human allegiance. In all the dialectic, Becket keeps groping after the ultimate law of God as after a mystery. He says to Henry:

> You're dividing us, and, what is more, forcing
> Yourself and me, indeed the whole kingdom,
> Into a kind of intrusion on the human mystery,
> Where we may not know what it is we're doing,
> What powers we are serving, or what is being made of us. (22)

What the ultimate will of God is like comes through to Becket in violent natural symbols:

> The vehement liberty of terror, which ignores our flesh,
> Is not the will,
> But it knows the will, returns to it in calm.
> Even when in rebellion it keeps
> The signature of light. In the avalanche of snow

The star-figure of the flake is there unchanged.
It was out of a whirlwind that God answered Job.
And here, too, in the whirl of our senses,
The way for this will has to be kept unthreatened. (41)

Becket does not presume that he and the church are the sum and substance of God's will; nevertheless, when the will of God is completely revealed, the honor of the church will be woven into its fabric. Therefore, when Henry equates "The will of the people" with "the will of God" (41), as though beyond a doubt Henry is doing the will of the people, Becket responds thus:

They have many wills: many lusts and many thirsts:
A will for death as well as a will for life.
But, quick or dormant, in th'm they have a longing
To be worked into the eternal fabric
By God's love. (41)

For Becket to give in to Henry would not only be a subjugation of the church by state, but surrendering a paradoxical view of reality for a non-paradoxical view. Henry's opinion: "One order is going to be saved: mine in this kingdom!" (42) Becket's opinion:

What you see as the freedom of the State
Within the law, I fear, as the enslavement
Of that other state of man, in which, and in
Which only, he can know his perfect freedom. (40)

In the name of the paradox within the will of God, Becket pushes the claims of the church against the state.

Henry will even allow Becket to turn the church toward pacifism, inner light, and anachronistically, Quakerism:

Very well; give up this world.
Contend against me like an opposite.
See that the spiritual power is powerful in the spirit.
Indeed, go on, be smitten with a great light
And relieve us all of a load of darkness.
Show us, my friend—we are hungry to see it—
The humility, the patience, and the poverty,
The movement into grace, the entire surrender
And sacrifice of the self. (32)

If not Quaker quietism, then a sacramentalism unrelated to everyday affairs would suit Henry fine:

> Perform the mystery, demonstrate
> The mysterious order: baptize us, reprove us,
> Absolve us, and bury us; but in so far
> As your body sweats like the rest of us,
> You owe me obedience. (33)

Simultaneous state-before-church and mystical withdrawal from the affairs of state amount to the same thing: a non-paradoxical view of God and humanity.

Learning to live with paradox and uncertainty is the only way for persons to grow spiritually, to discover more fully the will of God. It is also the essence of art, what Keats called "the negative capability."[13] The flesh and the spirit unite in an art work: the medium is physical, but the successful art work speaks of and to the spirit, and what it says cannot be reduced to propositions. In the rare person, the flesh and spirit unite so that the life becomes an art form.

Eleanor of Aquitaine in *Curtmantle* is that kind of person. Henry speaks of her as

> this woman
> Who had been the inspiration of poets
> Ever since I could understand language,
> And the haunter of male imagination
> Ever since I could understand sex. (16)

Her aesthetic laws keep time within her like her own heart; she governs "as music governs itself within,/By the silent order whose speech is all visible things" (78). In Fry's view the aesthetic vision gives a person the strength to live with paradox and uncertainty, and that Fry and Eleanor see eye to eye on aesthetics can best be shown by bringing forward parallel passages from Eleanor's speeches and from Fry's essay "Comedy."[14] Fry says that, "groaning as we may be, we move in the figure of a dance, and, so moving, we trace the outline of a mystery." Eleanor says repeatedly that she wants life to be a dance for her, an aesthetically prescribed way of life:

> My life is in Poitou with Richard. There
> At least, the warm sun will give me leave to smile
> And we shall make laws for sport and love

> And put a little light in the eyes of Europe. (61)
>
> . . . you need the sun to set your blood
> Flowing more freely than ever it can here. (61)
>
> They [the boys] shall show me how the world should be,
> And I will believe there can be such a world. (61)

Eleanor is trying to *unmortify*—it is Fry's word—herself; as Fry defines *unmortify* in "Comedy," she is attempting "to affirm life and assimilate death and persevere in joy." For comedy, in Fry's words, "believes in a universal cause for delight, even though knowledge of the cause is always twitched away from under us, which leaves us to rest on our own buoyancy." Her own buoyancy is what Eleanor means to discover:

> . . . at last
> I mean to wrench myself awake
> And open my eyes to my own reality. (61)

That reality is "in myself," Eleanor insists, "past, present, and to come" (61), and at this point Eleanor goes beyond Fry, who is careful not to make comedy the absolute vision. Just as Henry had pursued civil law as the true law, so Eleanor pursues the aesthetic law as the true law: "The true law hides like the marrow of the bone, Feeding us in secret" (81). But her vision of life, her aestheticism, is not the lovely-but-useless adornment Henry takes it for. Too much of Fry's comic theory has gone into her for that. She has a better chance of charming Henry into living with paradoxes than Becket has of arguing him into it.

Indeed, Becket has as much to learn from Eleanor as does Henry. For Eleanor knows, as Becket does not, that to live with insoluble paradoxes requires a comic vision. Given a sense of paradox but lacking a comic vision, one is tempted either to renounce the paradox (as Henry tempts Becket to renounce the paradox), or otherwise to become a humorless martyr for the sake of the paradox. Becket could learn from Eleanor how to sustain a paradox with comedy, with wit, for all of her life is a paradox. Louis was disappointed in her because she produced only daughters; Henry ignores her now that she has borne him sufficient sons. When Louis produces a male heir with his new queen to Henry's embarrassment, Eleanor defines her paradoxical position between the two kings with wit:

> When heaven makes one of its rare rejoinders
> I should have thought it the merest common civility
> For all of us to attempt a smile. (53)

She has learned to "appreciate/Life's more acid comments on human endeavour" (53), and it helps her to survive: she could be envious of the new queen, spiteful toward Louis, hateful toward the new French prince, defensive for her own English sons, impatient with Henry, but instead she smiles. From Act I on, both Henry and Becket are blind to the skill with which she stands poised between them both:

> You've drawn blood from Becket, Henry.
> The city sunshine, and the new English archbishop
> Are equally cold and pale.
> And besides, he has made a long journey for you.
> You should give him time to rest. (24)

Hard upon that she is saying to Becket:

> . . . be his
> In every particular. The free and fallen
> Spirits we may think we are,
> You and I and the nest of young eagles,
> Have our future state only in a world of Henry. (24)

If she sometimes urges Becket to fight back and "draw blood" (38), it is more her impatience with Henry's failure to see paradox than hatred of him. She has disciplined herself into a state of comic detachment so that she can "stand and be the curious onlooker/ While two unproved worlds fly at each other" (38). If Becket means to sustain a paradox, he could do worse than to learn from Eleanor how to manage it.

For while Henry recognizes no paradox at all and while Becket considers maintaining the paradox a grim duty, Eleanor sees paradox as a delight:

> Let me say this to the man who makes the world—
> And also to the man who makes himself the Church.
> Consider complexity, delight in difference.
> Fear, for God's sake, your exact words.
> Do you think you can draw lines on the living water?
> Together we might make a world of progress.

> Between us, by our three variants of human nature,
> You and Becket and me, we could be
> The complete reaching forward. Neither of you
> Will dare to understand it. Have I spoken too late? (47–48)

Eleanor does not quite understand Becket, of course. She perceives wrongly that he represents the church as Henry represents the state; in reality Becket presses the claims of the church because he knows the state has a good spokesman in Henry, just as when he was Henry's Chancellor he spoke strongly for Henry and the state because the church had a strong spokesman in Theobald (21). The quarrel between Henry and Becket is more than business "the size of two men" who are "in a rage" (48), as Eleanor thinks it is. But her myopia is minor compared to Henry's or Becket's. For she recognizes her need of the other two in order to achieve the complete reaching forward, but neither Henry nor Becket realizes that he needs her. Eleanor represents the position of the artist in the world.

The complete reaching forward does not occur because the characters are either hostile or indifferent toward each other. Yet the beginning of Act I, after the Prologue, could not augur better for a complete reaching forward. From a balcony Eleanor has watched Henry welcome Becket home from a mission in France; everyone is laughing below, and Eleanor wonders why. An obscene joke? A bawdy play? Wit would be too much to hope for from Henry, thinks Eleanor; it must have been horse play. "Both," says Marshal:

> There they were, the King and the Chancellor,
> Riding together along Cheapside, the crown
> And the croney, in great pleasure together.
> There was a fairly disgusting beggar-man,
> Best part naked, lifting up one of his crutches
> Across the King's path. 'Poor lousy fellow,'
> The King said, reining in his horse.—'Dear lord of justice',
> Said the beggar. He knew his onions; he understood
> Just how to come at the King's generosity.
> He said he was born at Le Mans, the same as the King.
> Everybody knows what affection the King has
> For his own birthplace. And then a hard-up story
> That jerked a quick tear out of the King. 'Christ,"

He said, 'we'll have no naked men. Christ's
Charity, Thomas, let him have your cloak!"
'Give him yours, Henry,' Becket said:
'This is *your* deed of grace.' 'It's too old, and too short',
Said the King. 'It would be no charity to his arse.'
And he made a grab at the Chancellor's cloak—cinnamon
Velvet, a new one—and they wrestled on horseback, to take it
And keep it, until every man round was laughing himself
To water, and the Chancellor gave in.
So the King threw down the cloak, obliterating
The beggar, and we all rode forward, happy. (10)

"A deed of grace, gracefully done,/And very delicately reported" (10), responds Eleanor. With Henry not only full of horse play, but turning witty, there may be room for a comic view of life in the English court, and what follows confirms it. Becket confesses with wry self-irony that he enjoys splendid pageantry (11), Henry twits Becket with his chastity, Eleanor twits Henry with his lechery (13), Henry mocks Eleanor for her vanity (17), but only after he has confessed his own shyness in courting her ("a cap in hand,/heart in mouth," 16); all three are wholly themselves, aware of the strengths and weaknesses of each other, and full of innocent laughter, though not always such gentle laughter, at themselves and at each other. Their laughter helps them cope with the very problem which most vexes them: Henry and Eleanor's guilt and ambivalence toward Louis of France. The three play a charade in which Becket takes the part of Louis with exaggerated piety, humility, and sexlessness. It is a non-violent means of coping with guilt, fear, and violence. They ought, of course, to be more aware that the laughableness of Louis is like their own. Eleanor is not entirely wise when she says that Philip is

Frayed to ribbons whether to be
A king or an archbishop. It was always so.
He could never co-ordinate the two worlds. (18)

Can she? Can anyone? Still, even less-than-perfect laughter is a more forgiving atmosphere than no laughter at all; and their laughter, not only at Philip but at themselves and at each other, produces an atmosphere in which moral change is possible. If only this atmosphere could last—frankness about weakness with laughter which tempers the judgment—one could almost believe that the three have a chance at being the complete reaching forward.

But in the midst of the merriment, Henry announces by the bye that Becket is the new Archbishop of Canterbury. Immediately the laughter ceases. Henry cannot understand that he and Becket from now on represent opposite polarities in a conflict larger than either man; in order to make the point clear, Becket resigns as Chancellor and refuses to have his clerics tried in secular courts. Becket's agreeing to ratify the articles of Common Law, and then his refusing do so, while perfectly comprehensible to someone attuned to paradox like Becket, is pretense, evasion, and wooliness to a person of Henry's literalness. Henry levies unreasonable taxes on the church by way of punishment; Becket flees to France for seven years, returns to England after a reconciliation with Henry, but immediately excommunicates all persons involved with the coronation of young Henry. Henry issues ambiguous orders in a rage, and Becket's murder follows.

Just as civil law and canon law show no sign of synthesis into God's law, Eleanor's aesthetic law ceases to react with the other two. She retreats to Poitou, "shaping her own dream of civilization" (77). All of Eleanor's wisdom about living with paradox, while it ought to be knitting Becket and Henry, canon and civil law, England and France, is used instead to support her Court of Love. The problem brought to her tribunal so that witty judgment can be passed on it: "Would the Love Court of Poitou consider/That true love can long survive in marriage?" (79). One can pardon Eleanor for using wit to resolve her feelings about two bad marriages, but one cannot pardon her for using wit as she does:

> Nevertheless, consider
> The nature of love. In love a man and woman
> Are newly minted as in the beginning of the world,
> Creating themselves out of each other's eyes,
> But in marriage, whatever world is made,
> Has the bones of the woman walled up in the foundations,
> No air to breathe, nor any light to move in. (79)

Eleanor uses her wit as an end in itself. But art is art and wit is legitimate wit only when they exist for the sake of the complete reaching forward. Art short-circuits when it becomes art-for-art's'sake.

And so what could have been the complete reaching forward in

Act I disintegrates gradually over the three acts; what could have evolved into a discovery of the law of God is fragmented into civil, canon, and aesthetic law, each being a law to itself. Lack of love is responsible for the fragmentation: lack of love for God and for the discovery of his law, and lack of love between the characters. "Thou shalt love the Lord thy God with all thy heart, mind, soul, and strength" and "thou shalt love thy neighbor as thyself" (Matthew 22:34–40): the moral law. Henry's amorous escapades are good-humored and innocent, except that they reduce Eleanor from her position as wife and queen to Henry's occasional whore. Becket's excommunication of Henry's friends does not take seriously that Henry was attempting to firm up the kingdom by passing the crown to Young Henry. Can Eleanor put her art-for-art's-sake theory more cruelly than she does to Henry: "Purpose, however wise, is hardly blessed./God thrives on chance and change" (82)? In short, all three are unwilling to get along with the others for the sake of the complete reaching forward. All three are immoral in failing to love.

The disintegration is reinforced among the children. When the disease of hostility begins between Henry, Becket, and Eleanor, it spreads to Young Henry, Richard, Geoffrey, John, and the illegitimate Roger—postponing the complete reaching forward for at least another generation. Henry himself spreads the polarization into the next generation when he has Young Henry crowned king: immediately John is trying on Young Henry's new coronation robes; Geoffrey is openly envious of Young Henry; Roger, though commendably loyal both to Henry and Young Henry, is as humorless throughout as Becket. In fact, in the tableau immediately preceding the final confrontation between Henry and Becket, all four legitimate sons draw swords against Roger and draw blood, thematically anticipating the martyrdom of Becket and showing that, though a new generation is on the way, the old situation still maintains (64). On his part, Young Henry is as grim and inflexible over the taunting of his brothers as Henry is toward Becket once the polarization sets in:

> What else could I have done?
> Sit like a girl and let them mock the crown?
> They were trying to make a laughing-stock of me,
> Said I was nothing but your shadow. (65)

If only the new generation had the willingness to make themselves and each other the laughing-stock, as Eleanor, Henry, and Becket do at the play's beginning, there would be hope.

The more is the pity, because the strengths of Henry, Eleanor, and Becket are the very strengths of the younger generation. Richard, his mother's son, catches the force of the aesthetic law; Geoffrey and Constance have a romantic marriage which can good-humoredly sustain the super-civilized cynicism of the Court of Love—a marriage reminiscent of Henry and Eleanor's early in the play; Roger has Becket's loyalty to conviction regardless of consequences; John combines his mother's love of fine clothes with his father's love of power; Young Henry has his father's concern for the stability of the realm and for civil law. As with the older generation, the moral law is empty without mutual love; aesthetic law expresses itself in triviality; canon law is humorless; civil law is inflexible; and the complete reaching forward is nowhere in sight at play's end. Nor was it in sight in 1961, nor is it today, though it remains a possibility.

Civil law is for Henry the will of God, and establishing it is for him as much reaching forward as needs to be done. The tragedy of Henry is that, like so many political reformers, he thinks he is establishing the New Jerusalem, but he does not establish it within the self, the only place where it can flourish. Henry is under the illusion that he is a simple man with a simple aim, but he is more complicated than anyone else. Because he is unaware of his own complexity, he is the victim of it:

> He was simple and royal (his nickname 'Curtmantle' derived from the plain short cloak he wore), direct and paradoxical, compassionate and hard, a man of intellect, a man of action, God-fearing, superstitious, blasphemous, far-seeing, short-sighted, affectionate, lustful, patient, volcanic, humble, over-riding. It is difficult to think of any facet of the man which at some time he didn't demonstrate, except chastity and sloth. (ix)

Henry sees no need to order the chaos within. His identity, the founder of law and order, does not grow from within; it is imposed from without, just as Henry thinks to impose law and order on the country. It is a synthetic, incomplete identity which hardly covers his bones. A second theme of the play, in addition to the theme of law, is "a progression toward a portrait of Henry, a search for his reality, moving through versions of 'Where is the King?' to the unresolved close of 'He was dead when they came to him'" (ix).

Where is the king, indeed? Does he himself know? The question is asked explicitly four times. Once in the Prologue it is asked by Richard Anesty, who has been fighting the courts for five years, been riding after the king for two months, cannot keep up with the itinerary of the royal inspection of troops, has lost two horses in the pursuit, finally reaches the fringes of the royal encampment, makes the mistake of sleeping, only to be awakened with the news that the king has left in the dead of night. "Where is the King?" (8) cries Anesty as the Prologue closes and camp breaks up in chaos.

After having agreed to give the church's sanction to the Common Law, Becket changes his mind and begins the permanent separation between himself and Henry. When Becket first announces his sanction of Common Law, he also calls "Where is the King?" and Eleanor responds with a speech about the chaotic conditions:

> Ask youself where it is you stand, saying
> Where is the King?
> Look round at the unreality of the light
> And the unreality of the faces in the light.
> You and he, you told him, would reach a place
> Where you might not know what is being made of you,
> Or understand the conclusion when it came.
> Certainly the familiar world has departed.
> A death-world is here, where every move
> Is magnified on to the fog's blind face
> And becomes the gesture of a giant. (44)

The fog is spiritual and psychological as much as it is physical.

The messenger who brings news of Becket's murder enters, pauses, and calls in the direction from whence he came: "You said I should find the King here" (73). The statement implies that he had asked "Where is the King?" and has been told. Even before the messenger arrives, Henry knows the news will come, and his speech anticipating the news is about the chaos within:

> Dear Christ, the day that any man would dread
> Is when life goes separate from the man,
> When he speaks what he doesn't say, and does

> What is not his doing, and an hour of the day
> Which is unimportant as it went by
> Comes back revealed as the satan of all hours,
> Which will never let the man go. And then
> He would see how the natural poisons in him
> Creep from everything he sees and touches
> As though saying, 'Here is the world you created
> In your own image.' But this is not the world
> He would have made. Sprung from the smallest fault,
> A hair-fine crack in the dam, the unattended
> Moment sweeps away the whole attempt,
> The heart, thoughts, belief, longing
> And intention of the man. It is infamous,
> This life is infamous, if it uses us
> Against our knowledge or will. (72–73)

The chaos is both inside of himself and around him. He cannot get the outside world and the inner world to correspond. He tries to impose his private plans for law and order on the outside world, willy-nilly; yet he refuses to impose law and order on his own private desires and conduct.

Young Henry and Geoffrey are dead; a coalition of the forces of France, Richard, and John (whom Henry expects to help him) are fighting against Henry at Le Mans, his birthplace. Marshal reports on the chaos without:

> We smashed the bridge, and as we started driving spiles into the fords the mist lifted. We saw the pavilions where Richard and the French army had spent the night spread along the edge of the wood only a few yards away from the river. When the King saw them, he turned to me as though to someone who should wake him from a nightmare (84).

Hard upon this a Captain shouts: "Where is the King?" Marshal brushes him off; the king is in no condition to receive callers, no matter how urgent their business. But the brush-off means more: the king is nowhere; outer and inner worlds have completely separated from each other; the chaos is complete.

Henry gives frantic orders to burn some houses along the river (fighting disorder with disorder), to "destroy cover and hold the enemy back" (84). The enemy: the only sons to whom he can leave a kingdom. Instead of a few houses being burned, the whole city of

Le Mans is burned when the wind changes. Refugees flee in all directions, some of them onto the stage. The chaos is the holocaust without and the fury within Henry, both of them metaphors for each other.

> There's no more to come from God! I've seen what God's mind is.
> He knew I loved this city,
> He knew if he ever looked into my heart,
> He knew I loved the city I was born in.
> . . . .
> I have burned my city, I have burned away
> My own beginning, the one place in the world
> Where memory could return untroubled, before
> The earth began to bleed wherever I walked.
> *He looks up to the smoke-obscured sky.*
> I meant the fires to save us! Do you think I kneel
> To a God who can turn a brutal wind
> To eat us up in fire? No,
> I renounce all part in you: no such hands
> As yours shall have my soul. I'll burn it
> Away like the city, I'll hurt you
> In the centre of your love, as you do me.
> Your eyes can sting like mine, and weep
> With the same helpless water.
> There's nothing left for either of us to save. (87)

Each time someone asks the question "Where is the King?" Fry is indicating a new stage in the chaos. When Anesty asks it, Henry's energetic tactics are making a chaos he does not even recognize; he sees only law and order. When Thomas asks it, it signals the beginning of the permanent breach between him and Henry; Henry does not see the chaos, only a troublesome enemy, once his friend. Even before the messenger comes with the news of Becket's murder, Henry is aware of the chaos, both within himself and outside. When the Captain asks "Where is the King?" Henry's despair is total, both for order within and outside himself.

The explicit theme of "Where is the King?" is supported by numerous entrances of characters coming in search of the king, though not using those precise words. The prostitute, Blae, comes looking for the king to confront him as the father of her illegitimate baby. She does not have to see the king: "I can tell who he is in the dark" (26). When Becket comes seeking the king at the beginning of Act II for the crucial confrontation, Eleanor says "The morning is . . . unwilling to appear," and Becket seems unable to say, until later in the act, "Where is the King?" Eleanor says it for him:

> Have you come to find the King?
> Today's a poor day for finding any man;
> Only sounds and voices, and half creations of the fog
> Which move like men but fade like spirits. (37)

Again at the beginning of Act III, when Henry is kneeling in prayer, doing penance at Canterbury, Foliot, summoning Henry for flogging, explicitly does not say "Where is the King?"

> Henry: Is it day?
>
> Foliot: The first hour, my lord, yes.
>
> Henry: The monks still awake to aim their lashing.
>
> Foliot: They're waiting for you, at the high altar. (77)

The omission of the words "Where is the King?" is eloquent in these instances and in others like them. Blae does not need to see the king, Becket postpones seeing the king as long as possible, and Foliot is sad for the king's sake.

Besides the omission of the words in the situations where we would expect them, there are other uses of the theme. Juxtaposition: The Prologue fades as Anesty cries three times in desperation, "Where is the King?"; hard upon it, Act I opens with Marshal saying to Eleanor: "The King's arrived in the yard, ma'am, with the Chancellor" (9). Thus opens the only scene in which Henry, Eleanor, and Becket are at peace with each other. For once we know where the king is. Contrast: Henry thinks he knows where he is at all times, but does not know. Becket, by contrast, has doubts:

> Becket: Tell me, Marshal, do you know yourself, who you are?
>
> Marshal: I daresay I could pick myself out among two or three men, if I took thought.
>
> Becket: You have the best of it. (24–25)

Applied to characters other than Henry:

> Henry [of Becket]: Where is he, then? Ever since his consecration
> He has turned his back on us, crouching down in Canterbury

> As though he had conquered a rock, struck his cross on it,
> And meant to keep a sulking stretch of water
> Between him and me. (30)

Geoffrey [of Constance, and her resistance to the cynicism of the Courts of Love]: There's my Constance! (79)

Henry [at his death, to Roger]: Go and call back that monk . . . (97)

The play is a dense network of "Where is. . . ?"

Henry is and is not there. In the complete reaching forward, humankind's chief task, Henry is a failure; but in the limited scope of his activity he is a success and is remembered as the founder of English law:

> Your laws are fixed on England: grumbled at
> Like the weather, but, like the weather, accepted
> As a source of strength . . . (94)

Henry's tragedy is that one can strengthen a community by means of civil law without belonging to that community; one cannot belong successfully to any community without the moral law (loving other people as one's self and doing to others as one would be done by), a sense of paradox (of the sort that must always be argued in good part between canon law and civil law, church and state, and all the other laws and institutions that claim our loyalty), and the aesthetic law (including the comic vision of one's self and others). Henry's flaw is that he mistakes civil law for the complete law of God. His life is as fragmentary as his perception of the law of God.

As Henry dies on an old crone's feather bed among refugees fleeing Le Mans, Roger, the faithful illegitimate son (legitimacy and illegitimacy, right and wrong being more complicated than Henry has ever been willing to admit), goes at his father's command to summon a priest. Henry dies complaining: "I don't know . . . if the laws will hold. It is all still to do" (97). Henry is no sooner dead than refugees strip his corpse of all valuables, with the old lady of the feather bed looking on. When Roger returns with Marshal and a monk, the old crone assures them that the refugees who stripped Henry's corpse did not kill him: "He was dead when they came to him" (99). Fry makes clear in the introduction that the statement is also an answer to the question "Where is the King?" This meaning is supported by what the plundering refugees say: "I wouldn't come close to a great king, but what we have here is a dead man. We've seen fifty like it or more. I'm thinking, we've had nothing from him yet, and he's lost us everything we had in this burning city. This dead fellow owes us a bit of justice" (98). Henry is a success as a king but a failure as a person. Where is the King indeed?

But if not perceiving the whole law of God is Henry's downfall, then Henry is not the only tragic figure in *Curtmantle*. Though Becket appreciates paradox and the process of dialectic within the whole law of God and though Eleanor understands that art and comedy are necessary to sustain paradox and dialectic, yet they both fail to perceive the whole law of God or to be the complete reaching forward. If Henry is a tragic figure, so are Becket and Eleanor. If Becket is a saint—not only in the technical, ecclesiastical sense, nor in Eliot's sense of Becket's proceeding from strength to strength, from insight to insight, but in the Quaker sense of an ordinary person trying to live a consistent Christian life—then Henry and Eleanor are also saints.

What Fry named as the two themes of *Curtmantle*—the portrait of Henry and the reconciliation of conflicting law—are really different aspects of one theme: the complete reaching forward, the next step in the moral evolution of humankind. When Fry was interviewed concerning *Curtmantle*, he made explicit that evolution is the theme of all of his plays:

> Just as the caterpillar pursues the shape of the butterfly, and the musician or poet is trying to express the form of the hidden order, so the human being is struggling to achieve the end, or form, which already exists for him. You can't move towards an end if the end isn't there already. I wrote about that in *Thor, with Angels*, in Merlin's speech, when he talks about the dreams coming out of the slumbering rock:
>
> Each dream answering to a shape
> Which was in dream before the shapes were shapen;
> Each growing obediently to a form,
> To its own sound, shrill or deep, to a life
> In water or air, in light or night or mould . . .

And later in the same speech he goes on about

> . . . the very obdurate pressure
> Edging men towards a shape beyond

> The shape they know. Now and then, by a spurt
> Of light, they manage the clumsy approximation,
> Overturn it, turn again, refashion
> Nearer the advising of their need.
> Always the shape lying over the life.

> It was encouraging to find recently in Pierre Teilhard de Chardin's *The Phenomenon of Man*, that he was saying, scientifically, what I've been tuning in to and trying to express in the plays—and before that in some poems—more or less since I started writing. Anyway, I need to use verse when a speech has to become—how shall I say?—like an object reflecting that inner shaping of the character, that process of evolution. Sometimes it's almost as if you're going through a process of evolution inside the speeches themselves.[15]

The irony in Fry's statement as applied to *Curtmantle* is that, while Fry seems optimistic about the possibility of the complete reaching forward, the play demonstrates why the complete reaching forward is not to be; we are no closer now to synthesizing the various conflicting laws than were Becket, Eleanor, and Henry. Fry is not really so naively pompous as to think that all viewers of his play will leave the theater prepared to take the complete step forward—or to think that he himself has already taken it. His creating a play is a metaphor for what the whole step forward will be like when it comes.

The same hope Fry nurtures for himself he nurtures for his audience; the same irony that qualifies his own hope qualifies his hope for the audience. Both Eliot and Anouilh are hopeful for themselves and ironic toward their audiences. St. John of the Cross never pretended that the dark night of the soul was for everyone; and though the progress of Becket and of the women of Canterbury through the dark night is Eliot's implied invitation to the audience to do likewise, he also makes clear that he does not consider his audience with the mystics but with the assassins, the knights justifying the murder in the language of twentieth-century business, politics, and journalism. Anouilh's secular Becket—not devoted to God, but to the honor of God, Becket's own construct—is to Henry what the play *Becket* is to the audience; just as Becket's coolness and control remind Henry of everything Henry can never be, so *Becket* reminds the audience what it can never be. *Becket* is Anouilh's Becket-like affront to the audience.

Neither Eliot nor Anouilh is as charitable to the audience as Fry—or as demanding, as insistent that change come. But aesthetic unity, not charity, is the issue.

Fry's technical device for unifying the two themes—the portrait of Henry and the reconciliation of the conflicting laws—is the character of Marshal. He is the narrator of the play, all of the action taking place in his consciousness as he remembers it years later. The transfer from life to memory is like the transfer from life to a play. In both, living people are metamorphosed into characters. Marshal mythologizes others, but he does not mythologize himself; he stylizes others into verse-speaking characters, though he himself continues to speak in prose. Marshal is an artist, but unlike Eleanor, he does not know he is an artist. When the next stage in humanity's moral evolution happens, it will be through an unselfconscious intuition which spreads to everyone and brings about the healing which Eleanor cannot; it will be through an intuition like Marshal's, who is neither a king nor a saint, but a middle-class bureaucrat, very much like us in the audience.

Now and then Marshal's characters lapse back into prose. The mob of the Prologue, the mob of the court and the mob of the bishops (Act II), the mob of refugees (Act III): all these mobs speak prose. Foliot, in a moment of hysteria for Becket's safety, speaks prose, as does Becket in reply (49). And Henry speaks prose in his final delirium. In short, when characters speak prose in the play, it is a moment of crisis for the characters and of total recall for Marshal, a moment so vivid that it appears in all its rawness; such brutish situations obtain that not even as pure a spirit as Marshal can turn them to poetry.

Nevertheless, Marshal is the preparation for the complete reaching forward. He is open enough to feel the presence of every character, now and again dropping his position outside of the action to undertake the handling of the illegitimate baby on Henry's behalf, to converse with Becket or Eleanor, and at the end, both in the action and outside of it at the moment, to remember the full irony of Henry's having said, "Christ, we'll have no naked men" (99). All the other characters, even Becket, close themselves too quickly and settle for one-sided understandings of the whole law of God. Marshal is the hope in *Curtmantle* . . . and the unity. Eliot's *Murder* is about the struggle of the mystic submitting his will to God; the characterization, the poetry, the wit, and the formal design are devices by which a thoroughly secular audience can be made to think about sainthood for an hour. The achievement is enormous, but the form and content are distinct; the form sugar-coats the content.

Form and content are not only distinct, but disturbingly at variance, in Anouilh's *Becket*. The form is elegantly tidy: the play ends where it begins, Henry being flogged by the monks of Canterbury at the very scene of Becket's murder, the whole play happening in Henry's memory just prior to the flogging. Henry submits to the flogging, not out of guilt, but to win the support of the Saxons against the Norman barons; Becket chooses the honor of God because it is the only weapon strong enough for a defeated Saxon to use against the Norman conquerors. Becket's father was a Saxon, his mother a Saracen, and thus even his Saxon honor is blemished; his mistress, Gwendolyn, is Welsh, perpetuating the blemish. No wonder Becket gives up Gwendolyn so easily to Henry; no wonder he grieves so little at her suicide. The play is as tidy as counterpoint, though what the play says points to a ragged, absurd world: no matter how great the hero, his declared reasons and his real reasons are not the same; at bottom everyone's motivations are grubby; coincidence does not reveal design, but accident. *Becket* takes place in the chaotic mind of Henry, and the profoundest discrepancy between form and content is the tidy form which Henry's rememberings take.

But the form and content of *Curtmantle* are not at variance. Some critics have argued that all of Fry's characters speak alike. Anyone on to Fry's overall poetic voice has no difficulty distinguishing the voices in spite of their similarities. In *Curtmantle* more than in some of the other plays, however, the similarity of voices is a positive strength, since the whole play takes place in Marshal's mind. Marshal's mind is the form of *Curtmantle*, the obdurate pressure edging the play towards a shape. Marshal's mind—aware of the needed synthesis between conflicting laws, aware of how synthesis might be achieved, aware of the tragedy of anyone who can take the complete step forward but who refuses through weakness and perversity, and aware that synthesis is not likely to be achieved soon—is also the content of *Curtmantle*. The content and the form are the same.[16]

THE ARTS IN THE BODY POLITIC 10

A Yard of Sun

A yard is neither a foot nor a mile. A cubic yard is just enough room to stand in. One cannot leap; one cannot extend both arms simultaneously as far as possible; one must crook one's knees and stoop one's shoulders. A yard is enough, but just barely enough, to give a person elbow room.

The Bruno family in Fry's play[1] had been, before the Second World War, a typical upward-mobile, lower-middle class family in Siena. This family has discovered after the war just how difficult it is for each member to occupy his own cubic yard without interfering with his brother's cubic yard. The Brunos are every family. In England or America they would be the Browns, and their name would be one of hundreds in any telephone directory. The Brunos represent the polarization in the family of humankind after the war. Roberto is the socialist, Luigi the ex-fascist, and Edmondo the capitalist. The tension between these brothers, intellectually and personally, is what gives the play its drive.

Roberto is the humorless revolutionary. Part of the resistance to fascists during the war, he is now a civilian doctor, but he treats the poor without proper pay. His patients admire his gentleness, but his family suffers from his ruthlessness. Roberto is ruthless with Luigi, who had been a Nazi during the war but is now ready to turn Christian Democrat, or anything else that circumstances seem to require. Luigi is ready to change political affiliations but not his light-hearted—and to Roberto, irresponsible—view of reality. In short, Roberto is ruthless with Luigi because he is not a socialist.

He is likewise ruthless with Edmondo, who has escaped from home and from the war, absconding with a neighbor's savings. Edmondo returns wealthy at the end of Act I for the first post-war palio, the traditional horse race between the several parishes of the city. Before his appearance he has through an agent anonymously rented the Palazzo del Traguardo from his father, the aging Angelino, who is the custodian. Edmondo's behind-the-scenes machinations have secured the best jockey in Christendom on behalf of the old parish. He has hardly arrived with his wife and impressive entourage, than he informs his family that his behind-the-scenes machinations had protected them during the war. Not long after that announcement, he arranges for model photographers to photograph Grazia Scapare, a neighbor girl. He makes his father an offer to finance remodeling the palazzo into a fine restaurant. But in spite of all of the good will and the material favors Edmondo brings his family, Roberto is ruthless with him, for Edmondo has become an international financier by supplying arms from Portugal for both the Allies and the Nazis. While Roberto is ruthlessly contemptuous of Luigi and Edmondo, Luigi admires Edmondo's business methods and considers Roberto's moral earnestness excessive. Edmondo makes it clear that he considers both brothers unambitious small fry; yet Roberto's contempt makes Edmondo feel guilty and unsure of himself. None of the brothers is at peace with the other two. Each is a universalist for his own ideology. All have military names: Roberto, "bright in fame," Edmondo, "protector of the wealth," and Luigi, "famous warrior."

Angelino is the widower-patriarch overseeing this family. He loves all of his sons, though never all at the same time. He loves them by turns. Angelino had made Edmondo's name taboo in the Bruno family after his theft, yet Angelino forgives all when the prodigal returns:

> The doctor said
> When they'd got you off the umbilical hook
> '*There's* a promising cranium.' The spirit
> Of prophecy was in him. . . (42–43)

When Roberto finally proposes marriage to Grazia, Angelino praises him: "Have you found your way of asking her, at last?/ I knew you were the one with the intelligence" (109). And when

Luigi wins the horse race, standing in for the stricken Cambriccio hired by Edmondo, Angelino says, "I always said/Luigi was the one to succeed. All he needed/Was the opportunity" (101). Obviously Angelino loves all three of his sons, but at the same time he is ashamed that one turned out to be a capitalistic thief, another a Nazi, and another a socialist.

Angelino's ethic is genuine enough, but outdated. A leather merchant, he had set aside some money for each son in order to make that son respectable, successful, and a credit to the family. Now Roberto has become a doctor, but he is not successful financially. Luigi has become a politician, but he backed the wrong party. Edmondo, the only son who did not use the money his father had set aside for him, brings home the success that Angelino so much wants to see; but Edmondo is a thief.

The difference between Angelino and his sons is the war. Angelino has suffered during the war (first Nazi officers and then American officers are billeted in the palazzo, all of them hard on the furniture and on the wine supply), but moral choices have not been thrust upon him as they were upon his sons. The opposition among his sons was bought on by the decisions made necessary by the war. Like Luigi, most Italians followed the government in spite of corrupt policies and violence. Those who resisted the government were usually socialists like Roberto, though not able to form a government less corrupt and less violent than the one they opposed. Some few turned the domestic and foreign strife into cold cash like Edmondo, but were immoral in the process. One can imagine Angelino as his parents' "angel"; his is a bourgeois standard of success. He does not know what it is to be heroically committed to any cause, but on the other hand, he is impeccably moral by his own lights. Angelino's ethical system was never meant to endure the ambiguities of war.

The Brunos are like the Browns, the Whites, the Greens, and the Smiths in the Anglo-Saxon world. Life after the war has rendered parental authority ineffectual. Inherited codes of behavior are no longer appropriate for returning soldiers who have seen into the heart of darkness, which their parents have not seen. Youth confronts age, the ideologies of the young contest against each other, violence confronts violence, and no end of the vain contest appears.

Peaceful coexistence is the best alternative, giving each his own cubic yard of sun. A cubic yard of sun allows some freedom, but not complete freedom. To prevent interference in one's own cubic yard, one must agree to stay out of the other fellow's. That means adopting a cramped position, means being less free than one could be, and means that Hobbes was right about the political state of humankind. Humankind, said Hobbes, exists in a state of natural warfare; to achieve freedom from warfare, each person must voluntarily give up some freedom. It is the pragmatic condition of modern society, but it is a far cry from the City of God, in which all the citizens are members one of another.

After a temporary reconciliation at the palio, each of the Bruno sons retreats to his own cubic yard of sun. Divide the world of sun into cubic yards, and the effect is a prison. The world is a prison which the Bruno sons enter voluntarily at play's end in order to be free from each other, in order to enjoy a minimum allotment of sun.

Like a set for a play of the Italian Renaissance, the set for *Yard* has for its vanishing point up-stage, the Palazzo entrance. The entrance to the right is the door to the Bruno Osteria and the entrance at the left is the door to the Scapare dwelling. All of the action of the play takes place on a street which leads to the Palazzo del Traguardo. The meaning of *traguardo* is "goal." The street leading to the "goal" suggests a race which has nothing to do with the palio.

Indeed, the Brunos are in a race with each other, and their goal is what to do with their treasures from the past, among them the Palazzo. Edmondo would use it, as he would all of his treasures, for the good of his family—by no means as selfish as he might be in wanting to make Angelino a restaurateur in it. Luigi would use it for the sake of the community or party. Roberto would use it for the sake of the poor, a clinic. The goal in the race of the Bruno brothers is what to do about the Palazzo del Traguardo and all it represents. Only the elderly Angelino seems to retreat from the race when he declines the offer to make it into a restaurant.

Angelino's declining the race makes him less like the Brunos and more like the Scapares across the street. For the Scapares have each escaped from the race, from the *civitas mundi*, of the Brunos. *Scapare*, from Latin *excappare*, means "escape," and having escaped from the race of the Brunos, the Scapares inherit the Palazzo's courtyard, full of sun. They inherit the full yard of sun because they know how to enjoy it.

True, Luigi Bruno takes account of the sun:

> I remember it [the palio].
> I swallowed the last black morsel of what I was dreaming as soon as it was light
> And said Here it is, we're all new men
> In a new world. I stood at the window, like Adam
> Looking out on the first garden. (5)

But, as Roberto reminds Luigi, he has not really earned the right to inherit the courtyard full of sun. Luigi would like to make a new beginning without escaping from the *civitas mundi*. If it were all to do again, he would again be a Nazi. His enthusiasm for the courtyard flooded with sun is empty. Only the Scapares can really enjoy the full yard of sun because they have escaped from the race of the *civitas mundi*.

Cesare Scapare had left his frigid, arthritic wife and infant son, Alfio, in Naples before the war, and had moved in with the warm-hearted Giosetta in Siena. He and Giosetta loved each other; but feelings of guilt for leaving his wife and son subjected him to bouts of depression. Even the birth of Giosetta's daughter, Grazia, did not solve the problem. During the war Cesare had been picked up by the Nazis and put into a concentration camp. His return to Siena coincides with the first post-war palio. He comes back for a joyful reunion with Giosetta and Grazia, but soon announces his plans to return to Naples to salvage what he can of his marriage. "Easing the sting of death in the next bunk" (100) is something Cesare knows about. "The sting of death is sin," as the Apostle Paul says (I Corinthians 15:56). Having heard the dying confessions of comrades, Cesare realizes that to conquer his own guilty depressions, he must decide not for preferences but for duty. In this decision he has escaped from the *civitas mundi* and is at peace with himself and world.

Cesare's alternative to Roberto's external political revolution is transformation from within:

> I never set
> So much value on us as I do now,
> Heart, mind, and vision: all we can call human,
> Not wolf, jackal, vulture, and pig.

> In the camp, you don't know what utopias
> We built out of some flicker of humanity.
> How, in what way, won't you forget?
> Don't for God's sake, reward us
> By staring so long at the gorgon's head
> It grips the muscles of your living face.
> We've been in the dirt. We don't want to be remembered
> By generations playing at mud-pies
> And calling it the true image of life—
> I'd rather come soon to the clean skull.
> Purify us, Roberto, purify us!
> Insist on all the powers that recover us! (103–104)

Escape from the rat-race of the *civitas mundi* is recovery and transformation. Nobody in the play escapes from more than does Cesare. His is the victory that overcomes the world. He is the true Caesar, the victor in the race for the new humanity.

Giosetta, "the joyful one," also escapes from the *civitas mundi*. After she has lived with Cesare during his bouts with guilt and depression, after she has waited for him faithfully for three years, Cesare rewards her: he goes back to his first wife. But the word *reward* is an ironic word belonging to the order of the *civitas mundi*. Giosetta is willing to let Cesare go to his first wife because she knows that he must go if he is to conquer his depressions. She agrees that it is not easy to let him go (100); but she does not need to control the people she loves, nor does her love need to be rewarded. Giosetta's detachment from what she loves allows her to be the painful reality principle to the Bruno family. When Angelino self-righteously criticizes Cesare behind his back as being certainly no hero and an irrational depressive at that, Giosetta diagnoses in brilliant detail the lack of heroism in the Bruno family, although immediately afterwards she makes it clear that she loves them all. She is as detached from things as she is from people, and when the Brunos are all quarreling about how much water is rationed to them (a flash flood has polluted the water system), Giosetta quietly solves things by allowing the Brunos the greater part of her ration. She can be detached from people and things because she is detached from her own rights. She can be truly charitable because she is not in the race of the *civitas mundi*. Like Cesare, she achieves her detachment in the process of resolving her guilt:

> If we could have married, it might have felt
> Something solid, divided and come together.
> In the early years whenever I went to confession
> And had to call our love a sin
> I felt I was being unfaithful to him with God.
> Cesare laughed, and said it was God who was jealous,
> Not him. But when they took him away
> I even thought it might be the punishment
> For our life together. It wasn't a good thought,
> To my mind, anyway. Only, if we were married . . . (55–56)

Guilt is a corrosive state of heart, but resolving a guilt is sure to make a person at once more detached, compassionate, and joyful than before. Giosetta escapes from the *civitas mundi* when she gives up Cesare.

Like Giosetta and Cesare, Alfio is aware of moral ambiguity. Alfio has a dual purpose in coming to Siena from Naples: He comes as the jockey for the parish most threatening to the Bruno's parish in the palio, and he comes in quest of a lost father, Cesare. When Cambriccio, the celebrity, falls ill, Luigi becomes the jockey for the Brunos' parish. Alfio had no chance to win against Cambriccio, but suddenly Alfio is the favored jockey against Luigi. Edmondo tries to bribe Alfio to lose the race to Luigi, and for a while seems to succeed. Alfio needs money to import cortisone from America for his mother's arthritis. A slave to the dilemmas of the *civitas mundi*, Alfio knows what guilt is like:

> I don't feel like company. I don't know
> Who I am any more. I'm not fit
> To be with other people, anyway. (82)

But when Alfio finds that his father may be present at the race, he knows at once that he cannot accept the bribe. He knows what guilt feels like, and thus he is not self-righteous about his decision not to take the bribe. Alfio is the "ensign-bearer" in the community of which his father is the Caesar.

Grazia is implicated with the others in the guilt of the *civitas mundi*. She is sure that her telling her friend Rosa Lavanti that Cesare was at home in hiding had been the reason for his arrest and imprisonment. She has lived with the guilt for three years; and when Edmondo organizes a modelling career for her which may lead to acting, Grazia's first reaction is to leap at the chance to get away from the scene of her guilt.

> Oh, I wish I could go away from here! I'm sick
> Of the smell of the war in our hair, on everything I touch.
> I want to be where nothing reminds me of anything.
> Rome! I could lose myself there, couldn't I
> Edmondo? I should feel better there.
> Not to be quite real, however absurd—
> A fancy person, someone else's invention,
> Whose clothes, even, aren't her own clothes.
> I'll go, if they invite me. (83)

At this point Grazia is allowing her guilt to pursue her. She is not really escaping it. Her going to Rome would make her "not quite real," and then her guilt would be not quite real either. If she went to Rome, her state would be like Alfio's when he accepts the bribe: "I don't know/Who I am any more" (82). Grazia escapes from her guilt at the same moment she escapes from the glitter of Rome. Both guilt and glitter are manifestations of the *civitas mundi*. The "grace" which is the true Grazia can emerge only when she has escaped from the race of the *civitas mundi*, in which the goal is false glitter and winning involves guilt.

The race of the *civitas mundi* is managed by a morally bankrupt bourgeois ethic. Based on propriety, the bourgeois ethic of Angelino and the pre-war world did not condemn or otherwise cope with the monstrous impropriety of the war. Protesting against the government or refusing to commit violence were not considered good form. Without the guidance of a wise older generation, the young people brought up during the war spun their own systems of ethics based on power and violence, and nothing checked them: capitalism, communism, and fascism. The Scapares escaped from the prison of the *civitas mundi* of the Brunos by a radical return to a personal morality based on integrity rather than on propriety.

Giosetta and Cesare forego the palio to sit together in the sun—a whole courtyard of it. "A good idea, the sun," says Cesare. "Yes," answers Giosetta, "it helps" (99). People do not need "to earn each other" in their system; getting along with each other is "given away free with the daylight" (98). At that moment, without even trying, the Scapares are winning the archetypal race of which the palio and all other races are imperfect imitations. They have won the race for a new humanity, the *civitas dei.* That community will not be completed until all break out of their confining cubic yard of sun to live in courtyards flooded with sun. Sitting in front of it, enjoying the sunshine on it, Giosetta and Cesare know how to use the Palazzo del Traguardo better than anybody else. It is at once their goal and their prize.

Communication between the two families and within the two families is helped along by, and sometimes would be impossible without, the aesthetic influence of Ana-Clara and of the palio.

The palio makes the Bruno family work as a unit in spite of differences. Edmondo's international contacts provide a celebrity jockey, Cambriccio, to represent the Bruno parish. Cambriccio falls ill, but unless Edmondo had fired up enthusiasm by engaging Cambriccio to begin with, the Bruno parish would not have had a chance at winning, winning being a matter of spirit as much as of skill. When Edmond's schemes to replace Cambriccio with another celebrity fall flat, Roberto suggests that Luigi ride. Roberto knows how to pick up a lost cause and make it go. His experience as resistance fighter during the war and as champion of the downtrodden afterwards qualifies him uniquely. When Edmondo's methods fail, Roberto can take over. Of course, anyone who wins as ambiguously as Luigi would curl up like a hedgehog in winter, and there still would be no victory to celebrate; Luigi falls off his horse, though the horse comes in first. He wins by a technicality, even though Alfio *rides* in first. After the humiliating defeat of the Nazis, Luigi needs any victory at all; he rises to the occasion. Carried on the shoulders of the men of the parish, he accepts the accolades of the community as his due. In spite of their irreconcilable differences, the three brothers achieve a temporary community by working for and achieving the victory at the palio.

In a less dramatic way, the palio serves to unite the Scapares permanently. Alfio comes to Siena from Naples in order to ride for the parish competing with the Bruno parish. Cesare does not come to Siena for the palio, but his return coincides with it.

More important, the palio serves to unite the Brunos and the Scapares to each other. Alfio's arrival prompts Angelino to assure Alfio that Cesare is certainly not the father-hero he is looking for, which assurance prompts Giosetta to launch into her scathing analysis of the Bruno family. Her analysis clears the air for a solid relationship between the two families. Edmondo's plan to make

Grazia a model and an actress is part of his palio largesse; Roberto's noticing Grazia at all as a woman is brought about by his annoyance at Edmondo's manipulating her as he would any commodity. Roberto's annoyance with Edmondo's largesse makes him ask why Grazia should want to leave, makes him discover her sense of guilt, and makes him capable of speaking the liberating word: "It's not your fault that the world's name is Hazard" (85). Roberto and Grazia would never have become engaged if it had not been for the palio. It takes Roberto's awareness of Edmondo's insensitivity to Grazia for Roberto to discover his own insensitivity to Grazia. Giosetta and Angelino have the duty of preparing the festive meal for all of the others on the eve of the palio, and this occupation gives them a chance to exchange more long thoughts about each other than they have for years. Luigi's glory is shared by Scapares and Brunos alike and all together in a magnificent, though brief, experience of community. The palio brings unity.

Ana-Clara serves the same function as the palio. Edmondo had planned for her to appear on the scene with him:

> Imagine what he wanted! I crouch in the car
> Till the whip cracks, and the brass brays,
> And in I shuffle, mad, in hot spangles.
> Haven't we done better than that, father-in-law? (39)

As Edmondo's wife, she would meet the same suspicion and downright hostility that Edmondo meets. She chooses the better way, the way of reconciliation. Edmondo has rented the Palazzo anonymously, Angelino and the rest of the family are expecting wealthy guests, and Ana-Clara arrives alone a good while before her husband. Before Edmondo arrives, all three of the Bruno men are thoroughly bewitched by her. She compliments Roberto for his physique immediately. She knows date and architect for the Palazzo, and name and birthday for Angelino. Her enthusiasm for the palio is like a native's. The men all love her and hold her in awe, especially when her staff of six servants appears. When Edmondo finally enters, it is as the husband of the woman the family already admires. Ana-Clara smooths the way for Edmondo's return home.

When Roberto takes her compliments as insults to a peasant, Ana-Clara does not let that put her off. When Roberto and Edmondo quarrel heatedly because of their opposite attitudes toward the war, and when Giosetta confronts Edmondo with Cesare's arrest, then Ana-Clara intercedes for her husband:

> Let me say this: no man born could have talked
> About you all with such relentless affection
> As Edmondo did, until I could hear you breathe.
> Even turn to the door expecting you to be there.
> You were more real than the world I grew up in.
> Any man can make a woman his wife,
> But Edmondo made me daughter and sister, too,
> As if I always had been, by the force of his memories.
> From the day I first met him his guiding thought
> Has been to come home with his arms crowded with blessings.
> It became my purpose, too. (44–45)

The rest of the family, Luigi most of all, is swept away by Ana-Clara; only Roberto remains invulnerable to Ana-Clara's charm and diplomacy. Hence Ana-Clara must devise other tactics than defending Edmondo to get the red sheep into the community.

Ana-Clara takes the offensive. Her first victory is getting Roberto to admit that he once loved Edmondo, and wants to still. Then she attacks, ever so gently but pointedly, Roberto's doctrinaire socialism. He has become such a puppet ideologist that his real self cannot appear:

> How can I tell, after two not entirely
> Poised encounters, where the line divides
> Your shalt from your shalt-not? Whether I shall find it
> Just, or merely got out of the handbook? (48)

With Roberto's ideological prejudices exposed, she renews her defense of Edmondo, though never abandoning her offensive tack. Roberto may be sizing up Edmondo and Ana-Clara, but Ana-Clara is doing her own sizing up as well:

> I can only say that Edmondo wants to please.
> You could start from there. You could suspend judgement
> On him, and perhaps on me till you know me better.—
> As I do on you, in spite of all provocation.
> You're an open question to me; we shall have
> To see how you answer, won't we? (48)

She leaves with a significant smile, compelling Roberto to watch her leave.

Ana-Clara knows all the wiles and devices of coquetry; she uses them all on Roberto, but her intention is not to be unfaithful to Edmondo. She realizes how envious Roberto is of the younger brother who is more successful than he. Luigi shows all the signs of being the baby brother in his hero-worship of Edmondo and in his refusal to take Roberto's seriousness seriously. Roberto shows all the signs of being the oldest brother, used to being on top. If he cannot be on top in wealth or in having a lovely wife, then he will be on top in moral outrage. Ana-Clara sees how much she will reduce Roberto's hostility if she lets him feel that he could take her away from Edmondo. Roberto's exaggerated moral superiority is only a crude defense against oppressive feelings of inferiority.

Next day Ana-Clara does Roberto's rounds with him. Roberto takes her along only partially because he is fascinated by her, but chiefly because it is his opportunity to show the fine lady how the other half lives. But Ana-Clara is less impressed by the poor than by Roberto's humanity when he is with the poor:

> If you lectured *them* as you lectured me on the way
> They would all think death a happy release. You came
> Far nearer to prodding my social conscience awake
> By letting me see they loved you, than with all
> That rhapsody of statistics. (61)

Ana-Clara makes Roberto see that his doctrinaire socialism will allow him to be kind to the poor, but to nobody else.

But Ana-Clara does more. She makes Roberto see that he cannot even recognize the poor when he sees them. Ana-Clara herself came from slums in Lisbon more desolate than any in Siena. A beggar at 5, mistress to an actor at 15, and mistress to a professor at 17, Ana-Clara finally has become Edmondo's wife: "Bless him, he could have bought/A real duchess, but he settled for silver-gilt" (67). Later, Ana-Clara tells Roberto that the moment she revealed to him her poor beginnings, something in him lost interest in her: "When I owned up to what I came from/I could see a view-halloo fade out of your eye" (94). Ana-Clara makes Roberto question whether he does not exploit people as much as do the capitalists he abhors.

Ana-Clara is ruthless in her analysis of Roberto though she

always keeps alive just enough erotic attraction in Roberto to keep the relationship going. In fact, Edmondo becomes the jealous husband, but he need not have worried. Ana-Clara will never leave Edmondo. For Edmondo does not have Roberto's chief fault, and Ana-Clara does not let Roberto get away without telling him what it is. Roberto is completely self-centered, in spite of his compulsive efforts on behalf of the poor. Roberto does not notice other people for what they are in themselves, but only for what they are to him. Edmondo, on the other hand,

> gives me the patience I need
> To make my mistakes, which you would never give me;
> And the leisure I need to realize myself,
> How far my mind, unhounded, and my free senses
> Will take me, which you would never give me. (94)

And she has the courage to confront Roberto with his real motive in paying attention to her. Ana-Clara knows that Roberto has been out to seduce her, "to lay the donnanobile/On her back in love or confusion" (94). And yet this Roberto complains about the unreality in Edmondo's life, so that Ana-Clara needs to make the point: "He was real enough to make you want to show him,/Or anyway show yourself, you could take me from him" (94).

But Ana-Clara is not all negative. She notices before Roberto himself notices that he loves Grazia:

> None of this has any significance
> Beside the plain fact that you love Grazia.
> I know. I saw it take you by surprise
> When you turned and rent Edmondo. You hadn't bothered
> To mark its gradual height on the kitchen door.
> It's much taller than you imagined, isn't it? (95)

Before this revelation to Roberto, Ana-Clara had already helped to liberate Grazia from her guilty compulsion to escape the neighborhood where she betrayed her father.

> It was love and joy made you tell Rosa.
> That's no betrayal. But when you let remorse
> Wound the light in you, *then* you betrayed him. (84)

Ana-Clara puts Grazia into a state of mind in which she can allow herself to be noticed and Roberto into a state of mind in which he can do the noticing, and thus she helps to unite the Scapares and the Brunos.

In absolving Grazia of guilt, Ana-Clara is also uniting the members of the Scapare family closer together. She does the same when she defends Alfio against Edmondo's bribes and against Angelino's cajolery not to take it so hard:

> Oh? And why shouldn't he? It *is* hard.
> It's impossibly hard. It's ethically, emotionally,
> Rationally disgustingly impossible.
> I'm on Alfio's side. (88)

Ana-Clara gently prods Alfio against bribery; which decision made, he is a worthier son to a returning father.

Like the palio, Ana-Clara serves to bring the Brunos closer to the Brunos, the Scapares closer to the Scapares, and the Brunos and the Scapares closer to each other. The influence of the palio and of Ana-Clara transforms the fragmented community for the duration of the palio into a unified community, all hostilities reconciled. For a moment all the characters step outside of their own cubic yards of sun. The palio over, all the Brunos retreat to their own cubic yards of sun again, but the retreat does not diminish the glory of the community as long as it lasts. Only among the Scapares does the glory become permanent.

Ana-Clara's share in the glory of the palio is frankly sensual:

> What I fancied I saw was common life,
> Particularly the common male, glorified!
> Striped, pied, blazoned and crested,
> Pausing and advancing like courting sunbirds—
> Indeed, the whole deliberate procession
> Like an unhurried lovemaking. Isn't is so?
> The first shock of the gun, and the trumpets
> That stop the heart, until it beats again
> With the rap of the kettle-drums, and the pouring in
> Of colour on the pale square. The huge voice
> Of the crowd is like the roar of blood in the ears.
> The Commune flag fluttering, while the Commune bell
> Jerks in the erect campanile,
> Like an alarm, and like a gloria; both.
> And all the time the banners ripple and leap,
> Circle the body, stroke and rouse

> With creating hands. Oh, it really is, you know,
> A lovemaking, a fishing in sensitive pools. (33)
>
> At last when the corporate body has been tautened
> Absolutely to expectation's limit
> There comes the violent release, the orgasm,
> The animal explosion of the horse race,
> Bare-backed and savage. After that—well, after that
> I am lost in the dispersing crowd, I give way
> To my siesta. (33)

Ana-Clara's description of the palio as she imagines it before she has even seen it shows how sensual she is and how sensual the palio is, since nowhere does Ana-Clara express disappointment with the palio afterwards.

And yet the sensuality of Ana-Clara and of the palio is sublimated to non-erotic ends. Human sensuality can be sublimated to non-erotic ends only when there are memories of a past which was not as good as it could have been and when there are hopes for a future better than the present.

Ana-Clara has had enough experiences in bed with enough men. What would it do for her to add Roberto to the list of the actor, the professor, and Edmondo? Ana-Clara has learned by experience that the hunger we experience as the hunger of sex is a stronger hunger than sex can satisfy. Experience has taught her that her sexuality must serve not only itself but also the purposes of the spirit if it is to be satisfying. That is why she sticks to Edmondo and renounces Roberto. That is why she prefers the "oblique seduction" (68) of watching Roberto dress wounds to the real thing. Ana-Clara has learned to use her sexuality in the cause of community.

Like Ana-Clara's wisdom, the wisdom of the palio is based on the past. The annual event celebrates the end of every war since the palio began, this year the end of World War II. Luigi describes it:

> You know how it all began?
> Four centuries ago, or nearly that,
> The city held out through a siege for months
> Until the skeleton third of the population,
> All that was left, pushed open the gates
> And let the enemy in.
> The parish companies were stripped of their arms

> But were 'armed in the spirit', so history says.
> Instead of being military defenders
> They became civil protectors of our liberties
> And the city straightened its vertebrae to a ramrod.
> And that's what we celebrate in the Palio:
> Pride in our flair for resurrection,
> Excitement, violence and rivalry,
> With the Mother of God as carnival queen. (32)

The first celebration of the palio was as ambiguous as the end of World War II. The third of the population which worked underground to let the enemies in are not unlike Roberto's underground fighters. The parish companies, who are stripped of arms when the siege is over and then turn into quite adequate civil protectors of liberty, are not unlike Luigi's own Nazis. It is not victory that is celebrated in the palio, but the war's being over. It is the perpetual possibility for all people to be members one of another. The palio is a humbling reminder that communities are fragile. The festivity is not diminished by being solemn; but it is solemn, for the festivity is sublimated into something like prayer: God make us one, if only during the palio. The city's flair for resurrection is always almost matched by the city's flair for hatred and violence.

The sensuality of Ana-Clara and the festivity of the palio are not only sublimated into solemnity by the past; they are also kept alive and nurtured by hope for the future: the perfect palio, or the community that lasts. Just as Ana-Clara has learned that the flesh awakens hungers stronger than sex can satisfy, so Angelino must learn that his hope for the palio was really the hope for a perfect, lasting palio. This palio, with his family around him and his parish winning, is beyond his wildest expectations, and yet it is not a perfect palio: ". . . everything came/Together, except, somehow, us, we didn't/come together" (89). This palio can only give a premonition of what a perfect palio would be like.

A more mature woman than Grazia ("grace"), Ana-Clara ("pure grace") has learned what Grazia still must learn: just how much of what she perceives as sexual desire is to be fulfilled by sexual experience and how much is to be fulfilled by contacts not possible to flesh. Therefore, Ana-Clara also understands just how much her desire for the palio is to be fulfilled by this particular palio and how much must wait for the ultimate and permanent palio. Unlike

Angelino, who is disillusioned that, good as the palio is, it is incomplete, Ana-Clara sees this particular palio, brief as it is, as a certain glimmering of the perfect palio to come. She describes the experience of the palio afterwards in terms taken from the Apocalypse of St. John, which says that "the city had no need of the sun or moon to shine upon it; for the glory of God gave it light, and its lamp was the Lamb. By its light shall the nations walk, and the kings of the earth shall bring into it all their splendour. The gates of the city shall never be shut by day, and there will be no night there" (Revelation 21:23–25). Ana-Clara can explain her experience of the palio only in apocalyptic language; the literal palio exists in time, but her hope makes her see more than the timebound, the particular, and the literal. Already before the palio she was expecting to see "common life . . . glorified," and she was expecting to hear in the bell both "an alarm and a gloria" (33). After the palio her view of it is still common and glorified, sensual and holy, which is to say apocalyptic:

> It's a great slow love-making, anyway,
> And left me vibrating like an instrument.
> So nearly the city had no need of the sun
> Or the moon to shine on it. I could almost see
> By the light that streamed from the trumpets
> And shimmered from the bell. The courting sun-birds,
> The birds of paradise, so nearly sang
> The indwelling music which created us. (107)

The palio Ana-Clara sees and the palio she hopes for are not identical. If they were, there would be no need for hope. But neither are the two totally different. The double vision of hope makes apocalyptic imagery necessary: the images must be everyday enough to be immediately recognized, but their combination must suggest a state of perfection never before experienced by anyone.

The lovelorn writers of letters and popular songs are wont to disguise their inability to express themselves by writing lines like "There are no words to tell you . . ." For a writer with an apocalyptic vision this is literally true, no matter how gifted the writer may be; there are no words for what the apocalyptic writer is compelled to communicate. Fry gives Ana-Clara two speeches, one before (33) and one after (107) the palio, both speeches saturated with apocalyptic language. The literal and the figurative languages intertwine to suggest states of being other than the literal, though related to it.

But Fry also has a more original, more theatrical method of suggesting the apocalyptic vision: the spectacle of the palio.

> The light swiftly fades to darkness. In the dark, the sound, gradually increasing, of an excited crowd, the emphatic ringing of the bell in the campanile. A gunshot. The roar of the crowd as the race begins. Above the dark stage light strikes on rippling banners. (96–97)

Fry can only point toward the desired effect by a stage direction, but the context of the play shows that as a spectacle, the palio can hardly be overdone. The audience must remember Ana-Clara's ecstatic description of the palio while it is going on; when she describes it in apocalyptic imagery later, the audience must recognize the palio they saw. It must be strong enough to support Ana-Clara's speeches about it, but it must also be spectacular enough to divert the warring Bruno brothers from their animosities into a temporary community. The heart of the play—the Christian gospel of forgiveness, reconciliation, community, and hope—lies embedded non-verbally in the spectacle, even though all the words preceding and following the spectacle are necessary if the audience is to see the gospel.

What the palio and Ana-Clara are to the characters of the play, the whole of *Yard* is to the audience. The palio and Ana-Clara are sensuous; any work of art also exists in a medium available to the senses; *Yard*'s medium is the theater. The palio and Ana-Clara sublimate their sensuality; any successful work of art does the same; *Yard*, too. Ana-Clara and the palio reveal unrecognized violence and hostility in the characters; the play reveals the same in an audience, provided it is willing to examine itself. Ana-Clara and the palio bring about a temporary community of love and respect between fascists, capitalists, and socialists; not only the stage, but the theater auditorium becomes, potentially, a yard of sun. Ana-Clara and the palio do not have the strength to make the community permanent; each member of the audience and each actor retreats to one's own cubic yard of sun once the performance is over, just as the characters do when the palio is over. But Ana-Clara and the palio reach out bravely toward the perfect and permanent community; the play also reaches out in hope. Ana-Clara and the palio together are a parable for how the arts affect the body politic.

More is necessary in the body politic than art, of course. Giosetta and Cesare, for example. Superficially, their renunciation of the palio and of each other seems parallel to Ana-Clara's renunciation. Cesare leaves Giosetta for his invalid wife just as Ana-Clara gives up Roberto for Edmondo. Both renunciations assume that the hungers experienced in sexual desire cannot be satisfied entirely by sexual experience; both renunciations are the outcome of personal suffering. Yet the renunciation of Cesare and Giosetta is based on a deliberate decision. Ana-Clara, on the other hand, seems to indulge the flesh even as she renounces it. She does not abandon coquetry forever, but makes it serve the ends of the community; she has not reasoned her way to this use of coquetry, but achieves it by intuition. Ana-Clara's freedom is the freedom of a dancer. The dancer subjects herself to the bondage of daily practice, but then achieves the freedom to indulge in the most sinuous, sensual dances. Cesare and Giosetta renounce the dance altogether and choose duty instead, because the tyranny of despair was attached to their dance. The path of duty and mortification of the flesh is the way of the saint. The way of paradoxical affirmation and renunciation of the flesh, of sublimating the flesh to the goals of the spirit is the way of the artist.

Both sainthood and art are necessary. For art lacks staying power. It can provide the intuitive insight, the temporary fulfillment, and the successful palio which suggests the perfect palio to come. It can keep hope alive. Art can provide the inspiration and the vision, but it does not have the spiritual power in itself to change the world permanently. Saints have the power to change themselves, and thus they have potential power to change the world. Often saints are so concerned with the inner life that they lack communication with the world they ought to be changing. The saints, Cesare and Giosetta, are the only two characters not at the palio. They recognize that their race for the *civitas dei* has little in common with the race of the Brunos for the *civitas mundi*; they sense that the palio race is not a great issue at all.

And yet the palio is indispensable for the purposes of Cesare and Giosetta. Ana-Clara understands better than Cesare and Giosetta that art needs sainthood and sainthood needs art. Intuitively, she sees Cesare's moral program for the world already partially fulfilled in the palio, a connection that would not have occurred to the saintly but reasonable Cesare:

> I'm still thinking
> About the future you see for us, as if
> Our variation to adapt to life
> Was hardly begun.—All through the afternoon
> I felt as though the barriers were breaking
> Between our world and another. (107)

Art must guide sainthood to appreciate progress in vision, whereas sainthood must insist that art never settle for less than the perfect and permanent solution to time's problems. Art can provide the momentary delight and the intuition of a perfect delight beyond the momentary one. Sainthood travels the painful, plodding steps between, changing the self and changing the world. Without art and sainthood, the body politic will remain hopelessly divided between myopic factions: in our time, capitalists, fascists, and socialists.

Not ignoring the need for the labors of the saint, *Yard* emphasizes the need for the innocent openness and acceptance found in art: the willing suspension of disbelief. Even the play's saint says it: "It's all/Given away free with the daylight . . ." (98).

Not to the strong is the victory for which the Brunos yearn. Not to the swift is the race.

THE PATTERN IN THE CARPET 11

A Diachronic View of the Form

The conceptual categories of Fry's earliest play, *Boy*, are parallel to the three stages of human life as viewed by Søren Kierkegaard: the aesthetic (read "enjoying") person, the ethical (read "self-denying") person, and the religious (read "renouncing the world for God and regaining it, resigned to its absurdity") person.[1] Cuthman begins life as Kierkegaard's aesthetic person, enjoying his life as a shepherd boy, keeping his flock inside of his charmed circle; progresses to the suffering phase of the ethical person, accepting deprivation, alienation, and death, and settling on his pilgrimage and his building project as a response; and finally ends with the "absurdity" of grace: an appearance by Jesus Christ as carpenter to repair Cuthman's ruined project.

The play which most closely resembles *Boy* in its use of the Kierkegaardian formula is *Thor*. Colgrin, although only an incidental and delightful adornment to the play, represents an aesthetic enjoyment of the flesh. The pagan community, devoted to defending the status quo and the honor of their dead-orthodox gods, regardless of pain to themselves, is made up of impeccably ethical persons. The only exceptions are Cymen and Martina, gradually turning from the status quo of dead orthodoxy to the paradoxes of Christianity; Hoel, the former Christian, rediscovering the paradoxes of Christianity; and Merlin, the mythic chorus, whose religious viewpoint resolves the paradoxes because it spans the centuries.

Putting a single character through the three Kierkegaardian

stages was an obvious formal scheme, but having done it once in *Boy*, Fry rightly abandoned it. While its transparency is just right for a saint's play, no play but a saint's play can possibly be the result when one character is shown progressing through Kierkegaard's three stages. *Thor* is not a saint's play; it captures a cross-section of society at the moment of its conversion from dead-orthodox paganism to Christianity, with various individuals caught at each of the three stages. Especially for the religious phase, it is an effective technique, since Kierkegaard says he has never found a single example of the religious person that he was sure of.[2] Fry presents Cymen and Martina barely discovering the religious dimension of life, so of course they are not mature examples of the Christian faith; but since maturity risks smugness, their immaturity is no evil thing. Hoel is rediscovering Christianity, but is so tentative and unsure that he, too, keeps smugness far away. And Merlin, a sure example of the religious person, is sure only because his quest spans the centuries.

In *Firstborn*, actually earlier than *Thor*, the two structures combine. It is a saint's play like *Boy*, for *Firstborn* is the story of Moses, his aesthetic youth in the Egyptian court alluded to repeatedly: "You have coarsened during your exile," Seti tells him (22). The exile refers to Moses' sojourn in the wilderness and his new coarseness refers to his angry return as ethical person: identifying with Israel, demonstrating the rights of his people. At play's end, his resignation to God, his acceptance of the absurd cruelties of life, his awareness that the death of Rameses is the condition fo the release of Israel, and his conviction that God is the God of Israel *and* of Egypt in ways he cannot understand: all of this makes Moses a religious person. *Firstborn* is a saint's play.

Like *Thor*, *Firstborn* also gives a cross-section of the society in which the changes are occurring, Israel. Shendi is the aesthetic person. Moses and Aaron are ethical persons through most of the play (with allusions to the aesthetic dimension in the earlier life of Moses), and both advance to the religious view of experience at play's end.

Going beyond *Thor* formally, *Firstborn* shows the enemy side, the Egyptian court, caught in the three phases of Kierkegaard: Teusret is the prenocent aesthetic person; Seti, the ethical person, with a tragic determination to deny himself for the sake of Egypt;

and Rameses, the religious person, resigned progressively to life's incongruities and desperately urging Seti to decide for Moses and God.

Almost too much is going on in *Firstborn* for the form to sustain. If one saint must be picked to make it a saint's play, the saint must be Moses. Rameses and Aaron are saints as well as Moses—Rameses throughout and Aaron at play's end—so that it can be seen as a play about three saints. Bitterness has made Anath on the Egyptian side and Miriam on the Hebrew side incapable of commitment; they vacillate between aesthetic, ethical, and religious positions, quite unlike anyone in *Boy* or *Thor*. Besides, there is the whole problem of how to regard coincidence: the aesthetic person's writing off coincidence with a single vision of reality with personal pleasure at the center; the ethical person's interpreting coincidence paradoxically with double vision, the literal view and a religious view, but still centering on one's self or cause; and the religious person's expanding that paradoxical view to include all sides of all questions. Doing all of this makes *Firstborn* the most ragged of the plays: saint's play, cross-section of the favored side, cross-section of the enemy side, and a theory of coincidence/miracle.

Phoenix could not be more compact. The objective characters and their subjective perceptions of each other find a tidy form. Each character progresses through all three Kierkegaardian phases: Doto has had a life of pleasure, has renounced it to die with her mistress, and ends the play drinking a toast to both masters, the dead and the living. Tegeus finds pleasure with Dynamene, encounters the threat of death, and accepts Dynamene's sacrifice of her husband's corpse. Dynamene looks back on a happy past (which looks less and less happy the farther she progresses), encounters grief and wills her own death in response to it, and then decides for life on paradoxical terms. To paraphrase Kierkegaard's categories in Fry's own words: ". . . the characters in a comedy must affirm life, assimilate death, and persevere in joy."[3] What they perceive about each other's progress is recorded in their changing each other's names or the meanings of the names. The content is as complicated as *Firstborn*, but the form is tidy.

For all of its complexity, *Sleep* is also a very simple form. Peter begins as an aesthetic man, David (conviction without authority) and Corporal Joe (authority without conviction) as ethical men, and Meadows as a religious man. At the end all have progressed into complete men.

The difference in design between *Sleep* and the plays discussed is that the hierarchy has been removed from Kierkegaard's categories. For Kierkegaard and for the earlier Fry, only the aesthetic person can become ethical; only the ethical, religious—in a prescribed order. In *Sleep* the prescribed order has fallen away. A complete person has all three faculties functioning in harmony, in interlocking segments, but anyone can begin anywhere. The burden is on David, ethical man, to generate aesthetics and faith, for instance; but the burden is just as heavy on Meadows, religious man, to generate ethics and aesthetics. Meadows, as religious man, is not automatically the moral center of the play. The moral center of the play is the interlocking community.

In fact, when one has liberated the Kierkegaardian categories from the strict progressions of aesthetics, ethics, and religion, one has the traditional categories of reason (or in its trivialized form, common sense) for ethics, faith for religion, and aesthetics. Faith, reason, and aesthetics have been the terms in which the plays have been discussed in the chapters on each play, since aesthetics, ethics, and religion as Kierkegaardian terms imply that order, while faith and reason traditionally imply an integration of complementary—though sometimes apparently contradictory—forces. The addition of aesthetics is Fry's contribution; it keeps the integrating process from Greek dualism and from canned formulations of the history of Christian thought.

In *Curtmantle*, the tragedy, Becket represents faith; Henry, reason; and Eleanor, aesthetics. The tragedy is that the three cannot get coordinated. Henry sees only reason in single vision, Becket sees only Henry's point of view and his own in double vision, and Eleanor sees how she, representing aesthetics, could bring the other two together if they considered aesthetics anything more than a useless adornment.

The seasonal comedies work with the same categories, though often with several very different characters for one point of view. In *Yard*, Ana-Clara and the palio represent aesthetics; the Scapares, the narrow escape into faith; the Brunos, reason, with capitalist, communist, and Nazi mentalities represented. In *Dark*, Gettner represents aesthetics; Gelda, faith; Peter, Janik, and Jakob various kinds of reason; and the countess, a perfect blend of all three qualities into the complete pacifist she is.

In *Venus Observed*, a more complex structure, all three of the duke's mistresses are segregated in the aesthetic category, adornments for the duke's delight: Rosabel, for sexual delight, Jessie, for domestic delight, and Hilda, for intellectual delight. The duke keeps his mistresses segregated in their aesthetic category because he keeps himself segregated in his reasonable category; he watches stars through a telescope and is just as coolly appreciative of his mistresses as of the stars. In one subplot, Reedbeck represents aesthetics and Dominic, reason. Among the servants, Reddleman, the lion tamer, represents aesthetics and Bates, the shrewd and crafty reason of a thief. Aesthetics versus reason is the dynamics of the groupings of characters, and each group generates faith by the working of the events of the play. The faith generated between the duke and his mistresses, in Reedbeck's family, and among the servants is all the result of Perpetua, who does not represent faith but is the cause of its generation in others. Perpetua, like the countess in *Dark*, is the perfect blend of faith, reason, and aesthetics; in her presence, people trapped in either reason or aesthetics generate its counterpart, and generate faith as a by-product.

Venus and *Lady* are earlier than *Dark* and *Yard*, yet they are more complicated in structure because they leave out one or more of the three polarities to be generated between characters and in the audience, a kind of X in the equation. *Dark* and *Yard* have a character apiece (or a group of characters) for each of the three polarities. Fry writes:

> I try to reach the meaning of the plays through the characters and their experience of living without imposing too much of my thoughts on them: in this way I hope they do some exploring for me. If they have any truth they should be able to surprise me. I don't want them to be manufactured out of Christian truths: but what is true will be waiting for them. Of course, this can only be partly so since my own experience conceives them, but I try to be as little conscious of that as possible. Perhaps some damage was done to *The Dark is Light Enough* because I thought the earlier comedies had been taken only on their entertainment level, and so I tried to be more explicit—pushed a bit too hard, maybe. What do you think?[4]

What I think is that the categories of Kierkegaard (aesthetics, ethics, and religion) are weak dramatically, since the religious person is always superior to the other two and the aesthetic person always inferior to the other two. I think that, in spite of such interesting characters as Cymen and Seti, the earlier plays (*Boy*, *Thor*, and *Firstborn*) are necessarily confined to type characters with inevitable victory going to the religious character; that Fry's later categories (aesthetics, faith, and reason)—implying no hierarchy and identifying a full human life as a full complement of all three qualities functioning together—that Fry's later categories make a genuine dramatic conflict possible; that these complementary qualities define the form for *Sleep*, *Curtmantle*, and the four seasonal comedies.

I think that *Lady*, one of the earlier of the seasonal comedies, has a design based not on characters being assigned to each of the three categories, but on the capability of a couple, each representing one of the categories, to generate the third quality in the relationship between them. Every relationship in *Venus* is a polarity between aesthetics and reason, with faith being generated. *Lady* is more complex. One of the lead couples represents faith and reason and generates aesthetics; the other lead couple represents aesthetics and reason and generates faith. In its greater complexity, *Lady* is the better play as well as the more popular one.

I also think that, while *Lady* is superior to *Venus*, *Lady* and *Venus* together are superior to the other seasonal comedies, *Dark* and *Yard*, because the categories in the latter are all provided and not left for the characters (and the audience) to generate.

Lady, I think, is one of Fry's four best plays. The others: *Phoenix*, because it is so classically tidy; *Sleep*, because it achieves the impossible—a poetic structure that requires dramatic presentation; and *Curtmantle*, because it presents a new theory of the universal human tragedy—the failure to achieve the complete reaching forward.

I also think that the aesthetics-reason-faith pattern (as well as the earlier aesthetic-moral-religious pattern) is not to be written off as a formula, but to be endorsed as a human archetype. The pattern is not there because, in the manner of murder mysteries, the author has hit on a winner and now keeps on repeating it with cosmetic changes. The plays point to an unresolved mystery of identity: that no person and no community can have a total identity until aesthetics, reason, and faith are integrated, without any barriers between. The barriers break down because of the absolute rule of God over all three, but how they break down is a mystery all Fry's plays struggle to discover. Formula has to do with a repetitive dramatic technique, but archetypal form has to do with a persistent philosophical/theological/personal problem.

That archetypal pattern and philosophical problem rather than uniform dramatic technique account for the plays' similarities can be shown by assessing the shift in position of the audience between the religious plays and the comedies. In *Thor*, Cymen wonders until the play's end what the odd changes taking place in him amount to: loving enemies, renouncing violence, and making a sacrament out of drinking a toast. Cymen does not know, but the audience knows; its chief interest is in the psychology of Cymen and in the satiric bite that the church, where the play is being performed, resembles more the pagan establishment portrayed in it than the church resembles the saintly Cymen. In *Yard*, as in all the seasonal comedies, the audience sees incomprehensible changes among characters, and it experiences these changes vicariously. In the latter, Fry makes the audience feel the essence of Christianity without using the terminology. The audience of the seasonal comedies is cast in the role of Cymen in *Thor*. There is no dramatic formula that the two have in common, but one archetypal problem lies at the heart of both.

Fry's single human problem is how to integrate body, mind, and spirit within the personality, or their contemporary counterparts, aesthetics, reason, and faith. This integration is the single human problem worth pursuing, dying for, or writing plays about, all other problems being red herrings cast up gratuitously by society. Whenever three people represent one archetypal polarity in the plays, this is particularly evident. The real issue of *Yard* is how to get the Brunos (reason), the Scapares (faith), and Ana-Clara's palio (aesthetics) integrated; still, the characters themselves, as well as the audience, all think the conflict is between the capitalist, the socialist, and the fascist Bruno brothers—all representing reason. That political problem is local, provincial, and admits of resolution. Long after history resolves the problem of capitalism, socialism, and fascism, the basic conflict between art, reason, and religion will still need in great part to be worked through. The three types of women composing the aesthetic dimension of the duke's life in

Venus—domesticity, intellect, or love—are again a red herring thrown up by society—another soluble problem. As is the problem of diplomatic aggression, personal aggression, or military aggression—Peter, Jakob, and Janik—in *Dark.* The mainspring of the comedy in all of these plays is the triviality of the problems we declare wars over and conduct crusades for and against. These problems divert society from the universal human problem, and that fact gives all of the comedies their bitter edge.

The difficulty with an archetypal pattern is that critics who do not notice it think that Fry writes two opposite kinds of plays. Fry has noticed:

> The three plays brought together in this volume, and *The Boy with a Cart,* which is not included here, fall easily into the category Religious, as distinct from the comedies, which more than once have been called Pagan. But if any are religious they are all religious, and if any are pagan they are all pagan. They reflect the world I know, as far as my understanding has taken me. The real difference is that the comedies were written to be played in a theatre; the others in, or not far from, a church.[5]

An archetypalist demonstrates the archetype best by writing as wide a variety of pieces as possible, in various styles and forms, with the result that some critics discern opposite patterns.

To glimpse the presence of an archetype without saying what it is or tracing how it works itself out in great variety leads another kind of critic to say that Fry writes only one play in one voice. There are basically only two kinds of plays. The issue is when to name God and when not to name him, since it is Fry's conviction that God does not need to be named to be worshipped:

> *Need* not be named, not never should be. Though I think that God being badly named is sometimes worse than his not being named at all. I had a go at saying something about this in a talk I gave a year or two ago: 'When I say God, God only knows what is summoned up in the mind of the man I'm speaking to. It may be some ogre or bearded Nanny of his childhood, or what Blake called "Nobodaddy,' or a threat to personal freedom, or a psychological compensation, or a vaguely pantheistic all-overness. The mystic Master Eckhart said: 'God is without name, for no one can say or understand anything of Him.' But he also said: 'God becomes God when the creatures

say *God*. In other words, the ineffable becomes tangible, Godhead becomes God through a relationship with the existence of man.'

When I wrote to you that God need not be named, I think I was thinking of friends who would certainly argue against the terminology of religion, but who express him very explicitly in their lives.

In that talk I went on to say: 'Thirteen hundred years earlier Christ had said, "The Kingdom of heaven is within you." What do we take this to mean? Does it mean that by faith and God's grace we can acquire an inward peace and security, and be free of the burden of the ego? This may certainly be part of the meaning; but it is not what the words say. If that were all, surely the words would run: "The Kingdom of Heaven *can be* within you." But they say, unconditionally, "*is* within you" —in our existence, in the very fact of our being alive. It does not depend on whether we acknowledge it, or whether we employ the word: *God*. Clearly an acknowledgment can make us more capable instruments, just as knowledge of psychological and physiological truths can assist us to health. But even unacknowledged, the kingdom of heaven is an active part of us, just as the body has its own self-curative capabilities, though our physiological knowledge be nil.'[6]

Generally the plays that name God are the religious plays, which work with the hierarchical Kierkegaardian categories: aesthetic, ethical, and religious. The plays that are written for the theater use the non-hierarchical categories of aesthetics, reason, and faith. The two exceptions are *Sleep*, which, though a religious play, uses the nonhierarchical categories of the theater plays, and *Phoenix*, which, though a theater play, shows all three characters going through the Kierkegaardian categories. Both are among Fry's best plays.

Curtmantle, also one of Fry's best, is his only tragedy, using the non-hierarchical categories of the comedies. *Lady* uses the categories proper to the comedies, but makes the audience find the unknown quantities in *two* equations: aesthetics + reason + X = integrity; reason + faith + Y = integrity; X = faith; Y = aesthetics. In his four best plays, Fry is testing the perimeters of the archetype, exploring.

The other plays are not only necessary to define the norm of the archetype so that the adventuresome experiments can take place against it, but are also much richer in ideas than has generally been assumed. Provision and division (*Boy*); single, double, and multiple vision (*Firstborn*); the paganism of any dead orthodoxy (*Thor*); the practicality and utility of aesthetics (*Yard*); the wickedness of stereotyping women (*Venus*); the similarity between Judas and Peter (*Dark*); all of these ideas would be lost if we restricted ourselves only to Fry's best. Much praised for the music of his poetry, Fry's ideas have been overlooked—just as a sophisticated music lover tends to overlook the musical coherence in popular music. Sir Thomas Browne in *Religio Medici* said there was "something in it of divinity,"—in that "vulgar and Tavern-Music"—"more than the ear discovers."[7] There is more of divinity in the music of Fry's plays than the critical ear has discovered.

THE FINAL JUDGMENT 12

The Lady's Not for Burning

The paradox of *Lady* is the twin theme of spring and apocalypse.[1] The time is that cruel month, April ("I've an April blindness"[2]), and *Lady* is the spring comedy in the seasonal tetralogy. The play opens with Thomas leaning in at the window, interrupting Richard at his figures; annoyed, Richard chooses (and Fry chooses for him), out of all possible oaths: "Damnation." Thomas replies: "Don't mention it. I've never seen a world/So festering with damnation" (3). Both personal and cosmic apocalypse are concerns of Thomas:

> How do you know that out there, in the day or night
> According to latitude, the entire world
> Isn't wanting to be hanged? Now you, for instance,
> Still damp from your cocoon, you're desperate
> To fly into any noose of the sun that should dangle
> Down from the sky. Life, forbye, is the way
> We flatten for the Michaelmas of our own particular
> Gallows. (5)

On a bright spring day, Thomas cannot wait for the final judgment:

> . . . I've drunk myself sick, and now, by Christ,
> I mean to sleep it off in a stupor of dust
> Till the morning after the day of judgement. (19)

That we and his fellow characters find Thomas strange for wishing for the apocalypse is because we "don't/make any allowance for individuality" (5). However, that Fry wishes for the apocalyptic Thomas to dominate his spring comedy is not so easily explained.

That explanation is the burden of this chapter.

The apocalyptic mood spreads from Thomas to everyone. Even the most secular and skeptical of the characters, Tappercoom, speculates about apocalypse:

> As for the Day of Judgement, we can be sure
> It's not due yet. What are we told the world
> Will be like? 'Boasters, blasphemers, without natural
> Affection, traitors, trucebreakers,' and the rest of it.
> Come, we've still a lot of backsliding ahead of us. (38)

Tappercoom's point is that apocalypse is not coming, but he is talking about it. Margaret actually dresses for it, as well as for her party. Everyone sits up late into the night, waiting for it.

Although the rumor spreads well later, its beginning is inauspicious:

> Humphrey: But if he could be the Devil—
> Thomas: Good boy! Shall I set
> Your minds at rest and give you proof? Come here.
> *[He whispers in Humphrey's ear.*
> Humphrey: That's not funny.
> Thomas: Not funny for the goats.
> Humphrey: I've heard it before. He says the Day of Judgement
> Is fixed for to-night.
> Margaret: Oh no. I have always been sure
> That when it comes it will come in the autumn.
> Heaven, I am quite sure, wouldn't disappoint
> The bulbs. (32–33)

By being whispered, the rumor has a better chance of spreading. That Thomas knows when the day of judgment is coming is the best possible evidence for his being the Devil. Thomas knows that on judgment day the Devil will be destroyed (Revelation 19:20; 20:10). He also knows that Cool Clary will rise to the occasion of fighting Armageddon. Thomas as the Devil will then be destroyed and Jennet, who is accused of the same crime that Thomas confesses to (the transformation/murder of Matthew Skipps), will not be burned. The time reference *tonight* in the rumor is a desperate attempt by Thomas to focus the community's hysteria on himself now; tomorrow morning Jennet may already have been burned as a witch. But the immediate response to the rumor is Margaret's bland observation about the bulbs. Thomas becomes even more desperate. Will a specific time reference make the rumor more convincing? "The Last Trump/Is timed for twenty-two forty hours precisely" (33). Thomas is intent on dying for Jennet.

The prediction is true in a way that Thomas does not intend, for what happens at twenty-two forty hours he could not have predicted in Act I. Act I takes place in the afternoon ("Out there, in the sparkling air, the sun and rain/Clash together . . ." 6); Act II is early evening, for though the stars are out ("And then/They saw the star fall over our roof . . ." 39) it is only about an hour later (36) than Act I. Act III is later the same night (63), perfectly compatible with twenty-two forty hours. The last judgment, the apocalypse, and the parousia turn out to be the arrival of Matthew Skipps in Act III.

Parousia, apocalypse, and judgment are thoughts which evoke terror. Actually, the judge who is merciful is exercising judgment just as much as the judge who punishes; the apocalypse is the destruction of the Devil and all his works, but is just as much the salvaging of good; the parousia is the second appearing of Christ as judge, but also as bridegroom (Revelation 12:1–7, 21:1–7). At twenty-two forty hours, the accidental arrival of Skipps renders the evil of the community innocuous, changes the imagined crime of Jennet into innocence, and completes the change in Thomas from the death wish to the will to love. Matthew Skipps is the *deus ex machina*, who, at his appearing, bears away the sins of the whole world.

Of the audience, too. While twenty-two forty is certainly compatible with the dramatic time of Act III, it is also rather close to the audience time at the arrival of Matthew Skipps, assuming that the performance begins at twenty hours, and assuming ten-minute intermissions between acts. *Lady* is not only a judgment by God, or by Fry, or by the audience, or by the characters on each other; the *Lady* event is also a judgment visited upon the audience.

Judgment implies a standard, and Fry's standard is the total integration of reason, art, and faith within the structures of society as well as within the life of the private individual. The society or individual that fails, falls under the apocalyptic judgment; which is to say, is condemned to a future as bad as the present, change for the better being impossible; which is to say, is trapped in winter without the possibility for spring.

Take the chaplain, for instance. He is the spokesman for faith; he justifies every stand he takes on the basis of scripture. As violinist, he provides the music at the party and continually asserts his love for his violin, calling it mistress and angel (47). As one of the learned and reasonable, he is called on, with the mayor and constable, to spy on Jennet, suspected of witchery. The chaplain feels no conflict among his religious, aesthetic, and rational functions.

The chaplain is not, however, the play's norm. His quoted texts are all out of context and, rather than directing his thought, provide a professionally pious rhetoric for sanctioning the decisions of the community. He says of the disillusioned Thomas, paraphrasing the Song of Solomon: ". . . he cannot be stayed with flagons, or comforted/With apples" (41). If only the chaplain could summon the power of the original: "My beloved is like a roe or a young hart: *behold, he standeth behind our wall, he looketh forth at the windows, shewing himself through the lattice* [italics SMW]." (The Song of Solomon 2:9). The chaplain's prophecy misses Thomas looking in at the windows, digresses, apologizes, and retracts:

> I imagine
> He finds the world not entirely salubrious.
> If he cannot be stayed with flagons, or comforted
> With apples—I quote, of course—or the light, the ocean,
> The ever-changing . . . I mean and stars, extraordinary
> How many, or some instrument or other—I am afraid
> I appear rhapsodical—but perhaps the addition
> Of your thumbscrew will not succeed either. The point
> I'm attempting to make is this one: he might be wooed
> From his aptitude for death by being happier;
> And what I was going to suggest, quite irresponsibly,
> Is that he might be invited to partake
> Of our festivities this evening. No,
> I see it astonishes you. (41–42)

The chaplain's plan wins out, but not before the educated establishment—the mayor, the constable, and the chaplain—spies on Thomas and Jennet. Again the chaplain has scriptural warrant: "The ears of them that hear/Shall hearken" (47). He has picked a passage from Isaiah which is not at all a scriptural justification for eavesdropping:

> Behold, a king shall reign in righteousness, and princes shall rule in judgment. And a man shall be as an hiding place from the wind, and a covert from the tempest; as rivers of water in a dry place, as the shadow of a great rock in a weary land. And the eyes of them that see shall not be dim, and the ears of them that hear shall hearken. The heart also of the rash shall understand knowledge, and the tongue of the stammerers shall be ready to speak plainly. (Isaiah 32:1–5)

The Peaceable Kingdom awaiting those who sustain the judgment of the apocalypse is the burden of the whole passage, which eludes the chaplain. What it means for Jennet to be condemned as a witch also eludes the chaplain. The text he chooses to comfort her:

> I exhort therefore, that, first of all, supplications, prayers, intercessions, and giving of thanks, be made for all men; For kings, and for all that are in authority; that we may lead a quiet and peaceable life in all godliness and honesty. (I Timothy 2:1–2)

Totally ignoring that he himself is a member of the tribunal which has just condemned her, he applies the text above to Jennet's condition:

> Bother such sadness. You understand, I'm sure:
> Those in authority over us. I should like
> To have been a musician but others decreed otherwise.
> And sin, whatever we might prefer, cannot
> Go altogether unregarded. (59)

When he cannot play as skillfully as he would like on his violin, he complains that he has treated the violin "with an abomination/ That maketh desolate:—the words, the words/Are from Daniel—" (72). The abomination in Daniel concerns the substitution of strange worship for the worship of God: ". . . and they shall take away the daily sacrifice, and they shall place the abomination that maketh desolate" (Daniel 11:31; 12:10). The chaplain does not realize that his attitude toward the violin *is* the abomination, making anything less than God his ultimate concern. The chaplain's faith does not give him a comprehensive view of life, but here and there provides a text to twist to his intuitions. Sometimes his intuitions are bad, like urging Jennet to bear her burning without making a fuss; sometimes they are good, like suggesting that the prisoners be invited to the party, which invitation leads to their liberation; good or bad, the chaplain's intuitions do not comprise a plan for the future.

The chaplain *has* faith, reason, and aesthetics, but fails the apocalyptic test of *integrating* them. The chaplain's aesthetic is sentimental; nobody who masters an instrument, with all of the hard work involved, ever refers to it as an angel. As reasonable voice in the community, as member of the council, he is tolerated but not taken seriously. As man of faith, he quotes texts all out of context and never questions the establishment. After torture and interrogation, Thomas and Jennet discuss whether the chaplain might help them:

> Jennet: Do you think he knows
> What has been happening to us?
> Thomas: Old angel-scraper?
> He knows all right. But he's subdued
> To the cloth he works in. (48)

The chaplain is unaware that the integration of self—faith, reason, and aesthetics—is a slow and painful process. He is as out of place as the only survivor of Eden would be in an evil society. He is trapped in the corrupt establishment and does not know he is trapped. His voice is laughable because it is totally out of touch with the evil in society and in himself; he is one of the persecutors in a witchery trial, yet thinks himself and the world good. While we laugh, we are moved, because his voice reminds us of an irretrievable innocence:

> It was very interesting: I was dreaming I stood
> On Jacob's ladder, waiting for the Gates to open.
> And the ladder was made entirely of diminished sevenths.
> I was surprised but not put out. Nothing
> Is altogether what we suppose it to be. (38)

Aesthetics divorced from the rest of life turns sentimental; religion divorced from the rest of life turns mystically romantic; reason divorced from the rest of life turns into voting with the majority, as common sense tends to do. Having faith, reason, and aesthetics but not integrating them turns the chaplain into a mystical, common-sensical, and sentimental fool.

All of the characters of *Lady*, except the two lead couples, are as broken, incomplete, and, hence, laughable as the chaplain. What is true of individuals is also true of society at large. With a flick of the kaleidoscope, the chaplain represents faith; the constable, Tappercoom, represents reason, reduced to law and order; and Tyson represents an aesthetic sensibility that wants to be left alone to enjoy itself. The chaplain's faith is totally ineffectual because, as Thomas says, ". . . he's subdued/To the cloth he works in" (48); the other two officials patronize him:

> Religion
> Has made an honest woman of the supernatural
> And we won't have it kicking over the traces again,
> Will we, Chaplain?— In the Land of Nod.
> Admirable man. (37)

Asleep or awake, the chaplain makes little difference to the decisions the other two officials make, except that it is the chaplain's whimsical idea that the prisoners be asked to the festivities of the evening. Tappercoom and Tyson acquiesce, not because they are changing their position but because the party may loosen Thomas up sufficiently to admit his innocence and Jennet to admit her guilt. Though the chaplain's suggestion is carried out, it does nothing to help the unfortunate couple; they are saved by the *deus ex machina* of the arrival of Matthew Skipps at play's end. The chaplain calls his own plan irresponsible (42), Tyson admits he hears "very little of what you have said, Chaplain" (42), and when the chaplain says he hopes to see the prisoners dancing, Tappercoom, thinking of how they will dance in the flames, says, "They shall, dear saint, they shall" (73). Tappercoom and Tyson treat the chaplain with condescension, as though only they can face horrors that he has not begun to contemplate. It is a picture of the church in the modern world.

Not that Tappercoom and Tyson have much reason to condescend to anybody. Naziism is the result of reason's—like Tappercoom's—degenerating into law-and-order fanaticism, which is the result of his reason's not being integrated with the rest of life: "Good is as good results" (47). Good has nothing to do with truth, but with what the state considers its best interests:

> We have put him to the merest thumbscrew, Tyson,
> Courteously and impartially, the purest
> Cajolery to coax him to deny
> These cock-and-bull murders for which there isn't a scrap
> Of evidence. (36)

Guilt or innocence is less important in planning an execution than are public revenues and balancing the budget:

> As a criminal the boy is a liability.
> I doubt very much if he could supply a farthing
> Towards the cost of his execution. (42)
>
> Your guilt, my boy,
> Is a confounded bore. (93)

If the ambience of *Lady* were not the forgiveness of laughter, the Nazi-like mentality of Tappercoom would make the blood turn chilly.

Tyson, the mayor, represents sentimentality, the direction aesthetic feelings take when they are abstracted from aesthetic form. Without form, aesthetic feelings cannot relate to God, to the body politic, or to anyone outside the self. Though Tyson seems to respect law and order, he actually uses it only superficially—to avoid painful decisions. When Thomas says, "You're about to become my gateway to eternal/Rest" (18), Tyson evades by using law:

> Dear sir, I haven't yet been notified
> Of your existence. As far as I'm concerned
> You don't exist. Therefore you are not entitled
> To any rest at all, eternal or temporary . . . (18)

When Thomas says he has come specifically to be hanged, Tyson again evades: "Have you filled in the necessary forms?" (18). When "irresponsible events" (21) press him to make decisions, he evades by repeating the formula "This will all be gone into at the proper time" (23, 27, 33; "discussed" used on 24). Tyson loves himself as mayor but has no stomach for the responsibilities of the office. His compassionate sentiments lack the reasonable form they require to affect action, even his own. Against his sentiments, he drifts into Tappercoom's program:

Ay, yes,
Jourdemayne; what are we to make of her?
Wealthy, they tell me. But on the other hand
Quite affectingly handsome. Sad, you know. (36–37)

Jennet's wealth, not her guilt, is a "reason" for her execution; her beauty, not her innocence, is a "reason" for her pardon. Like many aesthetes, some of them artists, Tyson decides against his aesthetic sentiments and for cash, though not without pain. Tappercoom finds him in tears at the party:

We must burn her,
Before she destroys our reason. Damnable glitter.
Tappercoom, we mustn't become bewildered
At our time of life. (71)

No proper argument and influence goes on among Tappercoom, Tyson, and the chaplain; a proper integration can, therefore, never occur.

Naziism is never the fault only of the Tappercooms of the world, but the fault as well of the artists and priests who do not render the necessary opposition. Naziism is more an example of society's stupidity than of its wickedness in *Lady*, which is at once Fry's supreme insult to Naziism and his way of coming to terms with it—even forgiving it.

The family does not necessarily integrate faith, reason, and aesthetics, a point worth making in a play which does after all celebrate two marriages, both of which achieve integration. Margaret and her twin sons, however, do not. As Tyson, her brother, represents aestheticism without form—hence sentimentality—so Margaret represents aestheticism without content, aestheticism as pure form, which degenerates into social form, which in turn degenerates into domestic form. She assures Thomas that the final judgment cannot come in April because God "wouldn't disappoint the bulbs" (33), nevertheless changes her dress for the occasion as she might for church (33), and speculates about whether her crystal service is sufficient for the "glorious company of the apostles" (40). She is not so much frightened as aesthetically offended by the mob in the street:

But the number of people gone mad in the street
Is particularly excessive. They were shaking
Our gate, and knocking off each other's hats

> And six fights simultaneously, and some
> Were singing psalm a hundred and forty—I think
> It's a hundred and forty—(39)

The words the crowd sings:

> Deliver me, O Lord, from the evil man; preserve me from the violent man: Which imagine mischiefs in the heart; continually they are gathered together for war. (Psalm 140:1–2)
>
> As for the head of those that compass me about, let the mischief of their own lips cover them. Let burning coals fall upon them: let them be cast into the fire; into deep pits, that they rise not up again. (Psalm 140:9–10)

The violent person from whom the crowd prays for deliverance and on whom the crowd prays fire is the innocent Jennet; obviously, it is the crowd that is violent. The delicious irony is that Margaret can understand the words of the psalm well enough to recognize which psalm it is, but does not understand the words well enough to understand how ridiculously the words apply in the present situation. Yet, she develops some sympathy for Jennet. Just as Jennet's beauty persuades Tyson to compassion, her social aplomb affects Margaret:

> How am I to prevent
> This girl, condemned as a heretic, from charming us
> With gentleness, consideration and gaiety?
> It makes orthodoxy seem almost irrelevant.
> But I expect they would tell us the soul can be as lost
> In loving-kindness as in anything else.
> Well, well; we must scramble for grace as best we can. (78)

The pun on *grace* makes what Jesus the Christ died to bring to earth simply another desirable social adornment. Margaret goes a step beyond art for art's sake into art for snobbery's sake. It happens when art becomes pure form.

Margaret's twin sons, Humphrey and Nicholas, represent bombastic legality and bombastic mysticism, respectively—legality being a corruption of reason and mysticism of faith. Their affirmations are bombastic because their sole motivation is sibling rivalry. Nicholas is interested in Alizon only when it is clear that Humphrey is about to marry her (8). As soon as Nicholas shows some interest in Jennet (24), Humphrey cools noticeably toward Alizon (31), and then both are interested in Jennet (43, 64, 67). Yet the rationalizations in which they hide their rivalries are related to false reason and false faith. Humphrey argues his official rights as the elder brother, for Jennet as for Alizon (16, 69); Nicholas pleads on the basis of supernatural revelation, for Jennet as for Alizon (15–17; 78–79).

Nicholas: What about the stars?

Humphrey: All right;
What about the stars? They flicker and flicker, like hell's
Light they flicker.

Nicholas: You dismal coprolite!
Haven't they said that I shall have Alizon Eliot?

Humphrey: Astral delirium, dear Nick. Officially
Alizon is mine. What is official
Is incontestable. It undercuts
The problematical world and sells us life
At a discount.—Without disrespect either
To you, mother, or to my officially
Dear one, I shall lie down. (15–16)

"They're inseparable," Margaret says of Humphrey and Nicholas, "really twin natures, utterly/Brothers, like the two ends of the same thought" (11). The thought is sibling rivalry, and Margaret's family is as far from achieving satisfactory synthesis of faith, reason, and aesthetics as is the chaplain within himself or the chaplain, Tyson, and Tappercoom within society.

Two couples in the play generate a proper synthesis within themselves. Alizon starts in a convent, a representative of faith; Richard starts as the mayor's pedantic secretary. From the moment of her release from the convent and intensified by her meeting Richard, Alizon develops an aesthetic awareness of the flesh, the same aesthetic awareness of the flesh developing simultaneously in the heretofore eminently reasonable Richard. At the play's beginning, Thomas had pursued aestheticism to existentialism—that common route of twentieth-century aesthetes—and is planning the existentialist's meaningful suicide to justify his existence; Jennet has pursued rationalism to the point of logical positivism. Thomas is where the arts were at the close of World

War II and Jennet where philosophy and science were. In interaction, Thomas and Jennet generate a religious view of reality between them.

Two couples are necessary: one lower-life couple and the other aristocratic; one nonintellectual and the other intellectual; one lacking the aesthetic dimension and the other lacking the religious dimension. Not only the intellectually elite are worth redemption, the play seems to say, and no bourgeois institution—like government (Richard) or church (Alizon)—is too pedantic for grace.

No sooner has she left the convent and stepped onstage into the mayor's office than Alizon is beginning to celebrate the flesh aesthetically in a way one would imagine to be foreign to the convent:

> Out there, in the sparkling air, the sun and rain
> Clash together like the cymbals clashing
> When David did his dance. I've an April blindness.
> You're hidden in a cloud of crimson Catherine-wheels. (6)

Michal, David's prudish wife, was offended at his dancing naked at the return of the ark to Israel (II Samuel 6:16, 20–23; I Chronicles 15:29). Though she learned the story in the convent, Alizon is certainly no prude to mention that dance in this context. The song to which David danced naked concerns the apocalyptic judgment turned merciful and happy: "Then shall the trees of the wood sing out at the presence of the Lord, because he cometh to judge the earth" (I Chronicles 16:23). Alizon's other religious reference also underscores the fiery judgment turned downright giddy: "Catherine-wheels." They are named after St. Catherine, who was martyred on a crimson wheel. Metaphorically, the word has come to refer to pinwheels of fireworks; for Alizon, they refer to April's blinding light. Like Fry himself in the whole of *Lady*, Alizon unites judgment and joy, spring and apocalypse. After she falls in love with Richard, her aesthetic awareness of the flesh does not eclipse her awareness of God, developed in the convent: "We must never leave each other now, or else/We should perplex the kindness of God" (76). When Richard predicts that the establishment may make trouble, she responds, "Then they will have/To outwit all that ever went to create us" (77).

Richard, on his part, will not budge from his bookkeeping to take part in a witch hunt at the play's opening, so devoted is he to his duties toward the mayor; yet he defies the mayor's order to fetch the constable (31). He follows the mayor's whimsical command to scrub the floor with a good grace (44), but defies the mayor's opinion by eloping with Alizon. So great is his respect for justice that when he and Alizon come upon Matthew Skipps alive, they abondon their elopement to free Jennet (89–90). Richard has great respect for civil law and social law; but above these laws Richard sees God's law, which also gives the flesh its aesthetic due and requires that Richard love his neighbor's flesh as his own, regardless what the authorities require. Reason is there from the start; Richard comes to appreciate faith through Alizon; and a newly-generated aesthetic awareness of the flesh is the basis for the solid love between Alizon and Richard at play's end.

Alizon and Richard are timeless characters, but Jennet and Thomas think contemporarily. Jennet is on the side of reason, and she believes in the progress of the human race throughout history:

> I am Jennet Jourdemayne
> And I believe in the human mind. Why play with me
> And make me afraid of you, as you did for a moment,
> I confess it. You can't believe—oh, surely, not
> When the centuries of the world are piled so high—
> You'll not believe what, in their innocence
> Those old credulous children in the street
> Imagine of me? (27)

For her the supernatural is irrational: "What, does everyone still knuckle/And suckle at the big breast of irrational fears?" (27). For she is the daughter of a late scientist:

> May I, Jennet Jourdemayne, the daughter
> Of a man who believed the universe was governed
> By certain laws, be allowed to speak?
> Here is such a storm of superstition
> And humbug and curious passions, where will you start
> To look for the truth? (34)

She has been disillusioned, she admits, by her father's chemistry:

> My father broke on the wheel of a dream; he was lost
> In a search. And so for me the actual!
> What I touch, what I see, what I know; the essential fact. (52)

Jennet's thought is typical of the resurgence of logical positivism after World War II; she is determined never again to be irrational, even if that means abolishing all mystery.

What Jennet is to Wittgenstein, Thomas is to Sartre: Thomas is an existentialist. He is "less respectable" (3) than Richard, the clerk; he is an outsider, who during the first act "looks in through a great window from the garden" (3); he is like the spring lover from the Song of Songs: "Behold, he standeth behind our wall, he looketh forth at the windows, shewing himself through the lattice. My beloved spake, and said unto me, 'Rise up, my love, my fair one, and come away. For, lo, the winter is past, the rain is over and gone; the flowers appear on the earth; the time of the singing of birds is come, and the voice of the turtle is heard in our land; the fig tree putteth forth her green figs, and the vines with the tender grape give a good smell. Arise, my love, my fair one, and come away'" (2:9–13). Thomas will be talking like that at play's end; but at the beginning, when he stands behind the wall, looking forth at the windows, he is alienated. He is a discharged soldier, disillusioned with the irrationality of a world "festering with damnation" (3), a world "unable to die"; and he is impatient with bourgeois blindness which does not find anything out of order:

> Oh, be disturbed,
> Be disturbed, madam, to the extent of a tut
> And I will thank God for civilization. (14)

He has given up his life in civilization before the play opens. Free from the collective and inherited essence of what it means to be a human being, he is free to exist without fear—even of death, which makes him think himself ready for suicide. He says to Tyson, with some accuracy:

> Your life, sir, is propelled
> By a dream of the fear of having nightmares; your love
> Is the fear of your single self; your world's history
> The fear of a possible leap by a possible antagonist
> Out of a possible shadow, or a not-improbable
> Skeleton out of your dead-certain cupboard. (28)

Having given up his life philosophically, he gives Jennet the courage to do the same:

> We'll suppose ourselves to be caddis-flies
> Who live one day. Do we waste the evening
> Commiserating with each other about
> The unhygienic condition of our worm-cases?
> For God's sake, shall we laugh? (49)

Thomas, worn out by paradox and mystery, thus confronts Jennet, the foe of all paradox and mystery. Considering the world rational on the eve of her execution, however, is too much even for Jennet. Thomas helps her modify her logical positivism:

> And as for you, you with no eyes, no ears,
> No senses, you the most superstitious
> Of all—(for what greater superstition
> Is there than the mumbo-jumbo of believing
> In reality?)—you should be swallowed whole by Time
> In the way that you swallow appearances.
> Horns, what a waste of effort it has been
> To give you Creation's vast and exquisite
> Dilemma!
>
> . . . .
>
> We have wasted paradox and mystery on you
> When all you ask us for, is cause and effect!—
> A copy of your birth-certificate was all you needed
> To make you at peace with Creation. (53)

While Thomas chides and comforts Jennet, he himself begins to change. Jaded by the dilemma of the universe, he now, for Jennet's sake, makes meaning out of the dilemma:

> Nothing can be seen
> In the thistle-down, but the rough-head thistle comes.
> Rest in that riddle. I can pass to you
> Generations of roses in this wrinkled berry.
> There: now you hold in your hand a race
> Of summer gardens, it lies under centuries
> Of petals. What is not, you have in your palm.
> Rest in the riddle, rest; why not? (55)

He needs to accept the advice he gives Jennet, of course, for while he recognizes the riddle, he does not rest in it. He still considers himself "a cake of dung. Is there a slut would hold/This in her arms and put her lips against it?" (58). "Sluts are only human," Jennet replies. Under the influence of Thomas, Jennet has developed an aesthetic awareness of the flesh, which is to say, an erotic attraction:

> You may be decay and a platitude
> Of flesh, but I have no other such memory of life.
> . . . .
> I have come suddenly
> Upon my heart and where it is I see no help for. (58)

With her new aesthetic awareness comes her new awareness of God as well.

> I've only one small silver night to spend
> So show me no luxuries. It will be enough
> If you spare me a spider, and when it spins I'll see
> The six days of Creation in a web
> And a fly caught on the seventh. And if the dew
> Should rise in the web, I may well die a Christian. (68)

A perfect, rational, and intricate world, like the web, was all she recognized before. The seventh day—God's day—is also the day the fly gets caught in the web—like humankind caught in the universe. Part of the riddle which Jennet experiences is that the encounter with evil is also the discovery of God. If the fall—personal or archetypal—is the loss of God, it is also the discovery of God in a totally new way. Having sensed how caught she is, she has taken her first step in the discovery of God. Yesterday she would have seen the dew rising in the web as the result of evaporation, condensation, surface tension, and tensile strength; today she sees the same dew in the same web as an emblem of her regeneration—her baptism. She has learned something about affirming life, assimilating death, and persevering in joy.[3]

So much has she changed that at play's end she assists vigorously in furthering the change of Thomas. She exposes his existentialism as adolescent self-dramatization. Jennet, capable of intuition quite alien to her cause-and-effect stage, diagnoses Thomas mercilessly:

> There was a soldier,
> Discharged and centreless, with a towering pride
> In his sensibility, and an endearing
> Disposition to be a hero, who wanted
> To make an example of himself to all
> Erring mankind, and falling in with a witch-hunt
> His good heart took the opportunity
> Of providing a diversion. O Thomas,
> It was very theatrical of you to choose the gallows. (89)

He has already known all about affirming life and assimilating death, as all existentialists do; now he must learn to persevere in joy. At the end of the play he has learned it:

> I know my limitations.
> When the landscape goes to seed, the wind is obsessed
> By to-morrow. (95)

The whole play is obsessed at the end with "tomorrow's dawn" —the meaning, incidentally of Jennet's last name: "Jourdemayne." Even if Skipps were not to appear and if the burning were held on schedule, Jennet, once devoted to the law of reason, would still have become aware of mystery, the essence of tomorrow. Thomas, the prophet of nihilism, would still have found purpose in the mystery of tomorrow.

What gives Fry's mysticism its peculiar flavor is its freedom from Platonic dichotomy: from flesh yearning to be one with spirit; from painful, because impossible, synthesis. Richard and Alizon start out representing the formal institutions of church (for faith) and petty government (for reason). Thomas and Jennet start out representing the substantive content of their respective attitudes: Thomas existentialism (for art and aesthetics) and Jennet positivism (for science and reason). What Richard and Alizon generate between them is not a merely formal aestheticism, like taking art lessons or buying a painting, but the substance of aesthetics:

> Alizon: Men are strange. It's almost unexpected
> To find they speak English. Do you think so too?
>
> Richard: Things happen to them.

Alizon: What things?

Richard: Machinations of nature;
As April does to the earth.

Alizon: I wish it were true!
Show me daffodils happening to a man!

Richard: Very easily. (8–9)

What Thomas and Jennet generate between them is not merely a conceptual religion, to complement their respective theories, but a visible social institution, the sacrament of marriage:

Jennet: Am I an inconvenience
To you?

Thomas: As inevitably as original sin.
And I shall be loath to forgo one day of you,
Even for the sake of my ultimate friendly death. (95)

Adding an aesthetic component to their formal faith and formal reason, Richard and Alizon automatically acquire a conceptual framework for all three. Adding a religious component to their substantive aesthetics and substantive reason, Thomas and Jennet acquire a formal framework for all three. The form-content duality is simply not the focus of Fry's attention. That duality disappears automatically when a couple (or a community, or an individual) functions fully in the religious, aesthetic, and intellectual spheres.

Fry is nowhere more unlike his friend and mentor T. S. Eliot than in avoiding the Platonic dichotomy. One form or another of the Platonic dichotomy is Eliot's constant preoccupation, from the subjective-objective dilemma of "Prufrock," through the body-soul ensnarlments of "Ash Wednesday," to the time-eternity paradoxes of *Four Quartets*. The Platonic dichotomy, in one or another manifestation, is Eliot's dominant philosophical problem; Fry's dominant problem is practical: how to live a full life with aesthetic, religious, and intellectual faculties all engaged. Eliot's protagonists progress toward resolving the Platonic dichotomy within the privacy of the heart, with help or hindrances from external relationships; Fry's characters progress toward fully engaging their aesthetic, religious, and intellectual faculties *only* in relationships with others. In spite of heroic efforts, Eliot's protagonists never fully achieve the unity between body and soul that they strive for; the Fry characters who function fully as aesthetic, religious, and intellectual people solve the body-soul dilemma as a by-product, because, for them, the dilemma disappears—that is, the dilemma turns out to have been a false one. An active struggle goes on within Eliot's characters; in Fry's characters, passively accepting the wholeness of life brings health, which makes fruitful activity possible. Eliot's characters synthesize opposites; Fry's characters accept complementary modes of experience.

Fry's protagonists generate between themselves whichever of the three essential components of life are lacking—faith, reason, or aesthetics—but the resolution of form and content, body and soul, is automatic. Richard and Alizon's stumbling into intellectual content in the process of generating the lacking aesthetic dimension of life rests alongside Thomas and Jennet's stumbling into an institutional form in the process of generating the lacking religious dimension of life. Fry takes the urgency out of the Platonic dichotomy. If Fry had assumed the more mystical and Platonized method of Eliot, the conflict would have been localized between Alizon and Richard on the one hand and Jennet and Thomas on the other, the first couple urging form and the second urging content. In the play Fry wrote, there is no conflict between form and content, body and soul.

But what of those charming characters who do not meet the exacting standards of a full life? They do not function in all three aspects, but only in one or two. Or all three aspects are present, but not in fruitful tension with each other, as in the disoriented chaplain. Nicholas, Humphrey, Tyson, Margaret, Tappercoom, and the chaplain are not elected into love, but it is clear that Fry is not damning them. Damning them would be the blasphemy of doing the work which God jealously reserves for himself; damning them would be treating them in the same way they treat Jennet; damning them would self-righteously ignore the similarity they bear to ourselves. Fry's laughter is forgiving laughter.

The work leaves us, then, with an implied definition of redemption: faith, reason, and aesthetics are necessary for whole human life. The body-soul dichotomy falls away when a whole life is achieved. Wholeness is achieved only in interaction with other people. Only whole people can sustain the judgment of the spring, can be as naturally and fully people as crocusses are crocusses.

The ending of *Lady* could not be better, and this study concludes with a look at Matthew Skipps and a look at the last line of the play.

The arrival of Matthew Skipps, whose alleged disappearance has led to all the hysteria, is very satisfying not only because it eradicates all suspicion of witchcraft and necessity for confession of murder but also because aesthetics, faith, and reason are so finely integrated in the scene. Skipps has been rendered pliant by drink, of course:

> Your young gentleman says Come in, so I comes in. Youse only has to say muck off, and I goes, wivout argument. (90)

Even if the wholeness is only an illusion for Skipps in his drunken state, the wholeness presented in the play can be no more than an illusion for the audience. To like the play but not to seek wholeness in life outside of the play is to be drunk on the play just as Skipps is on liquor. When Tappercoom tries to establish legal identity, Skipps answers reasonably enough, but his reason drifts into talk of faith, of baptism:

> Who give me that name? My granfathers and granmothers and all in authorority undrim. Baptized I blaming was, and I says to youse, baptized I am, and I says to youse, baptized I will be, wiv holy weeping and washing of teeth. And immersion upon us miserable offenders. Miserable offenders all—no offence meant. And if any of youse is not a miserable offender, as he's told to be by almighty and mercerable God, then I says to him Hands off my daughter, you bloody-minded heathen. (90)

When Skipps is informed that he has been considered dead since morning, he considers himself in heaven: "Alleluia! Alleluia! Alleluia!" and "Glory, amen" (91). Skipps, in his cups, believes in an everyday heaven, a reasonable heaven, made one with his aesthetics in his singing and one with his faith in his confession. Sinking into stupor, Skipps speaks truer than he knows: "Youse blessed saints don't realize: it takes it out of you, this life everlasting" (92). Skipps is so satisfying, not only because he serves as the *deus ex machina* to release Thomas and Jennet and not only because he is so funny when drunk. Skipps is so satisfying also because he gives the illusion of what it is like to be ready for spring, to be functioning—no matter how imperfectly—as reasonable, believing, and enjoying person, all at once.

The alternative to taking on this life everlasting which so "takes it out of you" is the status quo, which Fry makes us in the audience see more as laughable and stupid than as desperately wicked. Fry makes us identify with Richard and Alizon, Thomas and Jennet. We laugh at the others, forgivingly. Then, just before the end of the play, the judgment turns on us in the theater (or in the library, or classroom, or living room, reading the text):

> Thomas: Do you see those roofs and spires?
> There sleep hypocrisy, porcous pomposity, greed,
> And all possible nitwittery—are you suggesting fifty
> Years of that?
>
> Jennet: I was only suggesting fifty
> Years of me.
>
> Thomas: Girl, you haven't changed the world.
> Glimmer as you will, the world's not changed.
> I love you, but the world's not changed. Perhaps
> I could draw you up over my eyes for a time
> But the world sickens me still. (94)

If our faith, reason, and aesthetics were all functioning to make us whole, the world outside the theater would be noticeably improved. The audience, like it or not, is not with the two happy couples, but with the others. Emotionally and aesthetically we identify with the health of the couples, but in real life we shun their kind of health. Fry's final judgment for the audience comes when Thomas said it would, twenty-two forty hours exactly (33).

The whole play is summarized in the last line of the play, spoken by Thomas: "And God have mercy on our souls" (95). There is no doubt that God can have mercy, because he has had mercy. He has elected Thomas into love so that he can pray this prayer, unprayable for him at the play's start. The prayer is its own answer. Besides, "And may God have mercy on *your* soul" is the formula which concludes formal sentencing of a condemned criminal. Had Tyson or Tappercoom pronounced the death sentence on Thomas or Jennet, the sentence would have included these words. A severe judgment is visited on Jennet and Thomas, to go on living and developing, a fate more difficult in some ways than death. It is the same judgment visited on the audience. "And God have mercy on *our* souls," as the play has it, means the following: We condemn each other and accept each other, just as we condemn ourselves and accept ourselves. We have no illusions about ourselves or each other. We expect mercy for each other just as we expect it for ourselves. The judgment in the love makes the love unsentimental; the love in the judgment makes wickedness seem foolish and laughable as well as wicked.

And, finally, ending the play with "And God have mercy on our souls" makes *soul(s)* the first and the last word of the play. If it is a nod in the direction of the "well-made play" of the turn of the century, it is a very meaningful nod. Act I begins with Richard pedantically poring over the mayor's accounts and Thomas interrupting him:

> Thomas Soul!
>
> Richard: —and the plasterer, that's fifteen groats—
>
> Thomas: Hey, soul!
>
> Richard: —for stopping the draught in the privy—
>
> Thomas: Body!
>
> You calculating piece of clay! (3)

At the beginning Thomas sees strangers as one or the other; he gives them the benefit of the doubt until again they disappoint him. By his own lights, Thomas, the Platonic aesthete, is tolerant here; actually he is a Platonic snob toward the pedestrian Richard. The beauty of the *last* line of the play—"And God have mercy on our souls"—is that it coincides with the moment of erotic attraction and physical contact between Thomas and Jennet. Their growing love and understanding throughout the play has always been too loaded with irony to allow any physical contact. Here and there Humphrey and Nicholas may make a pass or twitch a corner of her garment, but a romantic kiss and embrace—yea, even a hand-holding—would be inappropriate between Thomas and Jennet until this line or shortly before it. The word *soul* at the end of the play is not distinct from the body but thoroughly one with it. In D. H. Lawrence's sense, the body has become the soul. D. H. Lawrence and Christopher Fry are very close to essential Christianity at this point, even though Christianity is often Platonized beyond recognition. The immortality of the soul and the evil of human flesh and of the material world are Platonic ideas borrowed by Christianity. Yet the oldest creeds of Christianity affirm the resurrection of the body (not the immortality of the soul), affirm the incarnation (investing human flesh with a dignity unknown in Platonism), and assume the creation account of Genesis (which presents God declaring the material world good, repeatedly). The unity of body and soul, not their duality, underlies the unity of humankind's reason, aesthetic sense, and sense of God—underlies *Lady* and all of Fry's plays.

The last line, "And God have mercy on our souls," is a judgment on the Platonized audience, which resists living the full human life and prefers blindness and violence and struggle. The last line is a genuine prayer for mercy so that we in the audience can undertake the living of a fuller human life, under God.

Readers are now urged, before reading the concluding chapters, to forget this study; to read, or study, or see again Fry's living *Lady*; to envision for themselves what living a full human life would be like; to ponder why crocus life is so much more complete as crocus life than human life is complete as human life; in so pondering, to prepare themselves for the final judgment of the spring; and next spring and every spring, may God have mercy on our souls.[4]

13 HOW MANY BEANS MAKE SIX

A Synchronic View of Fry's Theology

The arithmetic
Of cause and effect I've never understood.
How many beans make five is an immense
Question, depending on how many
Preliminary beans preceded them.
The Dark is Light Enough, p. 97.

If Fry's plays were canonical scripture, this study could thus far be construed as what theologians call "Biblical Theology," helping the texts speak for themselves. In this chapter this study turns to collation and summary, a process theologians call "Systematic Theology," pursued usually under six rubrics: The Doctrine of God, of the Human Person, of Christ, of Salvation, of the Church, and of the Eschaton. They are the rubrics to be employed here.

THE DOCTRINE OF GOD

For Christopher Fry, as for any theist, God is prior to people, both in time and in importance. In deriving a theology from his plays, however, this study has placed the emphasis on characters, on people; God is spoken of in some of the plays, but God is a character in none of them (except by dream logic in *Sleep*). For Fry, man, both humanity collectively and persons individually, is the image of God; to find from the plays what Fry's image of God is, we look at the human persons. For Fry, theology is the basis for anthropology; for us the process of finding Fry's theology is reversed. Deriving Fry's theology from his anthropology is a matter of method, not of metaphysics.

A trinity found again and again in Fry's anthropology: a law-and-order rationalist (like Henry in *Curtmantle*), a true believer (like Becket), and an artist (like Eleanor). When these begin to integrate, the result is a romantic comedy (as in the seasonal comedies); when through stupidity they resist integration, the result is farce (as in Cool Clary in *Lady*, apart from the lovers); and when they resist integration through wickedness, the result is tragedy (as in *Curtmantle*). The closer these polarities come to each other, the closer they are to God, in whom the three are one.

Fry's anthropological trinity resists clicking into the traditional formulation of the Trinity, however. In the traditional view, God the Father is the creator; God the Son, the redeemer; and God the Holy Ghost, the sanctifier, working within human hearts. In the traditional view, God the Father is the least mystical of the three: the first cause, the prime mover, the static logical principle, whose primary work was finished on the sixth day of creation and whose secondary work continues in his good providence. The most mystical of the three is traditionally seen as God the Holy Ghost, the indwelling presence, both in the individual heart and in the company of believers, the Church. Fry's view of creation, providence, and the Church makes God the Father the most mystical member of the Trinity and God the Holy Ghost the least mystical.

Fry's conception of God the Father as creator is much influenced by contemporary theories of evolution. Hence, God as creator is not only objectively transcendent, but also subjectively immanent. God the Father is "the indwelling music which created us" (*Yard*, p. 107). Creation is unfinished for Fry in at least two senses: 1. humankind must help God finish creating the world and 2. the evolutionary process is still underway. These two are not, in fact, very different. In the process of producing what still needs producing out of the given raw materials, humankind comes closer to achieving the next rung on the evolutionary ladder, comes closer to being like God. When Cymen in *Thor* says that "lonely flesh" is "welcome to creation" (p. 154), both meanings lurk there: we are to help God create the world and we are to allow God, through the creatures, to go on creating us. Either way the essential loneliness is gone.

Merlin's position in *Thor* is like God the Father's in the cosmos. The cycles and seasons of evolutionary creation resemble the seasons of the year, except they move so much more slowly. In a single lifetime we cannot discern the evolutionary cycles: retrogression in the evolutionary winter, the creative spurt forward in the evolutionary spring, the growth of summer, and the gradual cessation of growth in autumn. Each of the seasons in the evolutionary cycles lasts centuries. Those are the cycles into which humankind is invited when it is welcomed into creation. We are welcomed into the yearly cycle of seasons by birth; being welcomed into the evolutionary cycle of seasons requires a spiritual rebirth.

The Holy Ghost, traditionally the mystical indwelling presence within the individual and within the Church, is seen by Fry as the ordering principle in society. Any community, not only the Church, is made possible through the work of the Holy Ghost. Any community in which the members increasingly become members one of another is the true Church, whether or not God the Holy Ghost is mentioned or believed in. In this sense Henry in *Curtmantle* does the work of the Holy Ghost, giving England its system of common law, thus making England more of a community.

The Church as institution which names God and teaches about the trinity is an institution to be guarded and loved. Knowing the formulations about the trinity can be a help to a community, just as a medical school's curriculum of physiology and hygiene can be a help to a community's health, but health does not depend on the medical school. The Church which names God correctly and teaches impeccable doctrine but whose members are not members one of another is an apostate Church, as secular as General Motors is thought commonly to be. Any community in which the members are increasingly becoming members one of another is the Church, blessed by the Holy Ghost, even though it never names God—and even though that community is General Motors. The work of the Holy Ghost among us is as non-mystical as people getting along together. Fry's theology of the Holy Ghost gives particular urgency to the words of St. Paul that "the fruits of the Spirit is love, joy, peace, patience, kindness, goodness, faithfulness, gentleness, and self-control" (Galatians 5:22–23). In short, the work of the Holy Ghost among us is the promotion of non-violence.

The irony is that, like Henry, we make schemes for promoting non-violence that require violence for implementation. The most warlike states and individuals indulge their violence only on behalf of their sweetly reasonable demands: the new order, which will bring love, joy, peace, patience, and the other fruits of the Spirit to more people. This blindness to violence in the self makes violence such a "stubborn aberration" (*Sleep*, p. 207). The only way to resist violence is not by being violent but by submitting to the violence of other people voluntarily.

The Son of God resisted violence by enduring it and overcoming it, as all of us may. It is Fry's doctrine of the atonement and of the resurrection. The emphasis is away from the pecuniary formula: debts accounted to sinners by God the Judge and debts paid vicariously by Jesus Christ in the currency of blood. Nor is the emphasis in Fry's theory on Christ as an example of moral excellence, so common in liberal theology a half-century ago. In overcoming violence, Christ showed that death might be overcome and the next step in the evolutionary process taken. Darwinian biology, to which Fry's theory of creation otherwise owed so much, keeps looking forward to the next step in the evolutionary process; the next step in the evolutionary process has already been taken, according to Fry, in the resurrection of Jesus Christ, in a body that passed through walls and yet digested food. It is the kind of body that can be ours if we identify ourselves by faith with the person of Jesus Christ and then, non-violently, promote his non-violent purpose.

In addition to the doctrines of atonement and resurrection, also the doctrine of the incarnation involves the Son of God. The Godhead assuming perfect flesh is like the ultimate content taking on the most physical of forms. That is why any art work at all, when content finds its appropriate form, is an analogical repetition of the incarnation. In high art like Gettner's and in ordinary crafts like Cuthman's are echoes of the incarnation. In aesthetic delight like that of Ana-Clara, Eleanor, and Thomas ("What a wonderful thing is metaphor," *Lady*, p.5) is a human response approaching worship. The aesthetic experience is, for Fry, much more than a behaviorist's predictable response to a given stimulus; the aesthetic response—even if the work admired is pagan, blasphemous, and immoral—is like the worship of an incarnate God; in admiring the work and in worshiping the Lord, we admire and worship the form that is so appropriate to the content. It is not only the *doctrine* of the incarnation that makes aesthetics so important, but also the *fact* of it. The aesthetic experience arises not from theorizing but from breathing, from being alive at all. It is why all the aesthetes in Fry's plays are so engrossed in physicality, to mention only Ana-Clara, Eleanor of Aquitaine, and Thomas Mendip again. Only a God who calls physicality good could ever become incarnate; and physicality could be as good as it is only if its creator thought flesh worthy enough to take it on.

THE DOCTRINE OF THE HUMAN PERSON

Fry redefines sin as violence. Violence against another human being is always violence against God, since humankind is God's dearest creation. But then, God loves all he has made; violent squandering of natural resources is not only an insult to the resources, but to God. Fry's sacramental respect for the physical world results in a reinterpretation of the Genesis myth. The original command was not an arbitrary test-trap to catch humankind. The command also came out of God's respect for a particular tree he had made for a particular purpose—a purpose which requires double vision to appreciate, a vision taking God's attitude into account as well as one's own, one's own single vision coming down to, "I like it. Why can't I have it?" In short, the original sin was bad *division* of God's *provision*, as *Boy* employs the terms. Proper division, use of God's gifts, can only happen when humankind sees (or tries to see) God's point-of-view, as a provider, and then actively joins God in providing. God, in the incarnation, also joins humankind in the distinctively human task of dividing. So God and humankind work shoulder to shoulder as providers and dividers when things are right.

Proper division happens in two ways: 1. humankind must divide and analyze all the creatures possible, to see what they can contribute to human happiness, and 2. humankind must also see that the creatures on earth are fairly divided. The first of the two tasks is humankind's animal assignment. The survivor in the evolutionary struggle is the creature that uses its environment wisely, finding as many uses as possible for every lower creature. The second task is assigned when the animal takes on humanity when God lets humanity rule. Later, in the incarnation, God takes on humankind's task of division in both senses, and the distinction between provision and division, both kinds of division, falls away.

The Genesis account of the origin of sin is psychological in its orientation—what it felt like to humankind. Actually, the historical account must have gone something like this: Selfish division was all humankind knew at the start. Humankind needed it to survive the evolutionary struggle. Gaining what it wanted, not abstaining, was its prenocent animal method of evolving; serving its own comfort and advantage was its only motivation. In the command to abstain from a particular tree, God was actually revealing to humankind: humankind's animal nature. Humankind could not abstain from what it desired precisely because its survival until then had depended on desiring and having. Through the forbidden tree, humankind not so much fell as learned its fallenness, its animality, its lack of control of self. The human creature knew it was selfish and violent and in imperfect communication with God, and in that sense it had lost its animal innocence. Before, its division had been only to support itself and, if necessary, to kill its competition. Now, even in the interests of developing a relationship with God, the person cannot break the old habit of violently taking what is wanted. So too, killing the weaker was no new phenomenon in the evolutionary process, but when Cain killed Abel for the first time there was guilt because of a new consciousness of God. At the moment of the new consciousness of God, at that moment humankind had achieved the rung on the evolutionary ladder on which it was distinctively human. The discovery that its task was to be its brother's keeper, even if that meant abstaining from what it wanted, made it know good and evil, although it is too caught up in the animal struggle even now to choose the good consistently. What felt like a fall psychologically was actually an animal's evolving into the status of responsible humanity, even though it cannot live up to it.

Though division in the second sense is humankind's distinctive task, people fail at it in three forms of violence: 1. outright greediness, either for personal gain like Edmondo's or for the good of the State like David King's; 2. passive detachment from the goods of earth, either for personal escape like Peter Abel's or for a total redistribution of good, no matter who steals from whom, like Roberto's; 3. an unimpassioned drift to whatever position seems more comfortable, like Joe Adams in *Sleep* or like Luigi in *Yard*, no power emanating from them for change, even though Joe Adams is the corporal in charge and Luigi has been on the reigning Nazi side. Peter and Roberto are actively passive, passivity having become a positive program; but Luigi and Joe are passively active, tepid members of strong causes, half-heartedly going through the motions of allegiance. In all three there is an anti-trinity of unregenerate humanity: active attachment, passive detachment, and slothful indifference; these are negative parallels to reason, faith, and aesthetics, respectively.

THE DOCTRINE OF CHRIST

The next step in the evolutionary process was taken by Jesus Christ, who, as God, took on humanhood; not ceasing to provide, he joined humankind in dividing; not taking away humanity's dividing, he added to it the distinctive work of God, providing. In Jesus Christ the work of God and the work of humankind are totally one. Again and again he displayed his reasonable side, cleansing the temple and lecturing the pharisees; his intuitive awareness of God, his faith, as at the transfiguration or in the high-priestly prayer (John 16–18); and his aesthetic sensibility, telling parables and framing those cryptic paradoxes called beatitudes.

In this state, God and humanity totally united, Jesus Christ could submit himself to the violence left over from the earlier evolutionary struggle—to be divided by his predatory brothers—and survive the experience of death. The next step in the evolutionary process is the new body Jesus Christ acquired in his resurrection. Jesus Christ has sloughed off the last remnants of animality, of the law of the jungle, by submitting to the law of the jungle, and thus has achieved the unambiguous, uncompromised humanity that all of us may achieve.

This uncompromised humanity is what makes Christianity unique among the religions of the world. The other religions all aspire to sloughing off the essential animality of predatory competition, but only Christianity can show an example of anyone who so thoroughly sloughed off his animality that his body, though it died like any animal body, lived again. Though based on an animal body, it was no longer subject to the physical restraints of an animal body. Christianity is the only religion which has succeeded in the quest of all religions—

—including Judaism. Judaism, along with all other non-Christian religions, lacks the evidence of a resurrection, the next step forward in the evolutionary process. That puts Judaism at the level of all other religions, but it also puts all other religions on the level of Judaism. As Jesus Christ fulfilled Judaism, so Jesus Christ can fulfill every religion in the world. The Old Testament is a pagan scripture, anticipating the full revelation of the New Testament, just as any pagan scripture does. Just as Christianity and its New Testament fulfilled the Old Testament, so Christianity and its New Testament can fulfill any pagan scripture. The complete Bible is a paradigm of the first conquest of a pagan religion by Christianity, brought on by historical accident, since Jesus Christ was brought up in Judaism. Just as Christianity conquered Judaism, so it may fulfill and conquer any pagan religion—

—including itself. As soon as Christianity settles into orthodoxy, ceasing to struggle for the next level of being, Christianity itself settles into paganism again. There is no declared orthodoxy without the danger of dead orthodoxy, which deludes itself by thinking it has arrived. Only if Jesus Christ is the fulfillment of dead orthodox Christianity can he be the fulfillment of any pagan religion; only if Jesus Christ is the potential fulfillment of all the pagan religions of the world can he be the actual fulfillment of any, including dead orthodox Christianity—

—and the fulfillment of Greek dualism, so pervasive in the doctrine and creeds of orthodox Christianity. Fry so closely identifies body with soul as to obliterate the difference. Orthodox Christianity is more Greek than Christian in its dualism: body and soul, the primacy of the soul over the body, the human and divine natures of Christ. Yet, traditional Christianity also affirms, not the Greek idea of the immortality of the soul, but the resurrection of the body. It is this non-Greek strain in Christianity that Fry emphasizes.

THE DOCTRINE OF SALVATION

The escape from the *civitas mundi* into the *civitas dei* is made possible by the action of God, objectively in the incarnation, atonement, and resurrection of Jesus Christ, and subjectively within the hearts of individuals and in the collective spirits of communities, in the application of the incarnation, atonement, and resurrection to them. Preaching, sacraments, and the general ministry of the church are useful interpretive actions of God's work in the world, but not the cause of it. God, as the indwelling presence, causes individuals and communities to identify with the redemptive work of Jesus Christ. This identification means that they increasingly put behind themselves the competition and violence of the *civitas mundi*. All individuals and communities begin with a childish passive aggression, and some stay there. Some progress through an aggressive phase on behalf of a cause, and some progress even further to an aggressive phase on behalf of God. The final phase is enduring aggression, and when no arrested development impairs, we survive death from aggression just as Jesus Christ did.

Without violence there is no redemption, since any redemption without bloodshed and suffering ignores the fact that bloodshed and suffering are exactly what we are being redeemed from, a violence usually recognized when it is inflicted on us and unrecognized when we are inflicting it on others. Violence is our only means of redemption; otherwise we close our eyes and must be content with an illusion of redemption.

To think one is redeemed from violence without confronting violence within is always the result of myopia among the ways of knowing: reason, faith, and aesthetics. Such myopia—emphasizing one way of knowing at the expense of the rest—gets institutionalized and turns violent against the other institutionalized myopias. To make no progress away from the myopia is inevitable tragedy. To heal all myopia is Fry's concept of total comedy—impossible to sustain in our present state for more than a glimpse, as at the palio in *Yard*—and its definition is joy. In our present range of experience an objective, intellectual comedy must sustain us. Sin and evil, that is to say, must become laughing matters, though to say so does not mean "laughing away" or "laughter as ignoring," the usual meanings of "laughing matters." Laughter is a sure sign of forgiveness, God's forgiveness of us and our forgiveness of each other. If God has removed a particular sin from us as far as east is from west, then it is also far enough removed from us to let us see its foolishness. To the extent that we are not able to laugh at a sin, to that extent we are not willing to let God remove it as far as east is from west, to that extent we are hugging the sin closely to ourselves and living in a tragic pattern rather than in a comic one. In a parallel way, the evil we suffer from others is tragic as long as we do not see its foolishness as well as its wickedness. The comic response is analytical and forgiving, making comedy as profound as tragedy—though in a world where redemption cannot be perfect there will always be enough unresolved evil in human life to keep tragedy appropriate.

Nor is all laughter redemptive, comic laughter. The laughter of a baby tickled under its chin is like most of our laughter: an automatic physiological response to artificial stimulation. It is like the laughter of farce, not based on analysis, insight, or forgiveness. But the paradigm for comedy at its best is the gospel of Jesus Christ. The gospel is caught on to, just as a joke is. What is caught on to may be explained, but it is seldom the explanation that makes us laugh or believe the gospel.

Since total joy is beyond us, our comic quest on earth is always open-ended, keeping alive what has been found and stretching for more insight, hence more profound comedy, hence even more adventurous exploration. In this middle ground—being released from the tragic pattern of the *civitas mundi*, yet still not free of all violence, within us or around us—in this muddled world, the least violent option is always the most moral and the most comic (and to those observing from the vantage point of the *civitas mundi*, the most comical) alternative. From the vantage point of the *civitas dei*, one assumes forgiveness for one's self, provides a comic-forgiving context for others, and, forgiving the wickedness in violence, celebrates the foolishness in it with laughter. Even the least likely sinner, like Gettner, is capable of change given the comic-forgiving context.

Growth in forgiveness must be linked to the flesh or forgiveness becomes more and more cerebral, spiritual, and Greek. Linking forgiveness and comedy keeps the doctrine of forgiveness within the focus of the incarnation, of the fleshliness of our life on earth in God. Any growth in religious desire cannot occur without the flesh, in Fry's view, or without the physical world, the book of the creatures. Sex awakens within human beings hungers stronger than sex can satisfy. The hunger in sex is the disguised hunger for God. One learns through attachment to the creatures what love is; the more one loves the creatures, the greater the capacity for loving God. The false dichotomy of much Platonized theology, God versus the creatures, is foreign to Fry's thought, since it is through the creatures that a person learns to love at all. As the creatures show their inability to fully satisfy love, the lover learns to seek a perfect love in God.

God and humankind cooperate in the learning process. Both are active in each other's activity. Whatever God reveals, humankind must not merely passively accept but still needs to work at discovering for itself. Whatever humankind discovers, no matter how great its own industry and ingenuity, God reveals. Revelation requires, as does everything else in Fry's world, double vision to appreciate how human activity and divine activity do not have their own mutually exclusive autonomies.

Single vision is such habit in a world of common sense that to avoid committing ourselves to a teleology in interpreting our experiences we use the phrase "it was only a coincidence" to mean "there is no meaning in what happened to me." When someone we love is run over by a train, we temporarily take comfort in saying, "With God there are no coincidences." Grief past, we pick up our reasonable single vision again. So afraid is a certain school of philosophy of the hidden agenda of teleology that it will go only so far as to say "It is raining" and "The pavement is wet" but not so far as to say "The pavement is wet because it is raining." It is a coincidence, presumably, that it is raining and the pavement is wet. The philosophers who consider the falling rain and the wet pavement a coincidence, such philosophers would also consider it a coincidence that this morning's sunrise occurred at the precise time that yesterday's paper predicted. And the same defense against teleology would result in calling it a coincidence that Jesus said to the stormy sea, "Peace, be still," and that it was still. And while few of us would go as far as these philosophers in denying cause and effect, few of us also, if we were eye-witnesses, would accept the stilling of the storm by Jesus without resorting to the explanation of coincidence. The word *coincidence* is no explanation at all, of course. It simply means, "I refuse to study the matter further."

Every event can be seen as a coincidence or as a miracle, in Fry's view—and must be regarded in both ways simultaneously, with double vision, if we are to be released from an unpatterned chaos and led into a teleology. Nor is it enough to employ the terms alternatively: miracles in the Bible and in cases of fatal accidents to those we love, but coincidences the rest of the time.

What Fry has built into his plays as a teleology is often construed as coincidence. Increasingly over the last two centuries, our literature has been concerned with character, events being disposed to reveal individual idiosyncracies. Episodic events reveal character; and when the events themselves become plotted, our fear of teleology—especially a teleology that involves miracles—makes us dismiss such a plot as "full of coincidences." Yet Fry's purpose is to express a teleology, to reveal the miraculous aspect of even our predictable, everyday lives. The plays, therefore, constitute a kind of test for whether Fry has inducted us into a world where double vision is necessary or whether we find ourselves resorting, in fear of teleology, to the typical dismissal of miracles as coincidences. The plays are valuable for the cause of Christianity because they present a Christianity definite enough to accept or reject. In fact, the plays have the power to smell out from people who consider themselves Christians the admission that the gospel offends their sense of rationality, their single vision, which keeps humanity at an animal level in the evolutionary scale—a very sophisticated and complex animal, mind you, but an animal just the same—and keeps society a sophisticated jungle of survival of the fittest.

Religious humanity—the highest humanity—begins with the recognition of paradox in human experience, with double vision; then double vision grows into multiple vision, the recognition that even the simplest phenomenon (like how many beans make five) is an immense philosophical question with many apparently contradictory issues involved in its consideration. Just as Jesus saw all human experience from the parallel perspectives of reason (shown in his cleansing the temple and lecturing pharisees), of faith (shown in the eloquent mystical prayer in the sixteenth and seventeenth chapters in St. John's gospel), and of aesthetics (shown in his carefully crafted parables and in those gnomic proverbs, the beatitudes), so every Christian may and must increasingly integrate the elements in one's own life and thus become a more accurate bearer of the image of God. When all three of these are present but not well-integrated, the result is a clown like the Chaplain in *Lady*: good, but weak and totally ineffectual in leadership. When only one of the qualities is present, the result is a tragic character like Henry II in *Curtmantle* or Seti in *Firstborn*. When two of the qualities are present, in paradox with each other, the result is double vision, a paradoxical reading of reality, like that of Moses in *Firstborn*. When none of the three are present, the result is a subhuman existence like that of the Phipps brothers in *Boy*. When the three are present and well-integrated, the result is a saint with multiple vision, like Rosmarin in *Dark*.

Spiritual health, like physical health, is a grace granted and a condition attained through hard work, both, whether complete spiritual health (that is, multiple vision, sainthood) or partial spiritual health (that is, double vision). Whoever begins, however slightly, to work shoulder to shoulder with God has the beginning of double vision; such persons will also find themselves finally completely healthy, with multiple vision, with sainthood—either inside of time or outside of time.

People with multiple or double vision end up very differently from those with a secular single vision. At any given moment on earth, however, very few people have achieved multiple vision, and even those who have share, as one view among many, the secular viewpoint—as do those with the double paradoxical vision. The secular view is wrong because it is limited, but this view is part of what the paradoxical and multiple minds also see. For that reason, it is hard to distinguish the secular mind from the religious minds (double and multiple) at any one time. Intellectual and moral ambivalences keep the religious minds and the secular mind looking more alike for us now than in fact they are *sub species aeternitatis.*

THE DOCTRINE OF THE CHURCH

Spiritual progress must be made collectively by communities as well as by individuals. One cannot live happily with multiple vision unless the whole community shares that vision. Any group which makes spiritual progress is the church, even though the group is General Motors or General Mills. Any group which is not progressing to a double vision, let alone to a multiple vision of reality, is paganism, even though the group calls itself a Christian church. When a church loses its capacity for double and multiple vision, doctrinal matters may, in fact, matter a great deal, but the spiritual reality behind the doctrines is ignored.

A definition of heaven is a community that has achieved multiple vision, collectively, in all relationships within the community. Each member of the community has also achieved multiple vision. When a single individual makes much more progress than the rest of the community, the result is martyrdom. The supreme example is Jesus Christ, who achieved perfect multiple vision, thus achieving the next step in the evolutionary process on behalf of the community that killed him. Had he done what he did on his own behalf, the vision would not yet have been multiple. He loved the very community which murdered him—an example of the multiple vision.

What is needed now is not another Christ to demonstrate again what has already been demonstrated, that living by the multiple vision of faith is the entry into a reality so much more profound than everyday reality that it conquers everyday reality, including death and all lesser evils of everyday reality. What is needed now is general consciousness raising, because the danger is that individuals may either progress too fast and risk being martyrs or may naively wish themselves to be more Christlike than in fact they are and may hypocritically pretend to be so. Awareness that progress, both individual and collective, is indispensable and slow—that awareness is necessary for us to make our way with poise in the here-and-now. As Fry says, "For the most part we take creation for granted, or something only to be expected. Only to be expected: creation! Insensibility can't get nearer lunacy than that, though without some degree of it we could hardly get through our day-to-day lives."[1] Since what is needed is general consciousness raising, not the individual demonstration to show what can be achieved, individual ardor must cool to a temperature usable by the community. Henry II is a martyr, not only because of his myopic concern for reasonable law and order (to the neglect of aesthetics and faith), but also because he thought he could rush the community. Spiritual progress must be undertaken in the name of the group, not in the name of power and wanting to be the leader, since Jesus Christ is already the leader.

Although General Motors can theoretically do the work of the church as well as the church can, it is unlikely that General Motors will, because General Motors is even more myopically concerned with money-making common sense than is the church. Theoretically any institution can take over the tasks of the church—keeping the Christian gospel alive by word of mouth and by administration of the sacraments: baptism, conveying an identity and name on a person, and communion, eating and drinking together in celebration of the new identity. The church must allow itself to be threatened into thinking it can be replaced—by any institution that thinks of better ways of speaking the implications of the gospel, of conferring identity, and of breaking and sharing bread and wine equitably and with double vision, literal and non-literal meaning, simultaneously.

Spiritual progress, as *Thor* points out, is the result of God's work within individuals and communities and not the result of persuasion—persuasion often mistaken for grace in the polemical and dialectical history of Christianity. The proclamation of the word is necessary to explain the progress within a person or a community from single vision to double vision to multiple vision. The word is necessary to interpret spiritual awakening and progress, but preaching is not the cause.

Traditionally, the sacraments are seen as an ordinary meal and ordinary bathing elevated to holy significance. Affirming all of that, Fry adds the dimension of all meals and all bathings and all physical experiences turning holy. The symbolic movement is not only from ordinary experience to the sacraments, but also from communion and baptism to everyday experience again. Recall, in this connection, the imagery in the eating and drinking scene from *Phoenix*:

Dynamene: A mystery's in the world
Where a little liquid, with flavour, quality, and fume
Can be as no other, can hint and flute our senses
As though a music played in harvest hollows
And a movement was in the swathes of our memory.
Why should scent, why should flavour come
With such wings upon us? Parsley, for instance.

Tegeus: Seaweed.

Dynamene: Lime trees.

Doto: Horses.

Tegeus: Fruit in the fire. (20)

This set piece on the communion implies that the institution of communion in the world will not have done its work until all scent, all sense experience, all eating and drinking—until all of our life on earth in all of its physicality is seen in a religious context as well as in the literal context which we call reality.

Potentially, then, as was mentioned earlier, any institution—from the family to General Motors—can beat the church at its own game: explaining the changes that God is working within people and communities, and demonstrating how any physical experience is more than simply physical experience, that is, by word and sacrament. The church explains and demonstrates that every physical experience has at the very least a religious dimension in paradox with the literal one, and beyond that paradox an expanding multiple meaning. The church's task will not be finished until families and General Motors and all institutions in the world have taken over the job of the church: getting reason, faith, and aesthetics properly disposed. Since all institutions have myopic purposes—most commonly exalting reason above the other two faculties and then trivializing reason by using it only to make money—the church is in no imminent danger of being out of a job. To the extent that the church's own purpose turns secularly myopic—like, toward making money—to that extent the church needs to be threatened that any other institution could do the work of the church as well. Otherwise the church will turn pagan again in its smugness, thus becoming a prison for its members, as dead orthodoxy inevitably becomes: a violent dead orthodoxy, unaware of its own violence. To the extent that the church is not threatened by having other institutions achieve double vision and multiple vision, in word and act, to that extent the church is being most true to itself: is content to work itself out of its job, since the whole lump of society is being leavened. To the extent that the church sees itself as expendable, to that extent it can be an agent for bringing about Christ's Kingdom: a total life style, for individuals and communities, in which the multiple, open-ended vision of God's progressive creativity is the informing principle.

THE DOCTRINE OF THE ESCHATON

The perfect community, in which each member has achieved multiple vision, is both a state achieved through effort and a grace granted, no matter how little or how much one has achieved. Those who worked all day in Christ's parable, bearing the full heat of the day, got the same penny given to those who worked only one hour. It is interesting in this connection that Fry's first title for *Yard* was *The Heat of the Day.*

Christ achieved a preview of humankind's evolutionary breakthrough: time ceased to bind him as he approached the breakthrough of the resurrection, for he conversed with Elijah and Moses, centuries dead; space ceased to matter in the same way, for though after the resurrection his wounds were real enough for Thomas to examine empirically, he appeared among his disciples without passing through doors.

When humankind achieves the total evolutionary breakthrough —each person and the total community as well—time and space will cease to matter. The same grace will then be granted to all those, centuries dead, who, in their own limited experience, trapped as they were in their own corrupt institutions, could not come close to the breakthrough.

Those few who made no progress at all in the spiritual pilgrimage, die like the animals they are. The ancient cosmology of hell, heaven, and earth midway between them is superseded in Fry's thought by an evolutionary model of a renewed universe. The idea of hell was a pedagogical device to aid the coming of God's Kingdom, but it was not satisfactory even as a pedagogical device, for people served God for the wrong reasons and slowed their progress. The poet's not for—in favor of—burning.

Progress is still slow, and centuries will pass before violence is eliminated and all people are members one of another, at which point death and the urgency of time are also eliminated. Then all who have made any progress at all in their own generation's quest for God, from the origin of the human race until the present, will live again in a body like Christ's after his resurrection. The slowness of our progress makes the cause of eliminating violence, achieving multiple vision, and bringing in Christ's Kingdom very urgent indeed. All the past generations of the race wait for us— and our generation again disappoints them. But still, the first evolutionary breakthrough, Christ's, has occurred, and the rest will inevitably follow.

For the moment, death gives time not only its urgency, but also a peculiarly intense delight, Fry argues. Every delightful experience turns poignant as well as delightful because it will not always be available. "Death is a kind of love," Fry argues, because we treasure delight in a way that would be absurd if we had world enough and time. Though the glory of a greater simultaneity of past, present, and future will be part of human experience after the next major evolutionary progression, the glory of this phase of the human evolutionary progression is the present:

> One thought that is always turning up, surprising me afresh each time, is that I am aware of being alive, *now*. Of all the thousands of years when I might have lived and died, it is this

> moment which is present with me; *now*, of all times, that eternity is flying through my brevity; *now*, that I am aware of moving towards the mountain range of death and the mystery beyond it; *now*, that I can look out on the downland slope of my window as Henry Vaughan once looked out on his Breconshire hill.[2]

It is in the present that we can progress from single, to double, to multiple vision, and only in the present that we can do so.

The limitation of the terminology *single, double*, and *multiple vision* is that it implies only a way of looking at our lives in the world, an epistemology, rather than a total manner of living in it. The coming of the eschaton requires not only the community's seeing right and thinking straight, but also doing right and being straight. At this point Fry's thought approaches that of his friend, Charles Williams, the theory of exchange: the way Jesus could take on himself the sins of the whole world—past, present, and future—is the pattern for how individuals can take on themselves the burdens of their fellow human beings. Exchange is more than a sympathetic understanding of a fellow sufferer's misery; through prayer it is possible to assume the other's pain temporarily, to feel it as one's own because it has left the other person and become one's own. It is the way Jennet and Thomas bear each other's burdens, how the Bruno brothers adjust to each other for the sake of the palio, how Gettner absorbs the strength of the Countess into himself at her death, how the four prisoners dream themselves into community, how Perpetua makes everyone else in the play come true, and how Dynamene gives her husband's death the power of new life. All of the plays turn, in some sense, on the idea of exchange.

Similar as Fry's ideas are to that of the Inklings on this point of exchange, and particularly to C. S. Lewis and Charles Williams,[3] there remain enormous differences. For Lewis and Williams, the basis for that idea of exchange is a Platonic rationalism: there can be no true archetype without lesser types in the visible, everyday world. If Christ could bear our sins and miseries and thus remove them, there must be lesser senses in which we can bear and remove each other's sins and miseries. The typical validates the archetypical, and the archetype points up the inadequacy of the typical. "Bear ye one another's burden and thus fulfil the Law of Christ (Galatians 6:2) needs obeying by people to validate the Law of Christ as a law. The law of exchange by which humanity was redeemed by Christ in the atonement is not even an absolute law, unless we can see it repeated, partially and imperfectly, on the level of individuals to each other. The Royal Law of bearing each other's burdens is ontologically necessary for Lewis and Williams, regardless of eschatology, God himself bringing the eschaton about supernaturally.

"Bear ye one another's burdens and thus fulfil the Law of Christ" has an eschatological dimension for Fry. When the Royal Law of Christ is fulfilled, when everybody has grown adept at bearing the other's burden, the burdens will have disappeared and the eschaton will have come. For Williams and Lewis the theory of exchange is necessary logically, may or may not influence the lives of individuals existentially, and is independent from the eschaton. For Fry, the exchange is not logically necessary to round out a system; it is existentially necessary in human experience because it is by means of exchanges between persons that God will bring about the eschaton.

For early plays like *The Firstborn* the terminology of single, double, and multiple vision is totally adequate; for late plays like *A Yard of Sun* the terminology of single, double, and multiple vision is no longer adequate without the stipulation that vision is no longer to be construed in a narrowly epistemological sense, but rather something much more like what Williams and Lewis mean by *exchange*: refusing to exchange being like single vision, exchanging with one other person being like double vision, and exchanging with many people being like multiple vision. Until now under the rubric of the eschaton, I have avoided using the term *exchange* extensively, lest readers plug Fry's more existential Christianity into the more rationalistic Christianity of Williams and Lewis. The theology of Lewis and Williams has often been described, and making Fry ride their band wagon would be unfair to all three, the difference between Fry and the others on the eschaton being very clear indeed. For the others the eschaton is purely a grace granted; for Fry the eschaton is a grace granted, to be sure, but also a state to be achieved.

A tally of six doctrines implied in Fry's plays is as limited a response to Fry's theology as to answer the question "How many beans make five?" with an automatic, "Well, five, of course."

Unless the tally here sends readers back to the plays themselves to discover Fry's theology, this chapter—and this book—is wasted. The world of literary criticism and systematic theology is not the world of Chromis the colorful but of Virilius the bookkeeper, who wrote down the extremely complicated gods in seventy parallel columns. No matter. Should Chromis and Dynamene set up housekeeping, they will need to file income tax forms just like anybody else, and anybody who thinks about God at all needs some tally to keep the thoughts from turning random—to remember what those thoughts about God are.

DEFENDING GOD'S DEFENDER 14

Fry's theology, as described here, is neither liberal nor conservative. If the assignment of persons in the Trinity to task and personality is unconventional, the doctrine of the Trinity itself is traditional. If substituting *violence* for *sin* seems liberal, the desperateness of the affliction, the stubborn aberration, is worthy of a Calvinist's concern with depravity. Considering dead orthodoxy and Judaism to be equal to paganism is iconoclastic; insisting on the uniqueness of Christianity is orthodox. Calling Christianity unique because it claims the next step in the evolutionary process is iconoclastic; claiming the uniqueness of Christianity on the basis of the resurrection is orthodox. Claiming that any community that eliminates violence is the church (even if it seems to be a factory community) and that any community that allows violence to thrive is not the church (even if it is, nominally, a church), that seems typically liberal; actually, behind the iconoclasm is a minor prophet's concern that the institutional church, which Fry guards and loves, should eliminate nominal Christianity and become zealous for its cause. Eliminating violence as equal to redemption seems liberal do-goodism, the social gospel; developing double or multiple vision as the means to do it—developing the eye of faith—seems a reworking of the old Protestant idea of justification by faith. Heaven as a state to be worked for and achieved in the eschaton is like the liberal gospel of post-millenialism; heaven as a grace granted is the Christian hope expressed in an almost fundamentalist, pre-millenial ethos. Fry is neither, is both.

Christian theology in the Western world since the Renaissance has been hopelessly involved in liberal-conservative debates, liberals pressing for secularization of Christian ideas and conservatives reacting by clinging tenaciously to the status quo, finally yielding (on the flatness of the earth issue, say) only when liberals have focused on another icon (like biological evolution). Whenever liberals score another secular victory over conservatives, the guardians of supernaturalism, theology turns a shade more inimical to the supernatural interpretation of the Bible or of life. Since the 1920's the popular mind has equated liberal Christianity with do-goodism and conservative Christianity with militant doctrinalism. At a more sophisticated academic level, liberal theology demythologizes the Bible myths and conservative theology argues for the literalness of the scriptural account.

Not a professional theologian, Fry is neither a conservative nor a liberal and thus escapes the polemical trap. In the light of what he knows from the contemporary sciences, he must adjust his doctrine of the Trinity, and in the light of recent history, he must change his definition of sin. No matter, for his modification of traditional dogmas is never less supernatural than is the received orthodox view, nor does it ever ascribe more power to natural and/or psychological law and less to God than does the received orthodox view. Though liberal theologians will consider him conservative and conservative theologians will consider him liberal, he is neither. Nor is he bland and middle-of-the-road, attempting to offend no one. He begins by affirming what through the ages has been thought by Christians to be God's revelation to humankind, and then he adjusts it subtly to square with contemporary anthropology and cosmology. That adjustment is free from cant because it is not rooted in the polemic of irreverent iconoclasm on the one hand or of beleaguered orthodoxy on the other.

What gives rise to this unique ethos for doing theology is Fry's doctrine of God's revelation to humankind and humankind's response. "God does not need to be named to be worshipped," Fry has written to me repeatedly.[1] It is the reason his plays for the secular theater establishment, in which he does not name God, are intended to praise God just as much as the plays he has written for church. God's not needing to be named to be worshipped implies that there are no distinctions at all between sacred and secular, except in human limitation. Taking in the sacred dimension of the secular, as well as the secular dimension of the sacred, imposes a strain on our limited human sensibility, but God sees no distinction at all. He reveals himself progressively in many ways—in people and in the created universe as well as in the Bible and in the person of Jesus Christ. For Fry, creation is not a static given, nor is humanity a static given, nor is the process of humankind's redemption a static given. Sometimes we get contradictory signals from scientists (students of God's physical creation), church people (custodians of humankind's history of redemption), and artists (custodians of what humankind holds beautiful). But God gives no contradictory signals. Human reception of God's signals is faulty, and, hence, what we learn at the university seems often to contradict what we hear in church. Liberal theologians are too eager immediately to compromise on the side of the university, partly because their tenured chairs of theology are part of the university. Conservative theologians are too eager to listen only to the historical church, and the church typically knuckles under to the evidence from the university only after it has already lost credibility. But Fry is neither a liberal nor a conservative, a spokesman neither for the university nor for the church.

Fry's opinion is that humankind's ideas of God evolve as human persons evolve, and that tenet has a university ring to it; but humankind's ideas of God evolve so slowly that brash and iconoclastic confrontations are unintellectual responses to the whole truth. Every discovery in science ought to modify our idea of God a little, since God reveals himself in the physical world. Every breakthrough in the humanities ought to modify our idea of God a little, since God reveals himself not only *to* humankind, but also *through* humankind. That the university and the church are not close allies is a monument not only to liberal, secular apostasy, but also to a religious dogmatism grown insensitive to God's continuing revelation of himself in nature and history as well as in the Bible and in church.

From Fry's central tenet, that God does not need to be named to be worshipped, all the other modifications of orthodox dogma flow, as discussed in the preceding chapter. The truth of any of his single modifications of orthodox dogma is not as important as that Christians should not allow their idea of God to be trapped and static. Disagree with any of Fry's modifications of orthodoxy, whoever wishes to, but God must not be turned into the static graven image of dead orthodoxy by anyone who has confronted God as Fry presents him.

Freeing God—that is, freeing our conception of God—has been the purpose behind his plays. Behind the plots of his plays is a poetic structure, intimately connected with the plot structure. This poetic structure has been the concern of each of the chapters written on the plays in this book. This poetic structure is also, as has been shown, some statement about humankind's evolving idea of God, whether or not God is named in the play. The poetic structure suggested by the dramatic structure is sometimes more than the ear discovers listening to the plays. The poetic structure is first of all intuited and enjoyed, not analyzed, but analysis helps us discover what was intuited and enjoyed. The plays exist to liberate God from the liberal-conservative straitjacket.

That the poetry is in the plays for the sake of raising consciousness about God is incomprehensible to a certain kind of critic. God, they maintain, is in the plays for the sake of the poetry. Consider Denis Donoghue: "Mr. Fry's pronouncements on poetry, reality, and verse drama have been unsatisfactory. His most representative statement is that 'what we *call* reality is a false god, the dull eye of custom.' The echo from Wordsworth is interesting, but it leads to the dubious equation of Prose with Verisimilitude, and of Poetry with Truth."[2] Almost everything Mr. Donoghue says about Fry is backwards. The ordering ought to be like this: Verse drama now and then breaks into poetry (what I have called the poetic structure of the plays, behind the plot), and poetry now and then points to an open-ended reality—God's. By listing "poetry, reality, and verse drama" in that order, Donoghue at best obscures how these are related for Fry and at worst totally trivializes Fry's use of the word *reality*, as though poetry and reality exist for the sake of a peculiar and precious species of verse drama. The dubious equation of Wordsworth and Fry itself betrays Donoghue's lack of comprehension. True, both Fry and Wordsworth (*Ode*, VIII) deplore the stifling custom, but Wordsworth does it in the name of childhood's God which once was and Fry does it in the name of an evolving idea of God, God not yet fully known. A world-weary dismissal of Fry's original and inventive theology as just another try at Wordsworthian pantheism shows a basic lack of comprehension of Fry.

But Donoghue goes on: "There is no end to the prose possibilities, Mr. Fry says, to the expression of this actual appearance of life: 'And if you accept my proposition that reality is altogether different from our stale view of it, we can say that poetry is the language of reality.' The argument is charmingly simple: appearance, reality; actual, real; fact, miracle; prose, poetry."[3] Consider the faint praise of the earlier "interesting echo" and this "charmingly simple." The order of the argument is charmingly simple only when read in the order Donoghue reads it, with verse drama as the conclusion. As an art-for-art's-sake justification of verse drama the argument is indeed too simple. But Fry's argument runs the other way: beginning with Fry's distinction between verse and prose, the reader proceeds to the chief end of the plays: exploring the reality of God, an enterprise neither charming nor simple when undertaken as Fry does.

Donoghue continues thus:

> The same conception operates again in Mr. Fry's discussion of *The Lady's Not for Burning*. He set out, he declared, to write a play that would be first cousin to artificial comedy. But he could see no reason, writing such a comedy, why he should not treat of the world as he saw it, a world in which "we are all poised on the edge of eternity," a world which has "deep shadows of mystery," in which God is "anything but a sleeping partner." Why, Mr. Fry asks, should I use poetry instead of plain prose? Answer: "Well, if we have to be born into a world as wildly unprosaic as this one is, what else can be done, if we mean to be realistic?" The tone is hearty but evasive; the proposed insight has a characteristic way of slipping through one's fingers.[4]

Indeed, since Fry's chief task is exploring the ineffable and charting the intangible, no wonder his insight has a way of slipping through our fingers. The great tradition of Christianity has always maintained that God is ineffable and intangible, though it has then too often gone on to define exactly what is meant by ineffable and intangible, until, like Virilius the bookkeeper, it writes God down in seventy columns. That ought hardly be what Donoghue expects from Fry.

Donoghue goes on:

> But the most revealing factor is the stark opposition between "poetry" and "plain prose." We are back again with the

> Georgian verse dramatists, with Phillips, Flecker, and Bottomley, as if *Sweeney Agonistes*, the *Pisan Cantos*, and Yeats's Crazy Jane poems were still unwritten.[5]

The Georgian verse dramatists gave an impression of verse equalling mysticism, but the mysticism is of a pantheistic strain; none of them embodied in their plays a consistent and original system of theology as does Fry. All three of the positive models that Donoghue recommends for Fry's edification are of the wasteland school: Eliot at the time of *Sweeney* was fighting his way out of the existentialist wasteland to Christianity, Pound at the time of the *Cantos* was resigning himself to remaining locked in the pain of the wasteland forever, and Yeats at the time of the Crazy Jane poems was escaping from the wasteland into a private do-it-yourself mythology that eased the pain. Fry never inhabited the existentialist wasteland that these three writers inhabited. Would Fry have served English letters better than he did if he had faked a wasteland stance as all undergraduate journals did a generation ago? The models Donoghue offers Fry are particularly cruel, because they seem to imply that any poetry in our time is *per se* trivial unless it is wasteland poetry.

Fry's problem is not how to find a faith in a spiritual wasteland, or how to live without faith, but a parallel problem: how to keep an inherited faith from going dead orthodox. Once that problem is seen as an existential problem, the difference between wasteland poets and Fry diminishes enormously. Consider the similarities between *The Waste Land* and *Sleep of Prisoners*, for instance.

A basically sympathetic critic like William V. Spanos, though very different from Donoghue, also lacks a comprehensive orientation to the basic pattern of Fry's thought. The whole tradition of contemporary Christian verse drama, Spanos subsumes under the rubric of incarnation, especially as that doctrine was conceived by Charles Williams. The goodness of the flesh, the importance of history, the universal meaning embodied in the particular fact: these and other implications of the incarnation he sees in the verse plays of Eliot, Williams, Fry, and others. On this basis he finds *Sleep* to be Fry's best play and disparages the others:

> Now in the seasonal plays, Fry's idea of comedy turns out to be something quite different. In these, Fry is apparently reluctant to invoke the Incarnation. On the thematic level, the

> protagonists—Dynamene in *A Phoenix Too Frequent*, Thomas Mendip in *The Lady's Not for Burning*, the Duke in *Venus Observed*, and Richard Gettner in *The Dark Is Light Enough*—trace the comic pattern from contempt for the world and despair to affirmation of a sacramental universe, but the affirmation does not have its source in the discovery of the possibility that the Incarnation redeems time. As a result, the resolution of these plays becomes what Fry wishes to avoid at all costs: "a vulnerable optimism."[6]

Spanos seems not to be alert to the comprehensive range of Christian thought embodied in the Fry corpus. Finding the doctrine of incarnation, Spanos approves; missing it, he disapproves. Of all the playwrights Spanos treates in his monumental book, Fry suffers most from the self-imposed limitation. Even the doctrine of the incarnation is present in the secular comedies, though it is not explicitly mentioned; God, in Fry's theory does not need to be named to be worshipped and doctrines do not need to be named to be functionally present. Even a sympathetic critic like Spanos needs a more comprehensive view of Fry's theology and of Fry's method than simply the idea of incarnation.

Or take as another instance of the need for a comprehensive view of Fry's theology several sentences by a totally sympathetic critic, Gerald Weales: "This background [Church of England family, Quaker school] is probably in part responsible for Fry's refusal to treat the search for God as a painful and harrowing quest, but as a simple act of opening the eyes."[7] One wants to ask, opening the eyes to what exactly about God? Not just a pantheist's awareness of God's closeness, surely? Surely the opening of the eyes is to the God Fry was taught about in his youth, and surely the opening of the eyes to what was true and what was ephemeral in what he had been taught about God, and surely the opening of the eyes to what needed reinterpretation in what he had been taught. The "simple act of opening the eyes" does not do justice to the intricacy of Fry's theology. Or to take Weales a second time: ". . . the dancing excess of the playwright's language does sometimes seem to infect the violent moments of the plays with a cheerful unreality."[8] But then what we habitually take to be everyday reality is not the truest reality, in Fry's view. Perhaps being untrue to comon sense reality is Fry's way of breaking us through to a new understanding of God's reality as different from ours. Or to take a final example from Weales: "Fry's strained and straining metaphors are as much a part of his approach to man and God as Eliot's increasingly spare and prose-like verse is an indication of his attitude."[9] Does the sentence say that Fry's relationship to God is strained and Eliot's is not? Or does one use "strained and straining" metaphors only with such intimate friends that the sentence indicates comaradarie between Fry and God that is missing between Eliot and God? Not that Weales is deliberately ambiguous; rather, the meaning is so unclear to Weales himself that it will not come out clean, and what is lacking is a comprehensive view of Fry's relationship to God.

The kinder the critic, the more vapid Fry becomes. The kindest of all the critics is Derek Stanford:

> To put the matter positively, we can say that the poet is best understood in the light of the Anglican tradition. I choose this last word rather than write "in the light of Anglican Orthodoxy," since the points of reference to be made concern sensibility and imagination rather than intellectual belief. This is a rough and arbitrary distinction, but one which the purpose to which it is put possibly excuses and justifies, since Fry—as both a person and poet—lays more store by imagination than by the workings of intellect. Negatively, we can say that the poet—to quite an exceptional degree—has a cast of mind which modern thought of the last two centuries has left untouched. This, again, is comparatively stated. Nobody alive in these islands today can remain uninfluenced and unaware of the many material alterations and psychological shifts of perspective which recent ages have introduced. One must, however, try to distinguish between the acceptance of material improvements (to employ the modernist's terminology) and acceptance of materialsm as a set belief. This latter definite confession of faith is one that Fry has never made. The whole long sequence of post-Reformation thought: its puritanism, its cult of science, its rationalism and belief in progress, its economic hopes and atheist persuasion—seem to have passed him over like water over the feathers of a duck. This is not to suggest that Fry carries in his mind some picturesque idea of an 'olde and merrie' England in the rollicking manner of Chesterton. That he appears, imaginatively, to subscribe to an Elizabethan outlook is something we should never wish to deny. Its gusto, abundant magniloquence and vigour he sympathises with and shares; but for its sense of

> desperate intrigue, its Machiavellian double-handed dealing, its Erastian centralised politics he shows no interest or admiration. Religiously speaking, he seems to be nearer to the England of Vaughan or Traherne—the mystical half-pantheist landscape of the *Silex Scintillans* and *Centuries of Meditation*.[10]

Has friend ever made friend look more innocuous? "Promising," the reader wants to say, when *Anglican tradition* is chosen rather than *Anglican orthodoxy*, because the word *tradition* implies the possibility for renewal and advancement. Only that turns out not to be Stanford's reason for using the word: *tradition* is vague and imaginative while *orthodoxy* is precise and intellectual, and, we all know, Stanford seems to imply, how unintellectual and wooly Fry is. The burden of this book, *More Than the Ear Discovers*, has been to show how intellectually alert to the current political and religious situation Fry is (as well as imaginative, of course). Fry has a metahistorical program for the future, yet Stanford cages Fry four centuries in the past, far removed from the contemporary world, but is careful to point out how free Fry is from intrigue. What was it if not intrigue that made Fry use the secular theater establishment to advance his very unfashionable views? As Fry himself wrote me about *Phoenix*,

> It is true that I had been reading St. Paul at the time I read the Widow of Ephesus story in Jeremy Taylor, and discussing the epistles with friends in my army company (towards the end of the war). But I wrote the play out of my general state of mind at the time, without wishing for any precise definition: hoping that what truth there was in it would come across to an audience who had no knowledge of Paul's writings or much interest in Christianity. For the truth of Christianity, as we know, is that it is in life . . .

If Fry has been used and abused by the theater establishment, he also has done his share of using and abusing—a minor Machiavelli on behalf of his holier gospel, whether in church or theater, in season and out of season. While an aspect of Fry's voice is captured by evoking the mystical nature poets Vaughan and Traherne, to do that and no more ignores Sir Thomas Browne's prophetic and intellectual voice, muted and disguised for our ironic age, but there in Fry's voice, not to mention an aesthetic fastidiousness that puts one in mind of Herrick and the Tribe of Ben. When even as kind a friend as Stanford takes less than a comprehensive view of Fry, Fry gets trivialized.

Why, then, has Fry never made his theology explicit, rather than implying it and embodying it in the plays? To need to be told, in Fry's theory of revelation, argues against the truth of what one considered the revelation. Fry implies a revelation in the play, and if it is recognized as such by someone else, it becomes so much the more a revelation to Fry himself. If it is a true revelation, it will sound spontaneous chords in others, truth being its own best testimony. It is what Fry calls "the sensation of overtaking what had always been waiting for us":

> Let me repeat what I have just said: "the sensation of overtaking what had always been waiting for us." In the simplest form it is what growing up means. As children we carry in us the waiting adult. In the evolution of life on earth there has been a continuous pursuit from single cell to complex brain, from brain to deductive reason, from reason to creative intelligence. At each step life had overtaken what had been waiting for it. The first mud hut contained the blue-print of a cathedral; the first alarm cry or grunt of endearment held the vocabulary of King Lear. And unless we think evolution has given up and gone home, we must still carry within us other intuitions of what is waiting for us to comprehend. So when I ask myself "How far can a playwright explore beyond the primal emotions?" I pin my faith on these intuitions we have, or could discover in ourselves, intuitions of something other than physical life and outward appearances. It is the argument of a scene in *The Lady's Not for Burning*, when Thomas Mendip laughs at Jennet for her trust in "what I touch, what I see, what I know, the essential fact." He calls it the "mumbo-jumbo of believing in reality," by which he means the illusion we *call* reality.[12]

Everything humankind discovers, God reveals. Everything God reveals, humankind must still discover, sometimes at great pain and always with some effort. Accepting a revelation is never passive. Pointing to a revelation with a lecturer's pointer changes a revelation to a non-revelation.

This study may generate academic opposition because it does not present Fry's ideas adequately. But if in any sense this study has been a revelation, it *must* generate a more active and not merely academic opposition. One of the best arguments for the essential soundness of Fry's theology, in spite of some qualifications about particular ideas in it, is that it has kept the Gospel's power to offend.

NOTES

CHAPTER 1 PRELIMINARY NOTES AND QUERIES

[1]"How Lost, How Amazed, How Miraculous We Are," *Theatre Arts*, 36 (1952), 27; "Comedy," *Tulane Drama Review*, 4 (1960), 77–79; *Death* (Chichester: Chichester Cathedral Press, 1977); "Looking for a Language," MS, 1980.

[2]"Christopher Fry's *A Phoenix Too Frequent*: A Study in Source and Symbol," *Modern Drama*, 8 (1965), 293–302.

[3]"Enter Poet, Laughing," *Time*, 20 November 1950, pp. 58–64.

[4]"I think, maybe, the fact that during last October and November I finished the first draft of the first act of the new play, and started on the second, is due to a few people like you who have made sense of what I was up to. You ask about the play—well, it's the summer comedy: it takes place in Siena in 1946. The background is the first Palio after the war, and more than that I'm not prepared to say." Christopher Fry in a letter to SMW, 16 January 1967.

[5]Emil Roy, *Christopher Fry* (Carbondale and Edwardsville: Southern Illinois University Press, 1968).

[6]Nelvin Vos, "The Comic Victim-Victor," *The Drama of Comedy: Victim and Victor* (Richmond: Knox Press, 1966), pp. 74–99.

[7]Stanley M. Wiersma, *Christopher Fry; A Critical Essay* (Grand Rapids: Eerdmans Publishing Company, 1970), pp. 5–6.

[8]Christopher Fry, *Can You Find Me* (London: Oxford University Press, 1978), p. 17.

[9]See the letters to SMW quoted at the conclusion of Chapter 5 and of Chapter 11. The Quaker tone is unmistakable.

CHAPTER 2 SHOULDER TO SHOULDER WITH GOD: *The Boy with a Cart*

[1]Christopher Fry, *The Boy with A Cart* (London: Oxford University Press, 1939), p. 1. The prologue is found on pp. 1–2. This play is the only one to be discussed episode-by-episode in this book. Since the episodes are brief, the page notations for each episode will be given in the text, but not the page notations for every quotation from that episode.

[2]". . . there is an angle of experience where the dark is distilled into light: either here or hereafter, in or out of time: where our tragic fate finds itself with perfect pitch, and goes straight to the key which creation was composed in." Fry, "Comedy," 77.

CHAPTER 3 SINGLE, DOUBLE, AND MULTIPLE VISION *The Firstborn*

[1]Exodus 1–14. Biblical references are by book, chapter, and verse in the body of the text.

[2]Christopher Fry, *Three Plays* (London: Oxford University Press, 1968), pp. 1–95. First edition (London: Cambridge University Press, 1946). Future references to *The Firstborn* are by page number in the body of the text.

CHAPTER 4 *FRY'S* (Not Barth's) *KURZE ERKLÄRUNG DES ROMERBRIEFES* *A Phoenix Too Frequent*

[1]Christopher Fry, *A Phoenix Too Frequent* (London: Oxford University Press, 1949), a note under the Cast of Characters on an unnumbered introductory page. Henceforth, references to this work will be made by page number in the body of the text. First limited edition (London: Hollis & Carter, 1946).

[2]*Petronii Saturae*, ed. Franciscus Beucheler (Berolini: Apud Weidmannos, 1958), pp. 136–143 (Ch. 110–113).

[3]Jeremy Taylor, "A Peroration Concerning the Contingencies and Treatings of Our Departed Friends, After Death, in Order to Their Burial," *The Rule and Exercises of Holy Dying*, ed. Reginald Heber, in *The Whole Works of the Right Rev. Jeremy Taylor* (London: Rivington Press, 1828), IV, 562–565 (Section VIII).

[4]"Now the holly bears a berry, as blood it is red,
Then trust we our Saviour, who rose from the dead.
And Mary bore Jesus our Saviour for to be,
And the first tree in the greenwood, it was the holly, holly!"

"Sans Day Carol," stanza 4, *Oxford Book of Carols* (London: Oxford University Press, 1928), p. 75 (Carol 35).

"The holly bears a berry
As red as any blood,
And Mary bore sweet Jesus Christ
To do poor sinners good. . . ."
"The Holly and the Ivy," stanza 3, *Carols*, p. 81 (Carol 38).

[5]King James Version used throughout. References made by chapter and verse in the body of the text.

[6]The word *parable* refers henceforth in this study to Romans 7:1–14; the word *paragraph* refers to Romans 6:23.

The King James Version commonly prints each new verse beginning at the margin. Paragraphing is indicated by chapter headings. The original KJV (1611) had the following heading for Romans 6: "We may not liue in sinne, 2. for we are dead unto it, 3. as appeareth by our baptisme. 12. Let not sinne raigne any more, 18. because we have yeelded ourselues to the seruice of righteousness 23. and for that death is the wages of sinne." The original heading with modernized spelling is still published in some twentieth-century editions of the KJV, especially pulpit editions in which size and expense are no factors.

As early as 1648, however, the Daniel edition of the Cambridge Bible came out with abridged chapter headings. These abridgements have been used throughout the intervening centuries to conserve space and reduce cost, especially in editions meant for private use. The abridged heading for Romans 6, found in innumerable standard, early-twentieth-century British editions of the KJV, is as follows: "We may not live in sin, 12. not let sin reign any more. 23. Death the wages of sin." This study assumes that Fry used an edition with this common heading.

It is possible that Fry used the 1880–1881 revision of the KJV. If this is Fry's version, the third paragraph would include verses with a similar idea: 1–11, 12–14, and 15–23. This edition, however, won neither popular, ecclesiastical, nor literary approval. It seems unlikely that Fry would have used it.

This study owes a debt to Margaret T. Hills of the American Bible Society, who assisted in pursuing the elusive history of paragraphing in the KJV.

[7]"The moral masochist must act against his own interests, even to the point of destroying himself, in order to provoke punishment . . ." Leland E. Hinsie and Robert Jean Campbell, *Psychiatric Dictionary*, 3rd ed. (New York: Oxford University Press), "Masochism."

[8]Ovid, *Metamorphoses*, Book III.

[9]*Modern Drama*, 8 (1965), 293–302.

CHAPTER 5 CREATION'S WELCOME TO LONELY FLESH
Thor, with Angels

[1]Fry, *Three Plays*, pp. 97–154. Future references to *Thor* by page number in the body of the text. First published by Oxford University Press, 1949; first published in an acting edition by H. J. Goulden Ltd. for the Friends of Canterbury Cathedral, 1948.

Biblical references will also be made in the body of the text by book, chapter, and verse.

[2]This essay itself was delivered at a service in Calvin Seminary Chapel at noon on 30 January 1974. The essay was followed by a reading of *Thor* by the following cast: Howard Slenk as Cymen, Ervina Boeve as

Clodesuida, Mary Walters as Martina, Clark Van Halsema and Ron Martin as the sons, Kenneth W. Kuiper and Delwyn Nykamp as the brothers, Steve Vander Weele as Colgrin, Mildred Zylstra as Anna, Henry Baron as Hoel, John De Beer as Merlin, and Paul Koops as the messenger. Ann Janssen Noteboom directed the production and Jane Zylstra Ophoff provided the music.

[3]Even more specifically, *Thor* is Ash Wednesday Evensong with Commination. Commination is the curse of the church against all sinners and heretics; the ritual is performed on Ash Wednesday. The benediction for Commination: "The Lord bless us, and keep us; the Lord make his face to shine upon us and be gracious unto us; the Lord lift the light of his countenance upon us, and give us peace, now and for evermore. Amen" (Prayerbook, 1662). The only other use for this benediction in Anglican liturgy is baptism performed at home. When Cymen leaves to hear Augustine, he pronounces this benediction on his family: "Meanwhile, the silence keep you, the silence/Be gracious unto you and give you peace" (141). Remembering that Cymen has just overturned his pagan altar and cursed his pagan gods, one sees that the commination service for Ash Wednesday is the occasion for the play to be presented. Cymen overturns a Jutish altar, but the actor playing Cymen—*Thor* is produced in church—overturns an Anglican altar.

It is ironic that with Commination hardly over, Cymen's family crucify Hoel—though no more ironic than what happens always at Commination. The faithful cry *Amen* to the following: "Cursed is he that perverteth the judgement of the stranger. . . ." "Cursed is he that smiteth his neighbour secretly," and "Cursed is he that putteth his trust in man, and taketh man for his defense, and in his heart goeth from the Lord," among other maledictions. One wonders whether Commination has ever significantly slowed down the suspicion of strangers, dirt done behind somebody's back, or trusting humanity rather than God, even among the faithful who cry *Amen*? The faithful all think somebody else is intended.

CHAPTER 6 A MANIFESTO FOR WOMEN
Venus Observed

[1]Christopher Fry, *Venus Observed* (London: Oxford University Press, 1949). Future references to *Venus* by page number in the body of the text. Biblical references will also be made in the body of the text by book, chapter, and verse. The New English Bible is used for these references.

CHAPTER 7 FRY'S *WASTE LAND*
A Sleep of Prisoners

[1]*Hamlet* in *The Riverside Shakespeare*, ed. G. Blackmore Evans (Boston: Houghton Mifflin, 1974), p. 1155 (II, ii, 239-256). The *Hamlet* reference first applied to *Sleep* by Charles Huttar, Professor of English, Hope College, Holland, Michigan.

[2]Fry, *Three Plays*, pp. 155-211. All page references will be made in the body of the text. First published by Oxford University Press, 1951.

[3]Fry, "Foreword," *Three Plays*, p. vii.

[4]Northrop Frye, *An Anatomy of Criticism* (Princeton: Princeton University Press, 1957), pp. 247-248.

[5]John Ferguson, "Christopher Fry's *A Sleep of Prisoners*," *English*, 10 (1954), 42-47. Ferguson introduced the idea of *Sleep* as incarnational play. William V. Spanos, "Christopher Fry's *A Sleep of Prisoners*: the Choreography of Comedy," *Modern Drama*, 8 (1965), 58-72. Spanos interprets the incarnation as Fry's friend Charles Williams interpreted it, the Way of Affirmation, the celebration of God through the creatures and by the flesh. Han Itschert, "Christopher Fry: *A Sleep of Prisoners*," in *Das Moderne Englische Drama: Interpretationen*, ed. Horst Oppel (Berlin: Erich Schmidt Verlag, 1963), pp. 267-287. Itschert explicates the play moment by moment as it would unfold for a perfect audience concentrating perfectly on every detail. Roy, *Fry*, pp. 98-109. Roy puts the play into its historical context, relating it to contemporary plays, to the rest of the Fry corpus, and to broad intellectual and artistic movements.

[6]Frye, *Anatomy*, p. 366.

[7]Frye, *Anatomy*, pp. 315-326.

[8]Any standard commentary on Daniel 3:25. Henry Leighton Goudge, Alfred Guillaume, Charles Gord, *A New Commentary on Holy Scripture* (London: Society for Promoting Christian Knowledge, 1929), p. 549. The lengths to which St. Jerome needed to go to argue against the fourth figure as Jesus Christ shows how early (AD 400) that interpretation had already become imbedded.

[9]"In *A Sleep of Prisoners* I have tried to make a more simple statement, though in a complicated design where each of four men is seen through the sleeping thoughts of the others, and each, in his own dream, speaks as at heart he is, not as he believes himself to be. In the later part of Corporal Adams' dream the dream changes to a state of thought entered into by all the sleeping men, as though, sharing their prison life, they shared, for a few moments of the night, their sleeping life also." Christopher Fry, "Dedicatory Letter to Robert Gittings," *Three Plays*, p. 157.

[10]Roy, *Fry*, p. 98, quoting an interview from *The New York Times*,

"Drama in a House of Worship" (October 14, 1951) Sec. II, p. 2.

[11]Roy, *Fry*, p. 100; Frye, *Anatomy*, p. 167.

[12]Spanos, *"Sleep,"* pp. 59–62.

[13]Frye, *Anatomy*, pp. 136–138, 155–156.

[14]Itschert, *"Sleep,"* p. 279. Based on a letter from Christopher Fry to Hans Feist.

[15]How Christopher Fry articulates the technique of displacement non-technically: "It must be remembered that whatever they [the characters] represent in our thoughts, they are still the men themselves, making their prison a little world. He [Meadows] is a *figura Christi* in what he has taken unto himself, but remains Meadows the gardener." Letter from Christopher Fry to SMW, 16 January 1967.

[16]Frye, *Anatomy*, p. 283.

[17]On 11 April 1973, Mr. Fry and I discussed an early draft of this essay at tea at his home in Sussex. Peter and the donkey figuring soul and body, following the "brother ass" of St. Francis of Assisi, was Fry's own suggestion. Fry also confirmed what he had written to Hans Feist: the seashore donkey rides and the return to childhood (note 14). Why Fry neglected to mention the donkey as body in the Feist letter can best be explained by the many clues to childhood and donkey rides in the Edwina passage itself. In response to Feist's letter asking about the Edwina passage, Fry commented only on that passage. In conversation, when Fry was asked to explain the earlier speech of David about the "half-wit angel strapped to the back of a mule," specifically, whether David's speech related to the Edwina passage, then Fry responded with the St. Francis allusion. For the "brother ass" reference in St. Francis, see Edward A. Armstrong, *Saint Francis: Nature Mystic* (Berkeley: University of California Press, 1973), pp. 127–128.

[18]Roy, *Fry*, p. 99.

[19]Frye, *Anatomy*, p. 223.

[20]Frye, *Anatomy*, p. 235.

[21]Itschert, *"Sleep,"* pp. 267–269.

[22]James Woodfield, "'A Unity of Difference': Christopher Fry's Quest for Meaning," *English Studies in Canada*, 2 (1976), 97–108; "'The Figure of a Dance:' Christopher Fry's *A Phoenix Too Frequent*," *Ariel*, 9 (1978), 3–19.

[23]From the interview on 11 April 1973.

[24]Frye, *Anatomy*, p. 366.

[25]Frye, *Anatomy*, p. 273.

[26]On 11 April 1973, Fry stated that his intent in *Sleep* had been to write a play that corresponded to the theme-and-variations form in music.

[27]S. Baring Gould, "Now the Day is Over," (1865) in *Anglican Hymn*

Book (London: Church Book Room Press, 1965), hymn 59.

[28]Frye, *Anatomy*, p.272.

[29]Frye, *Anatomy*, pp. 250–251.

[30]Frye, *Anatomy*, p. 246.

[31]Taking the pattern of the crossover seriously occurred to me in a conversation with Robert Gittings (to whom Fry dedicated *Sleep*) when Gittings was a guest lecturer at Calvin College, June, 1974. Gittings insists the idea did not come from him.

[32]Frye, *Anatomy*, p. 250.

[33]Fry, "Comedy," p. 78.

[34]Itschert, "*Sleep*," p. 280.

[35]Fry's interpretation, 11 April 1973

[36]Frye, *Anatomy*, pp. 91–92, pp. 95–115.

[37]Frye, *Anatomy*, pp. 247–248.

[38]T. S. Eliot, *The Complete Poems and Plays: 1909–1950* (New York: Harcourt, Brace & World, 1958), p. 49 (line 389).

[39]Bernard Bergonzi, *T. S. Eliot* (New York: Macmillan, 1972) pp. 164–165.

[40]Frye, *Anatomy*, pp. 115–128.

CHAPTER 8 THE COMPLETE PACIFIST
The Dark is Light Enough

[1]Wiersma, *Fry*, pp. 13–17.

[2]Christopher Fry, *The Dark Is Light Enough* (London: Oxford University Press, 1954). Further references by page in the text.

[3]T. S. Eliot, *Four Quartets* (London: Faber and Faber, 1944), pp. 40–41.

[4]The Countess is already detached, in Eliot's sense, in the very first act:

> I seem to have gone floating out
> Of this interesting present
> To some remote evening, a no-man's country.
> Now it seems to me very strange
> You should all be so occupied in living. (22)
>
> It's the perfection of sleep
> To be awake to the dream.
> If I were going to live for ever
> This would be the way: unconcerned
> And yet reasonably fond. (23)

Her early detachment has made some critics observe a static quality in the play. The dynamism of the play lies not in the character of the Countess, however, but in the reaction of all the other characters to her stability.

CHAPTER 9 LAW, LAWS, AND THE LAW
Curtmantle

[1]W. Moelwyn Merchant, *Creed and Drama: An Essay in Religious Drama* (Philadelphia: Fortress Press, 1965), p. 108.

[2]Roy, *Fry*, p. 123.

[3]James Woodfield, "Christopher Fry's *Curtmantle*: The Forms of Unity," *Modern Drama*, 17 (1974), 308.

[4]Gerald Parker, "A Study of Christopher Fry's *Curtmantle*," *Dalhousie Review*, 43 (1963), 201.

[5]Christopher Fry, *Curtmantle* (London: Oxford University Press, 1961), pp. vii–ix [2nd Edition, 1965]. Further references to be found in the body of the text, in Arabic numerals for the play itself and in Roman numerals for Fry's introduction.

[6]Merchant, *Creed*, pp. 103–104.

[7]Woodfield, "Fry's *Curtmantle*," p. 313.

[8]Parker, pp. 203–205, 209–211.

[9]Roy, *Fry*, p. 131.

[10]Roy, *Fry*, p. 131.

[11]Roy, *Fry*, p. 129.

[12]Roy, *Fry*, p. 129.

[13] "It struck me what quality went to form a man of achievement, especially in literature—I mean *Negative Capability*, that is, when a man is capable of being in uncertainties, mysteries, doubts, without any irritable reaching after fact and reason." John Keats, *Letters*, ed. M. B. Forman, I (London: Oxford University Press, 1935), p. 77.

[14]Fry, "Comedy," pp. 77–79.

[15]Christopher Fry, "Talking of Henry," *Twentieth Century*, 169 (1961), 187–188.

[16]Without the influence of the Amsterdam philosopher Herman Dooyeweerd and his philosophy of law, the importance of *Curtmantle* would never have occurred to me. His students and disciples will recognize the similarity between the philosophy and the play. This essay discharges a debt of gratitude.

CHAPTER 10 THE ARTS IN THE BODY POLITIC
A Yard of Sun

[1]Christopher Fry, *A Yard of Sun* (London: Oxford University Press, 1970). All future references by page numbers in the body of the text.

Biblical references also made in the body of the text by book, chapter, and verse.

CHAPTER 11 THE PATTERN IN THE CARPET *A Diachronic View of the Form*

[1] *The Living Thoughts of Kierkegaard*, comp. by W. H. Auden (New York: David McKay Company, 1952), pp. 56–114.

[2]Auden, *Kierkegaard*, p. 110.

[3]Fry, "Comedy," pp. 77–79.

[4]Fry, letter to SMW, 5 September 1966.

[5]Fry, *Three Plays*, p. vii.

[6]Fry, letter to SMW, 21 October 1966.

[7]II, Section 9.

CHAPTER 12 THE FINAL JUDGMENT *The Lady's Not for Burning*

[1]At least three critics have gone in quest of the paradox in *Lady*. John Woodbury fashions an accurate definition of *Lady's* paradox—spring and imminent cataclysm—but then blunts that instrument before he gets to use it, by equating spring with the myth of Orpheus, by equating cataclysm with the story and theology of Christ, and by not following Fry's clues for discovering more precisely how the paradox works. "The Witch and the Nun," *Manitoba Arts Review*, 10 (1956), 41–54. Gunnar Urang finds the "comic climate" of *Lady* the ultimate paradox of Christianity: "God . . . in Christ reconciling the world unto himself"; Mr. Urang's definition is too broad and blunt an instrument with which to examine the work. "The Climate Is the Comedy," *The Christian Scholar*, 41 (1963), 61–86. Nelvin Vos sees *Lady* as the resolution to the paradox of Victor-Victim, Victim-Victor. Mr. Vos devises his definition primarily for articulating differences between Wilder, Ionesco, and Fry, not for dealing with *Lady* specifically. "Comic Victim-Victor," pp. 74–99.

[2]*Lady*, 2d. ed. (New York, 1958), p. 6. Future references made by page number in the body of the text, as the other plays are. The first edition: (London: Oxford University Press, 1949).

[3]"Somehow the comic characters have to unmortify themselves: to affirm life and assimilate death and persevere in joy." Fry, "Comedy," 78.

[4]This essay was first presented in its present form in the New World Theater at Dordt College, Sioux Center, Iowa, 3 March 1981, in connec-

tion with an abbreviated production of the play, directed by Verne Meyer, Professor of Drama.

CHAPTER 13 HOW MANY BEANS MAKE SIX
A Synchronic View of Fry's Theology

[1]Christopher Fry, *Death*, p. 4.

[2]Fry, *Death*, p. 8.

[3]Charles Williams, "The Way of Exchange," "The Way of Affirmation," "One Way of Love," "The Jews," "The Society of Jesus," and "Apologue on the Parable of the Wedding Garment," *The Image of the City* (London: Oxford University Press, 1958), pp. 147–154, 154–158, 159–161, 161–163, 163–165, and 166–168. C. S. Lewis, "Transposition," *Transposition and Other Addresses* (London: Geoffrey Bles, 1949), pp. 9–20.

CHAPTER 14 DEFENDING GOD'S DEFENDER

[1]Letters to SMW, 22 August 1966; 5 September 1966; 1 October 1966; 16 January 1967; 12 October 1969.

[2]Denis Donoghue, *The Third Voice: Modern British and American Verse Drama* (Princeton: Princeton University Press, 1959), p. 180. Fry, "Poetry in the Theatre," *Saturday Review*, 21 March 1953, p. 18.

[3]Donoghue, p. 180.

[4]Donoghue, p. 180–181.

[5]Donoghue, p. 180–181.

[6]William V. Spanos, *The Christian Tradition in Modern British Verse Drama* (New Brunswick: Rutgers University Press, 1967), p. 307.

[7]Gerald Weales, *Religion in Modern English Drama* (Philadelphia: University of Pennsylvania Press, 1961), p. 207.

[8]Weales, p. 223.

[9]Weales, p. 223.

[10]Derek Stanford, *Christopher Fry: An Appreciation* (London: Peter Nevill Limited, 1951), pp. 29–31.

[11]Fry to SMW, 22 August 1966.

[12]Christopher Fry, "Looking for a Language," MS, 1980, pp. 7–8.

INDEX